You've Just Been Supervisor ...Now What?

Bringing Safety to the Front Line

Meredith L. Onion

Michael F. O'Toole, PhD

National Safety Council

Itasca, Illinois

NATIONAL SAFETY COUNCIL
The mission of the National Safety Council is to educate and influence society to adopt safety, health and environmental policies, practices and procedures that prevent and mitigate human suffering and economic losses arising from preventable causes.

COPYRIGHT, WAIVER OF FIRST SALE DOCTRINE
The National Safety Council's materials are fully protected by the United States copyright laws and are solely for the noncommercial, internal use of the purchaser. Without the prior written consent of the National Safety Council, purchaser agrees that such materials shall not be rented, leased, loaned, sold, transferred, assigned, broadcast in any media form, publicly exhibited or used outside the organization of the purchaser, or reproduced, stored in a retrieval system, or transmitted in any form or by any means, electronic, mechanical photocopying, recording or otherwise. Use of these materials for training for which compensation is received is prohibited, unless authorized by the National Safety Council.

DISCLAIMER
Although the information and recommendations contained in this publication have been compiled from sources believed to be reliable, the National Safety Council makes no guarantee as to, and assumes no responsibility for, the correctness, sufficiency, or completeness of such information or recommendations. Other or additional safety measures may be required under particular circumstances.

Copyright © 2003 by the national Safety Council, Itasca, Illinois
All Rights Reserved
Printed in the United States of America
13 12 11   6 5 4

Library of Congress Cataloging-in-Publication Data

Onion, Meredith L.
  You've just been made the supervisor-- now what? : bringing safety to the front line / Meredith L. Onion, Michael F. O'Toole.
        p. cm.
Includes bibliographical references and index.
  ISBN 978-0-87912-219-5
  1. Supervision of employees. 2. Middle managers. 3. Career development. I. O'Toole, Michael F., 1952- II. Title.
  HF5549.12.O55 2003
  658.3'02--dc21

2003008204

1C0411   Product Number:17649-0000

Contents

1. What This Book Is About — 1
2. Juggling Act — 19
3. Supervisors, Employment and Workplace Law — 35
4. Partnering with Human Resources — 91
5. Supervising a Diverse Workforce — 117
6. Communication — 145
7. Attracting and Keeping Employees — 175
8. Leadership — 203
9. Supervising in a Union Environment — 235
10. Measuring Performance — 269
11. Developing Employee Skills and Careers — 295
12. Developing Your Own Skills and Career — 311

Appendix A: Safety in the Global Workplace — 335

Appendix B: Resources for Supervisors — 355

Preface

The world and the workplace are changing faster than books and publications can keep up. The world is shrinking due to faster and faster forms of communication and greater acceptance that we are all more "similar" than "dissimilar". It is a given that companies operate globally.

You've Just Been Made the Supervisor—Now What? Bringing Safety to the Front Line was written for anyone "supervising" people in a global organization. The book is designed to be used as (1) a handbook for the classroom or self-study and (2) a resource for problem-solving in the workplace. Each chapter discusses what supervisors can do to be effective in their work, particularly for those supervisors looking for some guidance in how to supervise people in a global organization. The three key aspects of supervisor responsibilities are addressed:

- supervising those who work for them effectively, efficiently and productively (human resources)
- supervising the flow of material, goods and services effectively, efficiently and productively (physical resources)
- carrying out both of these responsibilities safely and effectively and assuring that others do the same.

We will use the term "supervisor" broadly, referring to anyone who has one or more staff reporting to them. In reality, the title may be "supervisor," "manager" or "vice-president," but the basics of supervising people remain much the same.

Remember that a supervisor's "human resources" are the most critical part of supervisory responsibilities. Working safely and effectively as a team is the most challenging and rewarding task a supervisor faces in today's ever-changing, global workplace.

About the Authors

You've Just Been Made the Supervisor—Now What? Bringing Safety to the Front Line is an updated version of the 1990 National Safety Council publication OUT IN FRONT: Effective Supervision in the Workplace, by Leslie E. Dennis, PhD, and Meredith L. Onion. The primary authors/editors of this book are Meredith L. Onion and Michael F. O'Toole, PhD.

Meredith Onion has 15-plus years of experience as a Human Resource professional in for-profit companies, with a large non-profit association, a university and the government. She has supervised teams, in addition to training others in management development. Her most recent position was as Senior Vice-President, Deborah Snow Walsh, Inc., consulting with Fortune 100 companies to bring in diverse, executive leadership talent. She holds a Master of Science in Industrial Relations from Loyola University Chicago, and is a Certified Compensation Professional (CCP). She has traveled overseas to study industrial relations in Southeast Asia.

Michael F. O'Toole, PhD, is Associate Professor of Organizational Leadership and Supervision, received a BA in Psychology, and MA in Industrial Psychology from Western Michigan University, an MS from Northern Illinois University in Safety Engineering and a PhD from the University of Illinois at Chicago in Public Health. He currently teaches courses in safety, health, supervision and human resources. Before coming to Purdue University Calumet, he worked 20 years in private industry holding a variety of positions in Human Resources and Health and Safety. He continues to be active in trade and professional organizations dealing with regulations affecting industry. He actively consults for industry and businesses around the country.

Contributing Authors

Joy Colwell, JD (Chapter 3, Supervisors, Employment and Workplace Law, and Chapter 5, Supervising a Diverse Workforce)

Joy L. Colwell is an Assistant Professor of Organizational Leadership and Supervision. She teaches courses in conflict management, personnel law, and creativity and problem solving. She regularly provides training in negotiation and mediation. Joy received her undergraduate degree and her JD from the Indiana University School of Law in Bloomington, Indiana. She belongs to the Society for Professionals in Dispute Resolution and the Society for Human Resource Management.

Laura Horian (Appendix A, Safety in the Global Workplace)

Ms. Horian consults to improve individual and organizational performance. Her expertise is in focusing people on results, and developing strategies and a plan of action for achieving those results. She uses this process with: leaders to develop a corporate vision; with sales personnel in creating long-term customer satisfaction; and with safety leaders in reducing accidents and injuries.

Christopher Janicak, PhD, CSP, ARM (Chapter 10, Measuring Performance)

Christopher A. Janicak, PhD, CSP, ARM, is an Associate Professor of Safety at Indiana University of Pennsylvania, Department of Safety Studies. He received his Ph.D. from Loyola University in Research Methodology; his Master of Science degree in Industrial Technology/Industrial Safety Concentration from Illinois State University; and his Bachelor of Science degree in Health and Safety Studies (Occupational Safety and Health Education Concentration) from the University of Illinois at Urbana-

Champaign.

Dr. Janicak has more than 15 years of professional experience in occupational safety as a loss control consultant, safety manager and University professor. He has presented at national and international conferences, published a book and numerous articles in the field of occupational safety.

Carl Jenks, PhD (Chapter 9, Supervising in a Union Environment)

Dr. Jenks holds the rank of professor in the Department of Manufacturing Engineering Technologies and Supervision (METS) and teaches courses in organizational leadership and labor relations. His special interest is in labor arbitration, and he is on the Labor Panels of AAA and FMCS. He received his BS, MS, and PhD from Purdue University, West Lafayette and has served the Purdue system in both teaching and administration capacities for over thirty years. Dr. Jenks has academic, industrial, and military supervisory experience and frequently consults in the area of supervisory developmental programs.

John Lucas, PhD (Chapter 9, Supervising in a Union Environment)

John Lucas is an Assistant Professor of Management. Dr. Lucas was formerly the Industrial Relations Representative for Commonwealth Edison. He has experience in all facets of human resource management, including labor relations, benefits administration, human resource planning and health education. He received his Master of Science in Industrial Relations (MSIR) and PhD degrees from Loyola University Chicago. Dr. Lucas also holds the Professional Human Resource (PHR) license and is an active member of the Society for Human Resource Management and Northwest Indiana Personnel Association. He teaches a variety of human resource management courses including Labor Relations, Benefits Administration, Collective Bargaining, Compensation Management, and Human Resource Planning, Selection and Placement.

Alicia J. O'Brien (Chapter 6, Communication)

For 15 years, Alicia held various positions in the Human Resources group of a prominent national non-for profit organization. As a manager and consultant to staff at all levels of the organization she experienced first-hand the value of consistent and effective communication in the workplace. In her current role as Assistant Director, Board of Trustees, Alicia continues to promote the use of key communication vehicles as a way to educate and empower employees at every level. Her degree is in psychology with a concentration in organizational behavior.

George Sanders (Chapter 4, Partnering with Human Resources)

George Sanders is currently Director of Training and Development for United Stationers, the largest wholesale distributor of office products in North America. He is a former Director of Human Resources with Motorola Inc. George has more than 19 years of experience in global Human Resources working closely with all levels of supervision and management in Engineering, Manufacturing, and Sales/Marketing. George is a certified Senior Human Resources Professional (Society for Human Resource Management), and received his MA in European Diplomatic History from the University of Arizona.

Yang Shao, PhD (Chapter 8, Leadership)

Dr. Shao is an international Human Resources and Marketing professional with global experience with several Fortune 500 companies. Currently, she is Associate Director, Global People Development at Colgate-Palmolive, managing several key people and leadership development programs to ensure the identification, development and retention of global talents for the company. Prior joining Colgate, She was the Head of Strategic Staffing for the Pharmaceutical Research Institute for Bristol-Myers Squibb. Before that, she spent eight years at Dun & Bradstreet and held various international Human Resources and Marketing roles with increasing responsibility. Her last position there was Marketing Director, Asia/Pacific, Canada and

Latin America with responsibility for development and implementation of the strategic marketing plans for D&B across 16 countries in this division. Dr. Shao has in-depth knowledge of and is a frequent speaker at major national and international forums on business environment and leadership issues in emerging markets in Asia and Latin America. Dr. Shao was born and raised in Beijing, China. She received her PhD in Social Psychology from Rutgers University; an MS in Organizational Psychology from the Chinese Academy of Science; and a BS in Psychology from Beijing University. She also received executive education in Marketing Management from Columbia University.

Ather Williams, Jr (Appendix A, Safety in the Global Workplace)

Mr. Williams is the Vice President, Safety and Industrial Hygiene-Worldwide, Johnson & Johnson. His responsibilities include Global Workplace Safety and Global Fleet Safety. He has more than 30 years at Johnson & Johnson, with an extensive background in developing and driving manufacturing and safety strategies. Mr. Williams' activities reflect a philosophy of achieving business results through leadership, accountability and technological innovation.

Dedication

This book could not have been possible without Leslie E. Dennis, my co-author of *Out In Front*.

Thanks to all of our contributing authors for their expertise and willingness to share it. Thanks especially to my family–Dave, Alexandria, Connor and Aaron–for their love and support. Meredith Onion

1 What This Book Is About

by Meredith Onion

What Will I Learn in This Chapter?

Being an effective supervisor in today's complex, global organizations is critical in an organization's ability to be profitable and successful.

Whether you are brand new to being a supervisor or an "old-timer," if you work for a small to mid-sized company or a mega-Fortune 500 company, this book will help any supervisor.

- How you can best use this book.
- What is a *supervisor*?
- How the word "*supervisor*" is used in this book.
- What is the *supervisor's* role in a safe workplace?

What's the Definition of a 21st Century Supervisor?

It is ancient history that successful companies focus on the quality of the widget being produced. Competitive, highly successful companies focus on the people producing the widget and/or delivering the service to their customers. And the people producing the widgets are usually only as good as their supervisor allows them to be. Even the most motivated worker will fail or leave an organization if left to work for a bad supervisor. An example: professional athletes whose performances were lackluster when playing for poorly managed organizations. When traded to a well-managed club, they can and do become significant contributors to the team. But even teams with stellar performers (i.e., a Michael Jordan or Sammy Sosa) still can't make it to the NBA playoffs or the World Series unless they are on a well managed team. That's where you come in.

Supervision is an art. Just as some people are "natural born leaders," supervising people comes more naturally to some than others. But people can learn to become good supervisors. Often outstanding individual contributors in an organization are promoted into supervisory jobs as a result of their individual performances. It may just have happened to you—but it is a mistake to assume that just because someone is a good and productive employee that he or she will also be a good supervisor. Becoming a good supervisor takes education, training, and practice. With the help of this book and the resources it shares with you, learning how to supervise will be that much easier.

This book is about how supervisors are developed. It tells you about how to become a good supervisor, a workplace leader with all the skills you'll need. It is also will help supervisors who want to learn more about their work and effective ways to supervise. **When we say "*supervisor*" in this book, it means those people with direct line responsibility for the performance of other employees.** Depending on the organization, those people who supervise others can also be called: *foremen; managers, team leaders* and even *executives*.

In this book we use the word *supervisor* to cover all situations in which you are responsible for leading and directing another person or persons. The more fluid our organizations become, the more we are asked to take on different roles at different times. You may not officially have the title *supervisor*, but you may be asked to lead an ad hoc committee or team. These members may not officially report to you; but for the time this group is together, they will look to you as a leader. As the leader, you will need to know how to perform certain typical important supervisory responsibilities:

- effective communication
- leadership
- understanding the dynamics of the group and the diversity that is represented

The U.S. National Labor Relations Act defines a supervisor as:

"Any individual having authority, in the interest of the employer, to hire, transfer, suspend, lay off, recall, promote, discharge, assign, reward, or discipline other employees, or responsibility to direct them, or to adjust their grievances, or effectively to recommend such action, if in connection with the foregoing the exercise of such authority is not of a merely routine or clerical nature, but requires the use of independent judgment."

What Is the Difference Between a Supervisor and a Manager?

What is the difference between a supervisor and a manager? The American Management Association says that management is the matter of:

> "...guiding human and physical resources into dynamic organization units that attain their objectives to the satisfaction of those served and with a high degree of morale and sense of attainment on the part of those rendering the service."

Supervisors deal with the day-in, day-out problems of handling people and goods on the front line of the workforce. Managers may be a step removed from the front line. Managers often supervise *and* manage. The lines between these two positions can be muddy. In fact, much of the literature on supervision has material that covers subjects that have little to do with the day-to-day work of supervisors. This includes subjects ranging from profit margins to strategic planning to organizational development. Those are things that managers deal with (or should). A lot of books on supervision are simply rewritten books on management. They don't recognize that the work of the supervisor is different from the work of the manager, and that supervisors are very important to the organization in and of themselves.

There are some responsibilities that both managers and supervisors share, such as dealing with people, handling people problems, meeting goals and keeping things moving. There are other things, such as long-term strategic planning, that are clearly the province of management. Much of what a manager does relates to areas of work or business–finance, marketing, planning, sales, supplies, product improvement, productivity—rather than directly affecting the production of goods or services. The supervisor is caught up almost exclusively with the problems of keeping people directly engaged in the production of goods and services. Most of the time, the supervisor deals with people and people problems. Robots need technicians to keep them working. People need supervisors.

How Can You Succeed as a Supervisor?

This book will give you a good foundation for the basic skills you will need as a supervisor. But like any new skill, it will take practice and an interest in continually developing yourself, to become a successful supervisor. Use any and all resources available to you to continue learning.

- Get to know your organization. Even if you have worked for your employer for a long time, how much have you paid attention to its mission and goals?
- Learn what challenges the organization faces.
- What are the strategies for growth?
- What gives them the competitive edge?
- Is the organization successful?
- How does it measure up against the competition?
- Who is the competition and what have they done to be successful?
- What issues or challenges does your particular division or workgroup face?
- How can you contribute?
- What is your organization's definition of global?

Change is usually a constant in today's competitive, global organizations. Take a look around to see what type of change, or changes, your organization is going through.
- Have you recently been merged, acquired or spun-off?
- Has there been a restructuring, a downsizing, a de-layering or a re-engineering?
- Is there new leadership at the top?

Stay informed and never think you've learned everything there is to learn. "*Try to stay uncomfortable. Comfort breeds complacency and there's no time for complacency if you want to be a successful global competitor.*" (HR Management News, 11/1/2000)

Get to know your people. It is very unlikely that your workgroup or workplace is homogeneous. You will find diversity in race, gender, cultural practices, sexual preference as well as diversity of thought and what motivates each individual. Chapters 5 (Diversity), 6 (Communication) and 8 (Leadership) will go into more detail on these topics.

Spend some time thinking about the type of supervisor and leader you want to be.
- Who have you admired most as a leader?
- What behaviors have your current or former bosses had that you would like to model?
- What behaviors did you find not motivating and ineffective?
- Think about your own strengths and weaknesses and areas that you might like to develop.

What resources are available to help you become and continue to be a good supervisor?

- Does your organization have training programs?
- Do they have assessment tools or 360-degree feedback instruments that you can use?
- Do you have a mentor that can serve as a coach and a sounding board? If not, try to develop one. (See Chapter 12 for more on mentors).
- Ask your Human Resources group how they can be helpful.

If your organization doesn't have these types of resources, ask your boss if you can look into attending training programs outside of the organization.

This book will be useful in helping supervisors learn many of the basic skills and techniques of sound supervision. Each chapter focuses on a particular skill area. It is important to keep in mind as you read this book that safety always plays an important role in the worksite. Supervisors must set a good example for employees 24/7 on working safely, using safe procedures and equipment.

Safety—A Critical Function for All Supervisors

Safety is a must for all good supervision. The more supervisors emphasize creating a safer workplace for employees, the better the workplace becomes. This results in better morale and productivity. As the keeper of rules and procedures, the supervisor automatically becomes responsible for maintaining a safe and healthful workplace. Part of safety is following important rules and procedures and applying a bit of common sense. The supervisor's role in safety involves recognizing hazards in his or her areas of responsibility, and establishing procedures or rules to minimize the risk of injury or illness to his or her direct reports.

Supervisors and Safety

A supervisor had gone to see how a plumber was getting along with an emergency job. Just as the supervisor approached, the plumber working on a ladder to make a soldered connection between two pieces of pipe, flipped excess solder to the floor instead of wiping it off with a rag. Fortunately, the solder missed the helper standing below.

The helper was looking up, ready to hand up another copper sleeve. Neither employee was wearing safety glasses. The supervisor stopped the work and had the employees put on their safety glasses. The supervisor stressed the requirement to use safety glasses on the job at all times. The supervisor commented, *"When you're under pressure to get a job done like this one, it's easy to forget something like your safety glasses, but you need to realize that they are the best insurance you have against an eye injury."* The supervisor checked several times during the rest of the shift to see if the plumber and helper were wearing their safety glasses.

The direct cause of an accident in this case would have been the failure of the employees to follow the correct and safe work practices. However, an accident may have also been prevented by the supervisor making a point to observe employees from time to time, to ensure compliance with these rules and practices. In addition, as in this case, a supervisor must intervene when he or she observes employees not complying with the organization's policies, rules or established work practices.

Of special interest is the supervisor's approach to that intervention. It was neutral, nonaccusatory and simply dealt with the facts. The supervisor acted as an adult dealing with other adults to improve safety performance. Worker safety is a prime measure of a supervisor's effectiveness in most organizations.

As this example illustrates, the supervisor must establish levels of expectations for employees in the area of safety. Those expectations will include not only physical conditions such as housekeeping, guarding and material storage, but also the work practices of the employees they supervise. The supervisor must also be aware of observable human factors that can cause accidents, such as fatigue, substance abuse, stress or preoccupation with something that might be the task at hand as well as non-work related issues.

Safety is usually a matter of following simple but important rules, regulations and procedures. But supervisors can never forget that they are dealing with employees whose diverse backgrounds influence their own unique perceptions, beliefs and values. One of a supervisor's safety jobs is to make sure that employees understand the safety culture of their organization. That culture may reflect a simple compliance-with-regulations-approach or reflect a more proactive, *best-practice* course. Regardless of the specific values an organization holds, the job of a supervisor is to set the example by consistently following all safety rules, regulations and organization policies.

Through the examples of supervisors and managers, organizations speak volumes about the safety culture. If the supervisor takes a *"do as I say, not as I do"* approach, there should be little mystery if employees are observed not following safe work practices. It is within this type of safety culture, management is often found asking the question, *"Why are our employees getting hurt?"*

Hazards or Risks?

You may not always know why employees get injured on the job. But it helps to understand typical human behavior. The differences between hazards and risks and general information about our perceptions can shed some light on the subject. A "*hazard*" is a source of danger; something that has the inherent potential to cause harm or property damage. Gasoline is a hazard, grinding a tool is a hazard, climbing a ladder is a hazard. As a supervisor, one of your jobs is upholder of a safe and productive workplace. This includes actively seeking out hazards and eliminating as many as you can. Often this is not within the supervisor's authority, so it is important to seek resources and expertise from upper management to address the hazards.

"*Risks*" are the likelihood or probability that a hazard will cause harm. As individuals we are not very good at effectively perceiving risks as they relate to us. So why do employees perform unsafe acts or not follow established rules and procedures? That is the million dollar question! In most cases, individuals are motivated to do something based upon their history with that or similar activities. If good things follow a particular activity or bad things are avoided by engaging in the activity, there is an increased likelihood that the activity (behavior) will be repeated (Geller, 1996; Krause et al, 1990; McSween, 1995).

One example happened when an employee took a short-cut and violated a safe work procedure. Even so, nothing bad happened to her and no one else was hurt. In fact the employee completed her task early, allowing for a short break. This employee will be more likely to repeat this behavior in the future based upon this prior experience.

These natural consequences or outcomes conflict with established procedures intended to reduce the employee's exposure to a given hazard. Even though the probability of any one unsafe act resulting in an accident or injury is really very small, the problem for supervisors is that no one, including the employee, can predict the accident will happen. That means that supervisors must support and coach on the procedures that do reduce the risk of accidents or injury at all times.

The supervisor should be aware of hazardous conditions within the workplace and have a plan to reduce or eliminate the risks associated with those hazards. If that is not possible, then the supervisor must establish adequate precautions that warn employees of the hazards so they can act appropriately. Sometimes it is not possible to eliminate the hazards of equipment or of the materials that employees use to get their jobs done. In those cases, it is advisable and sometimes required as with hazardous chemicals, to properly label them so employees are aware of the potential dangers. It is also important for the supervisor to make sure that only authorized and trained employees operate equipment or work with hazardous chemicals. Finally, it is the supervisor's responsibility to ensure that appropriate personal protective equipment (PPE) is available and used while working with hazardous chemicals.

As the upholder of a safe, healthful and productive workplace, the supervisor must also be familiar with special requirements or regulations dealing with things like hazardous chemicals, confined spaces, lockout/tagout and other provisions of the Occupational Safety and Health Act (OSHAct). Depending on the type of business or industry the supervisor is working for, he or she also may have to be familiar with the federal requirements of the U.S. Department of Transportation (DOT), the U.S. Mine Safety and Health Administration (MSHA), U.S. Consumer Product Safety Commission (CPSC) and/or the U.S. Environmental Protection Agency (EPA). This book does not attempt to cover all of these regulatory agencies, although many of the legal aspects that must be understood by today's supervisor are mentioned in this book.

Case Study—Getting Promoted to Supervisor

Janice Rodriquez looked forward to the day she would be promoted to group leader. Working as a customer service representative (CSR) with the Oxmoor Group for 3 years, Janice was responsible for answering the Call Center calls from customers who were either ordering new merchandise or were calling to complain, ask questions, or check the status of their orders. She had received excellent training in how to handle customer calls; and did very well in this role. She received several compliments over the years from her boss on how effectively she dealt with the customers, even the most difficult ones. She was very patient and understanding and customers also complimented her, on how friendly and helpful she had been. Janet also had a good relationship with her co-workers. Several of the CSRs who started with the organization at the same time as Janet had become good friends over the last several years.

The day for her promotion had arrived. Janice's boss informed her that their current team leader would be leaving the organization, and Janice would be promoted to this position. Of course, Janice was very excited and honored by this recognition.

The next Monday Janice started as team leader. Her boss really didn't spend much time talking to her about how to be a supervisor. He spent a few minutes explaining that Janice wouldn't be spending as

Case Study

much time on the phones. Instead, she would have to take only the difficult calls. She would also have to spend time developing the weekly employee schedule, gathering information regarding new products that the CSRs would have to know about in order to service customers, and working with the organization's technical staff about any equipment difficulties they had. She was also going to be assigned to an ad hoc work group on reviewing the on-line database the CSRs used when answering calls. Janice's boss also mentioned she needed to hire three new CSR's for the three vacancies in the group. And on top of all of that, performance appraisals for two of her staff needed to be completed.

At first, this all sounded very exciting and challenging to Janice and she was energized by so many new types of responsibilities. But, she had never recruited employees before, she had never written and delivered a performance appraisal, and she had never worked directly with the technical staff before. Her boss seemed very, very busy and when she tried asking for some guidance, he really didn't seem to have much time for her.

Janice also began to notice that her coworkers and friends treated her differently since she was now "the boss." They no longer invited her to lunch. A couple of them started coming in late in the morning and when Janice tried talking to them about this, they brushed her off and made comments like, *"We used to cover for you when you were late."*

> Janice's enthusiasm about her promotion began to give way to feeling overwhelmed and longing for the good old days when she was just one of the CSRs.
> - What would you do if you were Janice?
> - What resources do you think might be available to help her make this transition into her new role?
> - How could Janice's boss have helped Janice succeed as a supervisor, even before she was promoted? What should he do for her now?

Conclusion

This book gives you a good start or some new information to help your career as a good supervisor. It's an overview for first-time supervisors; and has lots of resources for more experienced supervisors. For example, if your organization has had a pretty stable workforce, but you've recently lost one or two people and you have to recruit for the first time. Refer to Chapter 7 on "Attracting and Keeping Employees" for help. Each chapter in this book stands on its own, so that you can refer to it when needed.

Becoming a supervisor is a great honor...and carries with it great responsibilities. As a supervisor you will have an opportunity to make an impact—not only on the people you are supervising, but also on the organization as a whole. More and more organizations recognize that the key to global competitiveness is a strong and happy customer base. Customers won't be happy unless the organization's employees are happy. And the organization's employees will have the greatest ability to be safe, happy and productive if they are supervised by a strong leader like you.

References

Geller ES. *The Psychology of Safety: How to Improve Behaviors and Attitudes on the Job.* Radnor, PA: Chilton, 1996.

HR's role in charting the global future. *HR Management News,* Nov 1, 2000, pp 4-5.

Krause TR, Hidley JH, Hodsen SJ. *The Behavior-Based Safety Process: Managing Involvement for an Injury-Free Culture.* New York: Van Nostrand Reinhold, 1990.

McSween TE. *The Values-Based Safety Process: Improving Your Safety Culture with a Behavioral Approach.* New York: Van Nostrand Reinhold, 1995.

Review Questions

1. If I've been an effective line employee, won't I naturally be a good supervisor?

2. What resources are available to help me become a better supervisor?

3. Isn't safety a "management" responsibility?

2 A Juggling Act

by Meredith Onion

What Will I Learn in This Chapter?

This chapter covers the roles a supervisor plays—all are *on the front line* and important to the organization. The diversity of these roles keeps being a supervisor challenging, rewarding and exciting; and reinforces the supervisor's critical point-of-contact between the organization and individual employees. You will learn how to:

- juggle the roles of a successful supervisor
- balance these roles.

What Are the Roles of Supervisors Today?

We often say that the supervisor is on the front line; and this front-line role has become more important than ever before. Capital or financial resources are important in every company. But with the global expansion of many companies and the shrinking labor pool, intellectual assets (copyrights, trademarks and product patents) and human resources (employees) have become just as important for many companies. The strategic knowledge resources employees have can be the key in providing a company's competitive advantage.

Front-line supervisors help to manage this resource. They are the first to:
- learn of changing customer needs
- see competitors' marketing strategies in action
- encounter new regulatory initiatives.

Top management of an organization increasingly relies on the ability of its geographically and organizationally dispersed managers and supervisors to perceive, adapt and respond rapidly whenever necessary. Front-line supervisors play different roles in carrying out the everyday duties of the job. Each supervisor, at one time or another, must be:

1. **assessor** of industry trends and the effects on the organization
2. **leader** of the frontline
3. **keeper** of rules and procedures
4. **maintainer** of a safe and productive workplace
5. **trainer** of employees
6. **advocate** for the workforce
7. **representative** of the organization.

Each is important and a building block to being a successful supervisor. Like a solid foundation, if one of the building blocks is missing, the rest of the structure may crumble.

Assessor of Industry Trends

1. As a supervisor you should:
    - learn as much as you can about your particular industry.
    - know and keep current about changes and trends in your industry.
    - break down and learn the steps of each job your employees perform.
    - learn and show employees the safest ways to do their jobs.
    - work with the organization's safety and health practitioners to determine which personal protective equipment (PPE) is needed, how to properly fit and use the PPE.
    - be able to show employees how to use the PPE.

Think for a moment what kind of organization you work in? Does it provide a service or a product? The basic skills for good employee supervision are much the same, but in each different type of workplace there may be small differences in the way you supervise. For instance, if you work in manufacturing you may need different skills to supervise workers in a factory, versus the skills needed to supervise night-shift nurses in a hospital.

Dealing with Change in the Healthcare Setting

Each type of workplace has its own challenges; and supervisors should know about industry changes and how they can impact the workplace. For example, healthcare has changed a lot in the last 20 years. A shortage of qualified nurses and support staff is one change. To combat this nursing shortage, hospitals used new ways to attract new nurses. They offered more choices to nurses, including flexible schedules, part-time positions and on-site day care hoping to attract nursing professionals and buck the nursing shortage.

Another problem hospitals have is the government's changes to the Medicare and Medicaid systems. These changes created financial pressures and administrative nightmares for most hospitals. Today a hospital supervisor needs to (1) understand what effects on the hospital these changes have; (2) help his or her employees deal with changes; and (3) help hospital management create solutions to cope with these changes.

Dealing with Change in the Manufacturing Setting

The manufacturing sector is affected by (1) globalization, (2) poor economy (3) labor shortages, (4) rapidly changing technologies, (5) government regulations and (6) professional standards. An example is the boom of the technology industry in the 1990s that resulted in the bust of the 21st century. Another is how the fast-food industry, once a high-growth industry, has slowed; and now must accommodate changes in our eating habits and demand for healthier fast food.

These examples show how no industry stays the same, and sometimes the changes come quickly. Supervisors who keep current with industry changes can prove their value and contribute most to their organizations. Supervisors should learn constantly and pass on their knowledge to the employees.

- Always take advantage of opportunities to attend training in the organization, such as marketing and sales training meetings about new products and processes.
- Attend seminars on safety and how to supervise, as often as you can.
- Read about the kinds of products or services your organization produces, and about the industry.

- Keep up with local, national and international news.
- Share as much of this information with your team as you can
- Try to get them into brown bag lunch discussions about safety.

Leader of the Front Line

The organization's chief executive officers (CEOs) often seem to most profoundly influence the workplace. This is certainly true in most cases. But on a day-to-day basis, most employees will tell you that it is their immediate supervisor who impacts them and their work the most.

You are a focal point of the workplace. You direct, guide, encourage, reward, discipline, counsel and advise those who work for you. It is a very personal relationship; one that is an honor to hold. You provide a vision to those who work for you; this helps them focus their talents and energies on carrying out safe and productive work.

A good supervisor can inspire, help motivate, encourage safe work habits and procedures and make sure that the job gets done properly and safely. This means that supervisors affect employees, who ultimately affect productivity and profitability. The organization's products are manufactured and services delivered at the employee level—and safety is integral here. An organization can be profitable via its employee productivity and safety and the appropriate facility and equipment design. Supervisors must see that those elements mesh together safely.

Supervisors also affect the environment in which the work is carried out. If the workplace is dirty and disorganized, if things are unsafe or falling apart, you can try to blame it on the lack of money, the failure to buy new equipment or poorly trained workers. However, most people agree that the primary blame should be placed on bad supervision. Why? Because the supervisor is responsible for the direct, front-line management of the workplace, getting things done with the people and equipment available. It makes no difference if the work takes place in an office, manufacturing facility, retail store, laboratory or railroad yard–the responsibility of managing the front line is the supervisor's.

If that doesn't seem right, think of the differences in the fast-food chains you have visited. The name on the door may be the same, but depending on the location and the manager that runs that particular franchise, the service, cleanliness and quality of the food can be very different. Even within the same labor market, why is one staff friendly, efficient and accurate, while at the location down the street, the restaurant is unkempt, the "hot" food is cold and the staff can't ever seem to fill the order right the first time? Chances are, all of these factors are the direct result of a good or a poor supervisor.

Keeper of Rules and Procedures

Another role of the supervisor must be that of keeper of the rules and procedures. Keeper seems like a funny term, but it's actually right on target. The supervisor's job is to make sure everyone in the organization follows its rules, procedures and policies. Every organization has some rules and procedures that describe how it wants things handled, the objectives of the job, descriptions of duties, acceptable and unacceptable behaviors, the range of behavior between unacceptable and acceptable, the "way things are to be done around here," and so on.

Sometimes, these rules and procedures are set forth in detailed personnel manuals, policy handbooks or labor union agreements. Work orders and work assignments also set forth basic rules and procedures. It is important that the supervisor:
- know what the rules and procedures are.
- understand their purposes.
- communicate the rules and reasons to employees.

As the keeper of the rules and procedures, the supervisor is both the source of knowledge on the rules and the enforcer of those rules. When there is a labor agreement, the supervisor should know the contents of that agreement at least as well as the union shop steward. In a sense, both have some of the same job duties.

- Both the supervisor and the shop steward are obligated to see that the union agreement, the mutually accepted terms and conditions of employment, are met.
- Both the supervisor and the shop steward should know the rules of the labor agreement. If either is ignorant of the rules, trouble can develop.

Perhaps the most frequent cause of formal grievances under a labor agreement is the failure on the part of the steward, employee or supervisor to understand the rules of the labor agreement. If you, as a supervisor, take the position that the labor agreement is none of your business, you're in for trouble, and you may find the shop steward running your workplace. On the other hand, if you take the time to learn the agreement and how to apply it, you will have far less difficulty in dealing with the union and your employees.

The role of the supervisor is to communicate rules and procedures to staff and make sure they are understood. (Detailed information on communication will be covered in Chapter 6, Communication.) The critical point to remember is that the obligation to communicate rests first and foremost with the supervisor. The supervisor must communicate the rules and then listen and observe for understanding. Often it is helpful to ask your employees to repeat the gist of what you communicate to them as far as rules and procedures. Then you have the chance to see whether they listened to you and understood what you were saying.

Are the rules being followed? If not, maybe the employees simply forgot.

Other times, staff may try to find shortcuts around inconvenient rules and procedures—one of the most common causes of safety violations. Therefore, handing out the rules and then assuming they are being followed is not effective. The supervisor must be out on the floor, in the lab or at the loading dock to observe those whom you supervise. This is a constant, ongoing process. Direct and frequent observation of procedures and inspection of work is the only way you will ever know if the rules are really being followed. And your employees will respect you for doing your job.

Praising employees for their good or appropriate behavior is more often neglected than carried out. Yet, praise is an effective motivator. It is always a good idea to catch your employees doing things the right way! It is the supervisor's role to reinforce adherence to the rules. It is also your role to correct employees who are not in compliance. For many supervisors, both of these things seem difficult to do. Some supervisors tend to avoid confrontation with employees when they see objectionable behavior. They might prefer to wish away the problem rather than to confront it. That doesn't work. What works is to immediately confront the problem and suggest an immediate remedy. (There is more on this in Chapter 6, Communication, and Chapter 10, Measuring Performance).

Figure 2-1.

What if I have an employee that can't or won't follow a company rule based on cultural or religious beliefs?

This is a very good question about a situation that many supervisors may face given the diverse nature of today's workforce. The simple answer to this question is "it depends." Generally speaking, if the individual's cultural or religious beliefs can be accommodated without causing the company undo hardship or a safety hazard, the request should be accommodated. For example, a company may require a uniform that includes a hat. One of your employees can wear the whole uniform, but the hat, due to a cultural tradition of wearing a turban. This accommodation can probably be made without being too disruptive to the workplace. On the other hand, if a hard hat is required for safety reasons, the rule shouldn't be disregarded.

If your company has a Human Resources (HR) Department, any requests by employees that may violate company rules or procedures should be run by them first. If you don't have a HR Department, your boss should at least review the situation.

Maintainer of a Safe and Productive Workplace

Being the keeper of rules and procedures, you almost automatically become the maintainer of a safe workplace, since safety is usually a matter of regularly following simple but important rules and procedures and applying a little common sense. This includes working to prevent accidents. Supervisors must be aware of observable human factors that can cause accidents, such as fatigue, substance abuse, stress or preoccupation with something other than the task at hand.

The supervisor must also know of hazardous conditions in the workplace in order to correct them. If immediate correction isn't possible, the supervisor must warn employees and establish adequate precautions. Sometimes having hazardous materials around is unavoidable. If that's the case, label them, make sure the employees are aware of the dangers and make sure that only those authorized to work with or move the materials do so. It is also important to make sure that the organization keeps the Material Safety Data Sheets (MSDSs) available in a convenient location for each chemical stored in the facility and/or used in the manufacturing processes there. The MSDS is a guide to chemical exposure and the corrective steps to take to avoid overexposure. The worksite's MSDSs should be conveniently located and easily accessed by every employee at the worksite.

As the maintainer of a safe workplace, the supervisor also must be familiar with special requirements of hazardous materials, storage regulations, the Right-to-Know Act, the general provisions of the Occupational Safety and Health Act (OSHAct) and first aid procedures. If your company has a Human Resources Department, ask them if they provide any special training on these topics. If not, contact the U.S. Occupational Safety and Health Administration (OSHA), the National Safety Council or the National Institute for Occupational Safety and Health (NIOSH) for training and booklets on these subjects. See Appendix B, Resources for Supervisors, at the end of this book for more information.

Trainer of Employees

Supervisors have to do a lot of training. Some of it is direct, on-the-job training, such as teaching your new employee how to use the new accounting software. Another kind of training can be what is called *modeling*. People see how you act, how you move, how you dress, how you handle your job. Good or bad, you serve as a model for your staff and you train them with your actions. Obviously, you must set a good example.

Some supervisors once followed the "sink or swim" approach with new employees. Without training, most employees will sink. In today's tight, competitive labor market, allowing employees to fail as a result of no training, is a very costly mistake.

The most common ways supervisors provide training in the workplace is by:
- orienting and instructing new employees.
- setting a good example to follow.
- allowing employees to practice new skills.
- observing employee skills and providing positive feedback or corrections.

Supervisors also should orient employees to the goals and standards of the organization, the purpose of the employee's job and the performance expectations in that job. Supervisors should emphasize to new employees that safety is part of the job and will be a factor in performance evaluation.

Advocate for the Workforce

Because supervisors know the needs of their employees better than anyone else in management, they often find themselves serving as an advocate for the workforce. Supervisors can weed through any complaints or issues that employees have and decide which of these to handle directly and which ones may need to be communicated to upper management. Since it is one of your roles to get the best production from your team, you must be aware of any workplace factors that may negatively affect productivity.

Being an advocate means being attuned to employee needs. Listen, ask and gather information from employees. Establish many avenues for your employees to be able to communicate concerns or needs to you. Keep an open door policy and encourage your employees to talk to you freely about the job and any ideas they may have to improve the safety and productivity of your worksite.

The supervisor actually acts as a liaison or communication link between upper management and the workforce. This is a critical link, and without it, the company wouldn't be able to function. The supervisor represents the employees and their needs to upper management. Supervisors must insure that employees have the proper resources (i.e., computers, tools, uniforms, and safety equipment, etc.) to perform productively and safely.

Obviously, you must selectively express employee concerns with management. You must also manage your employee's expectations regarding their concerns. Just because you take one of their concerns to management, doesn't mean there will be an immediate solution. You may also find that management won't agree with the concern. That doesn't mean the problem has disappeared or that you should give up if you think the issue is important.

The best approach is to listen to management's concerns, do more homework, and see if you can make another proposal that would answer both your workgroup and management issues.

Sometimes, of course, you have to respect management's wishes and drop the issue. Management might not always be ready to make certain changes, even if you believe the changes to be good ones. Knowing your organization and when the time is right is also part of being a good supervisor.

Representative of the Organization

Supervisors must stand for and be able to communicate the company's objectives, vision and mission, priorities, expectations, concerns and even appreciation. Employees look to their supervisor for guidance on what the company really is doing, what it wants its employees to do and what it hopes to achieve.

Company policies must be the supervisor's policies, or ultimately employees will lose respect for the supervisor's authority. Taking a position such as, "*Well, that's what they told us to do, but I think we can do it my way instead,*" means you, the supervisor, do not respect company policies. You will ultimately be at odds with your manager, and you will lose. When you lose like that you also lose the respect of those you supervise.

As representative of the organization, it is your responsibility to make the company resources known and available to employees. Keep your employees informed about on-site training provided by your organization and encourage them to attend the training that you think will be beneficial for them. Be familiar with employee benefits. Know what kind of counseling is available for various personal problems such as substance abuse, marital problems, childcare and so on. To your employees, you are the representative of the organization and their personal connection with the company.

Figure 2-2.

What if there are a lot of things the company does that I disagree with? In fact, I'm looking for another job outside my current employer?

This is a tough situation to be in. First and foremost, remember to maintain your professionalism. This usually means keeping your own feelings to yourself and doing your best to represent the Company's wishes to employees. For example, due to financial constraints your organization has just reduced its health benefits. This change affects you as well, but it's never a good idea to act disgruntled in front of your employees.

If you decide to look for a new job, keep this decision confidential until you're ready to officially announce your resignation. And even then, never "burn the bridge" with your current employer by badmouthing management as you exit. It does nothing to enhance your professional reputation and remember, you will need a positive reference from all prior employers.

Case Study

Finer Points of Fast Food

Sarah Melton has recently been promoted to the second shift supervisor at the local fast-food restaurant in her inner city neighborhood. Most of her employees have been high school students. However, Sarah is having trouble with high turnover, employees showing up late (often not in uniform), and not following other basic rules and procedures. Sarah has also noticed that many of their non-English speaking customers have stopped frequenting their restaurant. All of her employees only speak English, and have a hard time serving their Polish-speaking customers.

It's even been hard for Sarah to get to work on time, due to her class schedule at the junior college. She thinks she has exhausted the labor pool of high school students but she has two vacancies on her shift that she needs to fill as soon as possible. There are no written rules and procedures—employees are expected to memorize what their supervisor tells them...

- What ideas do you have to help Sarah with hiring?
- How can she stop employees coming in late, if she also is guilty of the same thing?
- What can she do about employees who don't follow the fast food chain's other procedures?
- How can she help better serve the Polish-speaking customers, so the restaurant doesn't lose any more valuable customers?

Of course, you must also keep in mind that the supervisor is management, the company, in the eyes of many employees. It is always important to set an example that expresses a positive relationship with the organization.

Conclusion

As we've covered in the first two chapters of this book, the front-line responsibilities of the supervisor, regardless of the size of the organization or the industry, are extremely important to the organization. It truly is a juggling act for the supervisor to be able to handle the just the seven roles that this chapter has reviewed. But all of these roles are important; and with a little patience and practice, you will be on the way to becoming a great supervisor. Look at the case study to get some more ideas.

Review Questions

1. Why is the supervisor's role so important in today's companies with a knowledge-driven strategy?

2. What are the seven roles of a successful supervisor? What are the characteristics of each?

3 Supervisors, Employment and Workplace Law

by Joy Colwell, JD

What Will I Learn in This Chapter?

In this chapter we deal with some of the more difficult issues facing supervisors today, including:

- the most important laws that affect employees in U.S.-owned companies, like the antidiscrimination laws, minimum wage and overtime laws, and laws on workplace safety and union activities
- complying with employment or workplace law
- assuring your employees comply with the laws
- sending a consistent message that the law is the law and must be respected
- overviews of some voluntary standards and guidelines that affect supervisors

Employment Laws Affecting Your Employees

We will review key parts of two kinds of laws you must know about: *employment law* and *workplace law*. In this chapter we only look at the major laws. There are so many laws that provide grounds for a lawsuit by an employee that it is impossible to cover them all here. Some of these laws include:

- Title VII of the Civil Rights Act of 1964
- Age Discrimination in Employment Act
- Americans with Disabilities Act
- USERRA (concerning military status and obligations)
- Family and Medical Leave Act
- Bankruptcy Code (termination for having filed bankruptcy)
- Immigration Reform and Control Act (national origin discrimination)
- ERISA/COBRA (benefits)
- Constitution (First Amendment free speech rights, due process under the Fourteenth Amendment)
- 42 USC Section 1981 (race discrimination)
- Fair Labor Standards Act
- National Labor Relations Act
- OSHAct
- EPA regulations
- MSHA regulations
- DOT regulations
- U. S. Coast Guard regulations
- State laws on civil rights
- State tort laws, including wrongful discharge
- U. S. Rehabilitation Act of 1973

Employment law is the term generally used for federal and state laws that regulate possibly discriminatory employer behavior toward workers. This covers such laws as:
- Title VII of the Civil Rights Act of 1964
- Pregnancy Discrimination Act of 1978 (amendment to Title VII)
- Civil Rights Act of 1964 (EEOC)
- The Civil Rights Act of 1991
- Age Discrimination in Employment Act of 1967 (ADEA)
- Rehabilitation Act of 1973
- The Americans with Disabilities Act of 1990
- The Family and Medical Leave Act of 1993
- State laws dealing with discrimination in the workplace

Workplace law is the term generally applied to federal and state laws that regulate employer behavior in regard to democratic rights of workers: the relationship between the employer, employee and labor organization; and the relationship between the employer and employees. This covers such laws as:
- Williams-Steiger Occupational Safety and Health Act
- The Mine Safety and Health Act (MSHA)
- Department of Transportation (DOT) (Hours of work)
- The Environmental Protection Agency (EPA) (Community Right-to-Know)
- Fair Labor Standards Act, 1938 (FLSA)
- Equal Pay Act, 1963 (an amendment to the FLSA)
- National Labor Relations Act (NLRA)

There are many more workplace laws that impact on the employer and the employee, but these usually don't involve the supervisor. For example, the minimum wage laws are important, but supervisors do not usually set wages. These laws have been around for many years and are usually not questioned. So except the more recent equal pay provisions, they aren't covered. Various pension laws and regulations are in this same category. In this book you will only find those laws that are relevant to supervisors. We will describe why the laws exist, the impact of the laws and your role in complying with and enforcing them.

What's Involved, and Why Should We Be Concerned?

As a supervisor you must be familiar with key aspects of these laws because your employer expects that. It's a very important part of your job. If you violate the employment or workplace laws, or allow those you supervise to violate them, you expose your employer to potential financial liability and damage to reputation. You may also have some personal liability if you or those working under your supervision commit acts declared illegal by employment or workplace laws, and a complaint or lawsuit is filed.

Background of Employment Law

Many employment laws have been passed by federal, state and local governments over the past 50 years that seek to stop and to correct various forms of discrimination against specific groups or classes of people. These groups are collectively referred to as *"protected classes."* The laws generally prohibit employment practices that discriminate based on race, religion, national origin, gender, age or status as a minority, veteran or disabled person (Figure 3-1). These protected classes have been selected for special focused protection under the law, because it has been found that these particular people have been or are being discriminated against.

You May Not Discriminate in Employment Practices Against Any Protected Classes

Background of Workplace Law

Workplace laws have generally been passed by governments because it is in the public interest to assure employees of the following:

- minimum employment conditions regarding wages, hours, benefits and working conditions
- safe working conditions regarding practices, materials, equipment, processes and procedures
- the right to representation by a labor organization of the employee's own choosing

Governments generally intervened to impose workplace laws because they found that employers were not uniformly providing these conditions, and that the employer/employee or the employee/union relationship needed to be regulated. Since governments in our country are elected by the people to represent the people, and since most of the legislative bodies had to vote in favor of these laws, our employment and workplace laws reflect the wishes of a majority of the people. Courts only step in to interpret these laws by applying the statutes to individual cases

Figure 3-1. It's the Law

You may not discriminate in employment practices against any protected classes.

That means, **no discrimination** based on:

- race/color
- nationality
- sex
- religion
- age (anyone 40 and older)
- mental or physical handicap
- veteran status

that come before them. Courts do not write those statutes. Employment and workplace law is present at the federal, state and local levels. Supervisors need to know what the laws say and how to abide by them. Simply put, the law is the law and one part of being a supervisor is to see that the law is followed in the workplace. Not following the law may result in a supervisor's liability to an employee whose rights have been violated, in addition to the organization's liability.

Most would say: The law is the law, and it is right! The workplace and employment laws protect employees (and ultimately, everyone is an employee, including top management). They are not to make life difficult for supervisors and employers. The laws are designed to prohibit past and even present wrongdoing by employers. The law sets a *minimum standard of behavior,* which means that if your conduct as a supervisor, and your employer's conduct as an employer, fall below the standard set by the law, you and/or your employer can be liable in monetary damages for failure to follow the law. Employees may be entitled to some or all of the following remedies for employers' failures to follow the laws:

- reinstatement
- hire
- promotion
- transfer
- back pay
- lost overtime
- back benefits
- front pay
- compensatory damages
- punitive damages
- pre-judgment and/or post-judgment interest
- attorney's fees, and costs, as well as injunctive relief

The law sets out minimum standards of behavior, but it does not set forth guidelines for best management practices. Ultimately the law tries to ensure that employers look beyond superficial characteristics like age, gender, race, etc. and focus on each employee's skills, competencies, merits, etc.

We do need to recognize that these workplace and employment laws arose out of practices:

- endangering children's health and preventing their education by making them work long hours in unsafe conditions at below standard rates of pay.
- setting up employer-controlled unions to prevent employees from organizing their own union.
- paying minorities and females less for doing the same job as white men.
- discriminating in hiring practices based on a person's race, color, creed, national origin and sex.
- terminating older workers just because they were old or because the employer could hire younger workers for a lower salary or wage.
- endangering employees through unsafe working conditions or failure to inform them of hazardous conditions or chemicals.

Thus our country enacted workplace and employment laws to protect both its employees and employers.

Employment Law

Here we list the eight federal employment discrimination laws every supervisor should know. We also discuss some representative state laws that go beyond the federal laws.

1. Title VII of the Civil Rights Act of 1964

This is the most important employment law. It defines what employers can't do in the area of the civil rights of protected classes. It seeks to prevent any discriminatory practice based on race, color, religion, sex or national origin. Under Title VII, the employer commits an unlawful employment practice (discrimination) if the employer or an agent, such as a supervisor, uses a person's race, color, religion, sex or national origin as a basis for:

- failing or refusing to hire an applicant for employment.
- discharging or otherwise disciplining an employee.
- determining an employee's compensation, including fringe benefits or other terms and conditions or privileges of employment.
- limiting, segregating or classifying an employee or an applicant for employment in a way that would tend to deprive him/her of an employment opportunity or otherwise adversely affect his/her status as an employee.

According to our U.S. laws, you cannot discriminate against an employee or applicant for employment, because he or she opposed an employment practice unlawful under Title VII, or filed a suit or complaint under Title VII. In other words, the law protects employees who exercise their rights under this law, by prohibiting discrimination against them.

Some employment practices stem from outmoded ideas about the roles of men and women—this is simply against the law. For example, giving traveling assignments only to a man because it might be difficult for the

Figure 3-2. Title VII of the Civil Rights Act of 1964

An employer may not use a person's race, color, religion, sex or national origin as a basis for:

- not hiring an applicant for employment.
- discharging or disciplining an employee.
- setting an employee's wages, benefits or working conditions.
- dealing with an employee or job applicant in a way that would deprive him/her of a job opportunity.
- discrimination against an employee or job applicant because he/she opposed an unlawful employment practice.

woman's family is discriminatory. (It may be as difficult for the man's family.) More importantly, travel experience is often a requirement for advancing to higher-level jobs. Thus, such treatment is not just ancient history, it's discriminatory and illegal.

Other discriminatory employment practices can reflect a *subconscious bias* or prejudice of a supervisor or employer. For example, a rule that ethnic employees can't speak their own language (unless you can prove it actually affects operational efficiency or safety) is discriminatory. The rule, on its face, singles out the group involved and deprives them as a class (Figure 3-2).

2. Pregnancy Discrimination Act of 1978

This law is an amendment to Title VII and was adopted because many employers denied medical benefits and leave for pregnancy. The law has three very straightforward key principles that must be applied in the workplace (Figure 3-3).

1. A pregnant woman should be treated the same as any other applicant or employee.
2. Pregnancy should be treated the same as any other temporary disability.
3. A pregnant woman does need not to receive preferential treatment.

Figure 3-3. Pregnancy Discrimination Act, 1978 (Amendment to Title VII)

Three Rules for Supervisors:

1. A pregnant woman should be treated the same as any other applicant or employee.
2. Pregnancy is to be treated the same as any other temporary disability.
3. A pregnant woman does not need to be given preferential treatment.

3. U.S. Civil Rights Act of 1964 and Civil Rights Act of 1991

U.S. Civil Rights Act of 1964

Much more than Title VII was included in the U.S. Civil Rights Act of 1964. It is the basic law that seeks to correct a number of wrongs relating to voting rights, public access rights, education, etc. In addition to the Title VII provisions we have described, the Civil Rights Act also prohibits harassment in employment because of one's sex, race, color, religion or national origin. Sexual harassment has been a widely discussed issue, although all other forms of employment harassment of protected classes are covered under the same mandate, such as race, color, religion, national origin and age. Harassment, while not specifically mentioned in the law, is included in the mandate as a result of judicial interpretation. Putting it simply: it is unlawful to harass a person at work or in connection with work because of or with regard to sex, race, color, religion, national origin or age (Figure 3-4). While U.S. (federal) law does not prohibit simple teasing or offhand comments, a pattern of remarks, or serious incidents, may create a hostile work environment and create liability for discrimination. An employer's anti-harassment policy should make it clear that harassment based on race, sex, religion, national origin, age or disability will not be tolerated. See the section on sexual harassment later in this chapter for more information.

Figure 3-4. Civil Rights Act, 1964

It is against the law for: an employer an agent of an employer (such as a supervisor) a fellow employee to harass any employee because of or with regard to

- sex
- race
- color
- religion
- national origin
- age

U.S. Civil Rights Act of 1991

The Civil Rights Act of 1991 amends the Civil Rights Act of 1964. In addition to the remedies provided by the 1964 Act, it provides for compensatory and punitive damages for intentional acts of discrimination. Damages recoverable under the Act are limited, depending on the size (number of employees) of the

Table 3-A. Damages under the U.S. Civil Rights Act of 1991

Up to 100 employees	$ 50,000
100-200 employees	$100,000
201-500 employees	$200,000
501 or more employees	$300,000

organization. The highest limit on damages is $300,000.00. Employees complaining of discrimination are entitled to a jury trial.

4. U.S. Age Discrimination in Employment Act of 1967

The U.S. Age Discrimination in Employment Act of 1967 (ADEA) essentially extends Title VII coverage to the protected class of age those 40 years of age and older. Under ADEA, employers or their agents, such as supervisors, commit an unlawful employment practice if they use an individual's age as a basis for:

- failing or refusing to hire an applicant for employment.
- discharging or otherwise disciplining an employee.
- determining an employee's compensation or other terms, conditions or privileges of employment on age.
- limiting, segregating or classifying employees or applicants for employment in a way that would tend to deprive them of an employment opportunity or otherwise adversely affect their status as an employee.
- reducing the wage rate of an employee in order to comply with other requirements under the ADEA.
- discriminating against employees or applicants for employment because they opposed an employment practice unlawful under the ADEA, or because they filed a charge, testified, assisted or participated in an

---

Figure 3-5. Age Discrimination in Employment Act, 1967 (ADEA)

No one can:

- fail or refuse to hire an applicant for employment because of age.
- discharge or discipline an employee because of age.
- base an employee's compensation or other terms, conditions or privileges of employment on age.
- limit, segregate or classify employees or applicants for employment in a way that would tend to deprive them of a job or adversely affect their status as an employee because of age.
- reduce the wage rate of an employee to meet other requirements under the ADEA.
- discriminate against employees or applicants because they opposed an employment practice unlawful under ADEA or filed a charge, testified, assisted or participated in an investigation under ADEA.
- place an employment notice or advertisement indicating a preference limitation or specification based on age.

investigation, proceeding or litigation under the ADEA.
- selecting younger employees by employment notices or advertisements indicating a preference limitation or specification based on age (Figure 3-5).

5. The U.S. Rehabilitation Act of 1973

The U.S. Rehabilitation Act of 1973 covers the rights of disabled people; it establishes basic rights, including public access to facilities and the opportunity to perform a job in the federal sector (federal contractors or those who receive federal funds). In the workplace, the law calls for affirmative action for the disabled. It defines *disabled* as anyone who (1) has a physical or mental impairment, (2) has a record of such impairment or (3) is regarded as having such impairment. There can be challenges in matching existing abilities of disabled workers and available jobs. Most of those challenges come from not knowing how to design the job and worksite to accommodate workers with disabilities. Often organizations assume that doing so is very expensive, when usually an inexpensive fix will work. This Act clearly spells out the rules for employers and their supervisors to follow.

- DO evaluate disabled applicants in terms of accommodations, such as modifications in equipment that can be made to enable them to fill the job.
- DO see each disabled applicant as an individual with a unique combination of strengths and weaknesses and try to match this combination with a job in your unit.
- DO consider redesigning a job so a disabled worker can do it.
- DO give newly hired disabled employees close attention at first to see how they're adjusting to the job and then make job modifications, if necessary.
- DO let disabled employees know you expect a full day's work, just as you do from any other employee.

- **DO** consider disabled employees for promotion, just as you do other employees.
- **DO** consider a disabled applicant in terms of actual job requirements.
- **DO NOT** refuse to hire a disabled applicant who is otherwise qualified for the job.
- **DO NOT** automatically disqualify an applicant with a disability.
- **DO NOT** use rigid physical requirements that would disqualify disabled applicants, unless they're actually job-related.

Though it is not spelled out in the Act, we recommend that you take steps to promote acceptance of disabled employees by the other workers in your unit. For example, urge them to include disabled coworkers in coffee breaks and other social activities. This will encourage acceptance of disabled coworkers and prevent workplace situations that might lead to employee claims of discrimination.

6. U.S. Americans with Disabilities Act

The U.S. Americans with Disabilities Act (ADA) states that any organization with 15 or more employees can't discriminate in employment decisions against qualified persons with disabilities. (The ADA covers lots more, but we'll cover what affects you the supervisor directly). Employers must provide reasonable accommodation for workers with disabilities. A *qualified individual with a disability* is a person who meets the legitimate skill, experience, education or other requirements of the job, and who can perform the basic functions of the job, with or without a reasonable accommodation.

The definition of *disabled* is similar to that in the Rehabilitation Act. A person is disabled if he or she has a physical or mental impairment which substantially limits one or more major life activities, or has a record of such impairment, or is regarded as having such impairment. Whether a person

has a disability must take into account the effect of "*mitigating measures*"–
if a person has little or no difficulty performing any major life activity
because he or she uses a mitigating measure, then that person will not
meet the ADA's definition of disability. Examples of a mitigating measure
is taking medication to control an illness or using eyeglasses to correct a
visual problem.

What is *reasonable accommodation*? Reasonable accommodation can be:
- changes to the job application process.
- changes to the work environment or to the way a job is usually done.
- changes to equipment.
- changes to allow an employee with a disability to enjoy the equal benefits and privileges of employment (such as access to training).
- restructuring a job.
- unpaid leave.
- modified schedules.
- modified workplace policies.
- reassignment to a vacant position.

Reasonable accommodation is limited by the concept of *undue hardship*. This means that an employer is not required to provide an accommodation that causes undue hardship, or significant difficulty or expense. To figure out if an accommodation causes undue hardship, look at the:
- nature and cost of the accommodation needed.
- overall financial resources of the business.
- number of persons employed by the business.
- effect on the resources and expenses of the business.
- impact of the accommodation on the business.
- whether there are outside resources (such as government grants or funding) that can pay for the accommodation.

The ADA requires organizations to keep employees' medical information confidential. It also impacts pre-employment physicals and the questions that can be asked in an interview. An employer cannot ask before someone is hired whether, and to what extent, a candidate is disabled. An employer can ask if the employee can perform particular job functions; but such questions should focus on essential functions of the job. Medical examinations can be given only with a conditional job offer, and only if all entering employees in the category are required to have the examination.

It's up to the employee to let the employer/supervisor know that he or she needs an adjustment at work for a reason related to a medical condition. The employee does not need to refer to the Act or use the phrase "reasonable accommodation". An organization does not have to make the specific accommodation requested by the employee, so long as the chosen accommodation is effective. The organization also does not have to provide personal use items, such as eyeglasses, wheelchairs, etc., to the employee.

The requirements of the ADA can overlap with workers' compensation laws, so be sure to consult your HR department, or get legal advice when there are questions.

7. U.S. Family and Medical Leave Act of 1993

The U.S. Family and Medical Leave Act of 1993 (FMLA) requires covered employers to provide up to 12 weeks of unpaid leave during any 12-month period to qualifying employees. The Act entitles employees to take reasonable leave for:

- medical reasons.
- birth or adoption of a child
- the care of a child, spouse or parent who has a serious health condition.

The Act applies to employers with 50 or more employees. There is also an "*hours of service requirement*" for employees (1,250 hours in the previous 12-month period). The intersection of the FMLA and ADA laws can cause complicated legal issues. Be sure to consult your HR department or obtain legal advice for questions in this area.

8. State and Local Laws

All states, most major cities and many large counties have adopted stringent employment laws generally patterned after the U.S. (federal) laws; but these state and local laws often extend rights to areas not covered by the federal laws. Sometimes these laws increase rights or benefits for protected classes or add more penalties against employers for violations of the laws. Because we don't have the space to cover all laws enacted by all U.S. states, cities and counties, we will use some employments laws from the states of Illinois and California, as examples of how state laws can get more specific than U.S. (federal) laws.

Example: Illinois Employment Law

The State of Illinois has a Human Rights Act that spells out many protections for employees. It's modeled on the 1991 U.S. Civil Rights Act, but adds some specific areas. Under the Illinois Human Rights Act an organization commits an unlawful employment practice if it considers certain things in connection with hiring decisions. Specifically, employers may not (1) refuse to hire on the basis of or (2) segregate or act without respect to any protected classes in any of the following employment actions:
- recruitment
- hiring
- promotion
- renewal of employment
- selection for training or apprenticeship

- discharge
- discipline
- tenure
- terms, conditions or privileges of employment.

Illinois law prohibits discrimination or employment decisions based on:
- race
- color
- religion
- national origin
- ancestry
- age (40 years old or older)
- sex
- marital status
- disability (physical or mental)
- unfavorable discharge from military service
- military status
- sexual harassment
- use of lawful products (such as tobacco).

If you compare these to the laws shown in Figures 3-1 to 3-5, you'll see many additional categories, such as marital status and unfavorable discharge. That Illinois' law has more items covered and details of categories is common in state employment laws. This is just one of Illinois' employment laws.

Example: California Employment Law

The State of California has lots of employment laws, most of them patterned after the federal laws, but again, the state laws significantly extend or specify employee rights. For example, California prohibits discrimination on the

grounds of:
- race
- religious creed
- color
- national origin
- ancestry
- physical or mental disability
- medical condition
- marital status
- pregnancy, childbirth, or related medical condition
- sex
- sexual orientation
- age (40 years old and older)
- political activities or affiliations
- involvement in AIDS research.

Looking at the State of California sexual harassment law, we see that California prohibits sexual harassment in employment and defines harassment with detail as follows.

> *"Harassment is:*
> 1. *verbal harassment, such as epithets, derogatory comments or slurs;*
> 2. *physical harassment, such as assault, impeding or blocking movement, or any physical interference with normal work or movement;*
> 3. *visual forms of harassment, such as derogatory posters, cartoons or drawings;*
> 4. *demand for sexual favors, such as unwanted sexual advances that condition an employment benefit upon an exchange of favors."*

That's pretty clear, isn't it? It's important for a supervisor to be aware of

> ### Figure 3-6. What Is Discrimination?
>
> It's legal to discriminate **among employees**; it's not legal to discriminate **against employees**.
>
> In hiring, promotion and other areas of employment, you may discriminate between employees on the basis of:
> - skills
> - education
> - experience
> - ability
> - personal preference.
>
> But this discrimination cannot be based on:
> - race
> - color
> - national origin
> - sex
> - religion
> - age
> - mental or physical handicap
> - veteran status.

state and local laws and regulations on employment. The combination of federal, state and local laws that regulate the protection of employee classes means they are really protected, and it is part of your job to see to it that the laws are respected and obeyed by you and your staff.

What Does This Mean to You?

Discrimination

Discrimination, as described in the various employment laws, is against the law (Figure 3-6). Legally, discrimination means all actions taken against individuals in the protected classes that have the effect of treating them disadvantageously and differently from other people not in the same category (Figure 3-7). Protected classes, again, are based on race, color, national origin, sex, religion, age, mental or physical disability and veteran status.

It's really not hard to know or sense when an employer is discriminating against employees in a manner that is against the law, but it's often hard to prove. That's why governments set up agencies such as the U.S. Equal Employment Opportunity Commission (EEOC) to enforce the law and provide assistance to employees who feel they have been the victims of discrimination. Most local governments (states, counties and cities) also have organizations to assist in enforcing their equal employment opportunity laws.

Generally, these agencies and the courts use three major principles to determine if employers discriminated against employees:

1. *The principle of discrimination by effect, even if not intended.* Certain acts can constitute unlawful discrimination because of their effect on protected classes, even if not purposeful or intended.

    For example, a company has a policy of following the EEO law and there are significant numbers of African-Americans in the natural hiring area of the company. African-Americans did apply for various jobs with the company, but it turns out that over a period of time (usually years) the company did not hire any African-Americans. There is a presumption that discrimination has occurred, whether the company intended it or not.

> **Figure 3-7. Discrimination in Employment**
>
> Discrimination: actions against protected classes which treat them disadvantageously and differently from other people.

2. *The principle of unequal or disparate treatment has evolved from EEO law enforcement.* If similarly situated or equally qualified persons receive unequal treatment, discrimination has occurred. If the person who has suffered such discrimination is in a protected class, then the action was unlawful.

    For example, assume that Jim and Jane are both laboratory technicians in a pharmaceutical company and have been employed for about the same length of time. They do very similar work, with a few minor differences in duties. Jim, however, earns $1.50 per hour more than Jane. On its face, that's unequal or disparate treatment of a member of a protected class.

3. *The principle of unequal or disparate impact.* When a practice or procedure appears neutral on its face, but when applied it has a greater effect on

members of a protected class, it constitutes unequal or disparate impact. A neutral rule or policy has a discriminatory effect.

For example, a company adopts a medical policy that does not pay benefits covering liver transplants, heart transplants or pregnancy (before the Pregnancy Discrimination Act of 1978). Men and women have livers and hearts, so that's equal. However, not many men get pregnant, so there is an unequal or disparate impact on a protected class. In fact, that's an example of why the Pregnancy Discrimination Act of 1978 was adopted. Or consider the case of a minimum height requirement for a job. Since women are generally shorter than men, few or no women will qualify for the job. Unless the minimum height is required for appropriate job performance, the height requirement may be discriminatory on the basis of gender, even though it does not refer to gender at all.

It is through the application of these three principles that EEO enforcement agencies determine whether the law is being broken in those cases where it is difficult to prove (Figure 3-8).

> ### Figure 3-8. Proving the Hard Cases
>
> Three key principles used by EEO enforcement agencies to establish discrimination when it's not so obvious:
>
> **1. Discrimination by effect, even if not intended**
> Certain acts can be unlawful discrimination because of their effect on protected classes, even if the effect was not purposeful or intended.
>
> **2. Unequal or disparate treatment**
> If similarly situated or equally qualified persons receive unequal treatment, discrimination has occurred. If the suffering person is in a protected class, then the action was unlawful.
>
> **3. Unequal or disparate impact**
> When a practice or procedure appears neutral on its face, but its application falls more heavily on members of a protected class, it is unlawful.

Stereotypes

One key thing the law emphasizes is that employment decisions cannot be based on stereotypes or class assumptions. You must not assume certain kinds of people are better at some things or do not like to do other things. For example, you must not assume that women would not be interested in a manual job performed out of doors, (women and men both have been doing that sort of work for centuries), or that women aren't interested in long-range career paths, or that women have a much higher turnover rate than men (not true.). Those are all stereotypes that have no foundation in fact. Thinking based on stereotypes will almost always get you in real trouble both in terms of the law and because they will often lead you to select the wrong people for a job. All employment-related decisions must be based on individual merit rather than stereotypes or class assumptions (Figure 3-9).

Figure 3-9. Get Rid of Stereotypes

All employment-related decisions must be based on individual merit rather than stereotypes or class assumptions.

Reasonable Accommodation for Religious Discrimination or Disability Under the Rehabilitation Act

Problems relating to discrimination against the disabled under the Rehabilitation Act or people practicing a particular religion almost always involve reasonable accommodation. Under the law, an employer must provide reasonable accommodation in these two cases. This means that the job environment and schedules must be tailored to make it possible for disabled or religious people to work where reasonably practical. This should be done without unreasonable hardship to the employer and/or fellow workers. As an example, non-Christian employees should be allowed to celebrate their religious holidays if Christian employees are allowed to celebrate Christian holidays (Figure 3-10). The law on reasonable accommodation under the ADA requires that employers generally go further in accommodating needs of their disabled employees than employers need to go to accommodate employee's religious practices. See the preceding section on the Rehabilitation Act to see which employers are covered by that Act.

> **Figure 3-10. Reasonable Accommodation of Religion and Handicaps Under the Rehabilitation Act**
>
> - Adjust the job environment and schedules to the needs of disabled or religious workers where reasonably practical.
>
> - This should be done without unreasonable hardship to the employer and/or fellow workers.

The question is: What is reasonable? It is what it seems it would be. For example, if your business happened to have its peak periods on Friday evenings and all day Saturday, and you required that everybody work these days, you could probably make a case that letting anyone off then is unreasonable. But if any employees were allowed off Friday evening and Saturday, it would certainly be unreasonable to refuse to give that time off to an employee who observes those times as their Sabbath—for example, Jewish, Muslim or Seventh Day Adventist employees. For them, Friday evening and Saturday are days of rest; the same as Sunday is to many Christians. An employer can claim undue hardship for religious accommodation if allowing the accommodation requires more than ordinary administrative costs. It also is undue hardship if the accommodation requires changing a bona fide seniority system by denying another employee a job or shift preference guaranteed by the seniority system.

Accommodating a job and/or the workplace for disabled workers is treated similarly under the Rehabilitation Act. If a blind person applies for a job as a typist, and shows that with special equipment he/she can perform the work, the employer should be able to reasonably accommodate this. The equipment may take a little more space, and the effort may take a little longer, but that is what reasonable accommodation implies. Employers are not required to accommodate in these instances if accommodation creates unreasonable costs or unreasonable hardship to the employer or fellow workers. (See the previous discussion of the ADA, about higher standards for accommodations under that Act).

Sexual Harassment

The laws regarding sexual harassment sometimes give some male supervisors and managers particular problems. They can mix up personal feelings and needs with appropriate workplace behavior. Many supervisors find it difficult to enforce appropriate behavior on this issue because of what they may see as custom and practice. However, the reality is that sexual harassment in the workplace is against the law. The inappropriate behavior must be corrected or the offending employee dismissed. In addition, the company and its agent (often a supervisor as an individual) can be held liable for wrongs committed by the offender.

The Equal Employment Opportunity Commission (EEOC) provides very clear guidelines on sex harassment:

> *"Unwelcome sexual advances, requests for sexual favors and other verbal or physical conduct of a sexual nature constitute sexual harassment when (1) submission to such conduct is made a condition of employment, (2) submission to or rejection of such conduct is used as the basis for employment decisions or (3) such conduct has the purpose or effect of unreasonably interfering with an individual's work performance or creating an intimidating, hostile or offensive working environment."*

The first two of these three guidelines are obvious, and most people understand them. The third guideline takes matters a step further. The question isn't whether the offender intended a sexual remark to be harassing; it is how the reasonable employee who was the object of the remark perceived it. The moral of that is clear: Cut it out. Your organization should have:

1. A clear-cut policy for handling sexual harassment claims.
2. There should be more than one person available who you can report

> ### Figure 3-11. Rules for Avoiding Harassment Charges
>
> - DO set a good example as a supervisor.
> - DO take complaints seriously, even if your first judgment is that the complaint is trivial or unwarranted.
> - DO investigate complaints and take corrective action.
> - DO know your company's policy on harassment of employees and communicate this to your staff.
> - DO treat these matters confidentially and delicately.
> - DO make sure that your employees know how to file a grievance or complaint and that they are encouraged to do so if harassment is occurring.
> - DO NOT use your position as supervisor to request personal favors of any kind.
> - DO NOT wait for a complaint if you personally observe offensive behavior.

harassment claims to.

3. Harassment claims should be investigated thoroughly and promptly, with the appropriate action taken.

If an organization does not have a policy for reporting and investigating sexual harassment claims or does not address employees' claims of harassment, it and the employees involved (including the supervisor) may be held legally liable.

Age and Other Forms of Harassment

Complaints under the U.S. Age Discrimination in Employment Act (ADEA) are growing rapidly. This is because of the changing workforce—older people who choose to stay in the workforce as they learn and use their rights under ADEA. Under the ADEA, an employer has an affirmative duty to keep the work environment free from age harassment, including intimidation or insults. Illegal age harassment may involve direct bias, such as a supervisor telling jokes about older employees and stating that, "*You can't teach an old dog new tricks*". Other forms of harassment include assigning an older employee to less desirable work, calling someone "*Pops*," or making other negative references to the individual's age. Just as with other forms of harassment, an employer is liable for harassment by co-workers as well as by supervisors.

The following guidelines will help you avoid age discrimination:
- Disregard age in making all personnel decisions, whether it's hiring,

promotion, termination or job duties and assignments.
- Review policy to be sure it does not discriminate against those over age 40, even if the policy is applied neutrally to all employees, unless you are prepared to prove it's a necessity on the job. (Example: high physical standards required for a job.)
- Avoid age-based criteria in hiring selection, such as young and attractive, youthful appearance or recent college graduate.
- Prepare a written explanation of why an older employee was rejected for promotion stating the business reason for the rejection.
- If an older employee is terminated for poor performance or some factor other than age, have full documentation to support this action.

Employers must not retaliate against employees for filing discrimination or other employment law complaints, if an employee feels discriminated against, he/she has the right to bring up the matter with the supervisor, other persons in management or a government agency. Any retaliation for making a complaint is strictly illegal. Whether the retaliation is obvious (discharge) or subtle (denying a merit increase due to an employee's uncooperativeness), it is illegal. Complaints should not be viewed as a sign of disloyalty. They should be taken seriously and investigated objectively.

Questions About Harassment

Essentially, harassment is illegal. That means harassment related to race, sex, age, disability, etc. If you see an employee harassing another employee, confront the behavior and stop it. Check your own habits. For example, calling white employees by last names, but African-American employees by first names is a common form of harassment because it is demeaning, intentional or not (Figure 3-11).

Let's take a look at some of the questions you might have about harassment in the workplace. These questions are based on a list developed by the Equal Employment Advisory Council, an organization that assists employers in enforcing the Equal Employment Opportunity laws.

Q What should I tell my employees about harassment?

A Tell employees that harassment of any form (racial, sexual, national origin, etc.) is a violation of the company's policy on discrimination. Refer them to the letter on company bulletin boards or the company policy manual that spells out the implications of this policy. Pass on to them the definition of harassment given in this chapter and offer to answer any questions they may have on the subject.

Q What impact does harassment have on our workforce?

A Aside from obvious legal liabilities, it reduces the effectiveness and productivity of the workforce. It may also increase turnover and cause an organization to lose good employees. When people are not accepted or feel intimidated by the majority members of a work group, they are not motivated toward the full development of their potential or commitment to the company.

Q How does harassment differ from discrimination?

A For all practical purposes, they are the same. Harassment is a form of discrimination and is an unlawful practice.

Q When may male/female interpersonal relationships constitute harassment?

A Many actions can constitute harassment but a good rule to remember in this case is that harassment is present when one or the other individual indicates advances or attentions are unwanted and such advances or attentions continue. Touching, patting, and poking can all be harassment. If someone says stop, then stop.

Q How do you handle situations where two employees are dating, going steady, etc.?

A This has nothing to do with harassment. It is possible that employees working together may be romantically attracted to each other, and as long as this relationship does not interfere with their individual job performances, it is not a matter of company concern. If their relationship ends, and one employee keeps making unwelcome advances to another, then it is harassment.

Q What do you do in a situation where an employee complains of harassment but only gives general information and will not reveal specific names or events?

A Record the complaint. In absence of more complete details, conduct a low-key investigation to determine the possible basis for the complaint. Advise the employee of the actions taken. As a normal rule, such complaints should be viewed as an early warning signal since the offending behavior is likely to be repeated. An employee may not want to stir up trouble for another employee but if no changes occur, he/she may feel compelled to file a specific complaint. If there is any possibility that harassment is involved, one way to defuse this situation is to remind all employees in the work group of the company's policy.

Q What is likely to happen if a supervisor does not take the employee's complaint seriously?

A The supervisor places the company in jeopardy of being found in intentional violation of the law by an EEO enforcement agency. In such instances the enforcement agency could take the position that the company was placed on notice and intentionally failed to act. Supervisors should take any comments or statements seriously no matter how casual, and report the incident to the company's EEO Officer.

Q What do you do about a complaint of harassment that is occurring off the job?

A As a general rule, the company should not become involved with the private lives of employees. However, supervisors may be viewed as company representatives when off the job, depending upon the circumstances. If the complaint alleges harassment by a supervisor or manager, you should report it, and the company should look into the matter. If the harassment is occurring between peer employees and does not involve a supervisor or manager, the company normally should not become involved. In such cases, special attention should be paid to the working relationship of the involved employees to assure that there is no carry-over harassment at the work site. However, harassment between peers—whether it happens at a business lunch, traveling on company business or at a company event held off company property—should concern you.

Q What do you do when you receive a complaint from an employee who you think is mad at another employee and trying to get him/her in trouble?

A Accept the complaint; do not make assumptions. Each complaint should be considered bona fide until you have the results of a company investigation.

Q What do you do if you determine that an employee has made a false accusation?

A Handle it like other employee disputes. Do not accuse the employee of lying unless you have undisputed evidence. The best way is to tell the employee that you were unable to substantiate the claim and can take no further actions until the employee can provide additional evidence.

Q Should employees be permitted to use ethnic, racial or commonly used slurs where it has been a common practice to use these terms in a give-and-take manner?

A Some employees may tolerate this practice because they do not want to rock the boat, but that doesn't mean that they might not be deeply offended by such language. This practice should not be permitted and is totally unacceptable. A single slur may be enough to find a hostile work environment.

Q Are contractors' employees and other noncompany workers at the work site covered by the company's harassment guidelines?

A Yes. They are expected to meet the same behavior standards as company employees.

Q Can an employee file a lawsuit against a supervisor or co-workers directly without first filing a charge of harassment with an EEO enforcement agency?

A Yes. Individuals can be sued for personal liability under various federal and state statutes for actions such as assault, battery, emotional distress, etc.

Avoiding Employment Law Claims

As a supervisor, one of your jobs is to maintain the workplace so that employment law claims do not arise (Figure 3-12). Sometimes it's hard but here are a few guidelines that will help your organization to avoid employment law claims. First, consider your state of mind.

- Make sure you apply all rules equally to everyone.
- Always send consistent signals and be honest in your appraisals.
- Avoid delaying decisions or ignoring problems.
- Assume everyone wants to advance in the job and with the company.
- Give clear instructions and warnings of consequences.
- Always hear the employee's side of the story before taking action.
- Avoid reaching conclusions on the basis of emotions (subjective feelings about employees); try to stick with objective facts.
- Clearly explain decisions to those employees affected.
- Keep those communication channels open!

Second, be aware that there are certain activities or times in which you need to be sensitive to discrimination issues. These include most of the major employment status actions you take, namely:
- interviewing, hiring and orientation.
- carrying out a performance appraisal.
- making decisions about promotions.
- changing duties and assignments.
- revising work and employee schedules.
- changing working conditions.
- handling gripes, grievances and complaints.
- making decisions involving discipline and discharge.
- settling disputes between you and an employee or between employees.

> **Figure 3-12. EEOC Claims Against Employers**
>
> The following are a few examples of EEOC cases against employers that the employers lost:
> - using unlawful hiring criteria adversely affecting women and minorities, such as arrest records, height, weight and family status.
> - imposing an education requirement without showing its job relatedness.
> - relegating women and minorities to low-paid and undesirable jobs.
> - excluding minorities from supervisory, sales, skilled and technical jobs.
> - laying off female employees while retaining males with less seniority.
> - limiting females from overtime work.
> - using stiffer promotion criteria for women/minorities.

Employment law claims or charges of discrimination arise when an employee feels unfairly or insensitively treated. Understanding that you are supervising in a democratic workplace is a first step toward sensitivity. The second step is to realize that for most minority and protected-class workers, the workplace is still dominated by white men. Even if you, their supervisor, are a member of a protected class, it is likely that most of the other supervisors and managers they see are not from a protected class. So you need to be sensitive to the reality of the workplace from their point of view.

The best way to express that sensitivity is precisely what we have been describing in this chapter and throughout this book. As the supervisor, you must be honest, fair and communicate clearly and candidly. You must also always be objective when you evaluate individuals and situations. Above all, show that you have regard for every employee's personal dignity and worth. That will help avoid complaints and make for a good supervisor.

Disciplining a Protected Class Employee

The subject of disciplining employees is covered in detail in Chapter 10, Measuring Performance. In that chapter, we cover the need for using progressive discipline as one approach to improve employee performance. Proper discipline procedure is the same for all employees, whether they are in a protected or not. To help you avoid facing employment law charges or claims, we will summarize the basic principles involved in effective disciplinary action for any employees with performance problems.

- Clearly communicate your expectations.
- Try to rehabilitate the employee through training, coaching and detailed performance expectations.
- Document (write down, record) your efforts and the employee's response.
- Apply equal treatment (same standards and expectations to all employees).
- Discharge, if necessary, should be the final step of a progressive disciplinary process (which can include steps like warnings, probation or suspension).

Sound, equitable, considerate and fair supervision should apply to everyone. For supervisors, the beginning of good employee relations is recognizing each employee's individuality and knowing that he or she will respond most favorably when treated with respect and thoughtfulness.

Affirmative Action

As a supervisor, you should familiarize yourself with your company's

affirmative action plan and help to see that the goals are met. Most companies are required to have affirmative action plans. An *affirmative action plan* generally consists of:
- an equal employment opportunity statement.
- appointment of an Equal Employment Opportunity officer who will have responsibility for implementation of the plan.
- a procedure for disseminating the policy both internally and externally.
- a workforce self-analysis to see where the employer is underutilizing protected classes (This is a process in which an organization examines the make-up of the workforce by job class [executive, professional, technician, etc.] to see how the distribution of "protected class" employees compared to the organization "employment " base. If there is a big difference or gap, then the organization could target those job categories affirmatively before getting into trouble with the EEOC.)
- a corrective plan of action.
- a self-audit and reporting system to see how well the corrective action is working.

The idea of affirmative action is that employers should monitor their use of protected class employees to see if their workforces reflect the makeup of local labor pools. The idea is that employers must act in a fair manner, and co-workers must act similarly.

Affirmative action laws extend the rights of reasonable treatment. It helps accelerate participation of the protected classes in the workforce. It is meant to be a proactive measure rather than a reactive measure. Affirmative action seeks to undo the wrongs of the past and present by adopting policies that will in a positive way advance members of the protected classes in the workplace.

Affirmative action plans usually require that companies identify areas in which protected class workers are "underutilized". Such areas can be identified by comparing the numbers of protected class workers to workers who are not in a protected class in the regional hiring area and within the various jobs in the company. An *affirmative action plan* is made to address the problem and seek an appropriate balance among employees.

These plans generally:
- call for reasonable and reachable goals (not quotas).
- show how these goals will be reached.
- give timetables for achieving them.

The use of quotas, "set asides" and preferential treatment to make the workplace more diverse is more controversial and harder to defend legally. An affirmative action plan does not provide for the lowering of performance or conduct standards.

Affirmative action programs may be required as a remedy under Title VII, for example, or may be required of employers who do business with the federal government (federal contractors). The U.S. policy on affirmative action is mandated by Presidential Executive Order (E.O. 11246), instituted in 1965. However, that concept is an evolving one, and promoting Affirmative action for protected classes has sometimes resulted in charges of reverse discrimination.

Reverse Discrimination

Reverse discrimination refers to the negative impact that affirmative action plans can have on the non-protected class. Although you have to consider complaints from employees about reverse discrimination, lawsuits against organizations for reverse discrimination are still rare. They are most likely to have problems when an improper affirmative action plan is started or when the plan contains quotas, etc. Note that if an affirmative action plan is temporary (designed to solve specific existing problems), most organizations can avoid reverse discrimination claims.

Workplace Law

Workplace law requires that employees work in a safe workplace, that they are paid a decent wage for their labor, and that they are assured certain basic conditions of work and rights to representation. There are many workplace laws. We have tried to select those laws that will impact supervisors the most. We have not gone into great detail on safety laws, since the National Safety Council has other books and courses that cover these subjects in great detail (the *Supervisors' Safety Manual*, the *Basics of Safety and Health*, etc.; visit the website www.nsc.org for more information).

OSHA Regulations & the OSHAct

The Williams-Steiger Occupational Safety and Health Act of 1970, known as the OSHAct, became effective April 1971, when the Occupational Safety and Health Administration (OSHA) was created. The OSHAct establishes the right to a safe workplace. Its regulations determine what conditions and exposure levels are safe and an enforcement procedure to see that safe standards are followed. OSHA's jurisdiction extends to most, but not all workplaces in the United States and U.S. Territories. In addition to federal OSHA, there are some states that have their own state-level OSHA offices. Check the OSHA website (www.dol.gov) for more information.

Most of the OSHA standards began as voluntary professional guidelines. Some were created by the American Conference of Governmental Industrial Hygienists (ACGIH Threshold Limit Values (TLVs)), the American National Standards Institute (ANSI), or the National Fire Protection Association

(NFPA). The NFPA is responsible for writing, modifying and maintaining the National Electric Code (NEC). When the OSHAct was created, guidelines like the NEC were adopted into the *U.S. Code of Federal Regulations* and became the basis for the original OSHA standards.

Each employer has clear obligations under the OSHAct to provide employees with a safe and healthy workplace. See Figure 3-13.

As a supervisor, these become your obligations. Remember that a supervisor is directly responsible for the safety of his or her employees (Figure 3-13) and enforcing safety regulations.

> Figure 3-13. OSHAct of 1970
>
> OSHA says employers must:
> - *Furnish to each employee both employment and a place of employment that are free from recognized hazards causing or likely to cause death or serious harm to employees.*
> - *Comply with occupational safety and health standards established by OSHA.*
> - *Furnish to each employee both employment and a place of employment that are free from recognized hazards causing or likely to cause death or serious harm to employees.*
> - *Comply with occupational safety and health standards promulgated by the Act.*

OSHA's Mission

As OSHA's mission has developed, its emphasis has changed, but in the 1970 OSHAct the U.S. Congress directed OSHA to:

- encourage organizations to reduce workplace hazards and implement new or improve existing workplace safety and health programs.
- conduct and underwrite research in occupational safety and health, and develop new solutions to workplace safety and health problems.
- establish separate but dependent responsibilities and rights for employers and employees for the achievement of better safety and health conditions.
- maintain a reporting and record keeping system to monitor job-related injuries and illnesses.
- develop mandatory job safety and health standards.
- provide for the development, analysis, evaluation and approval of the state occupational safety and health programs.

OSHA also monitors maintenance of the general sanitation and working conditions of the workplace. This means OSHA also looks at things like housekeeping, extermination and efforts to maintain a healthy and reasonably clean workplace.

Five Categories of Violations

The U.S. Congress determined and OSHA established the details on its five categories of occupational safety/health violations or potential hazards. You need to be aware of these, and the level of importance each has.

1. **Imminent Danger.** This covers any conditions or practices that could be expected to cause immediate death or serious physical harm. In such circumstances, the company can be shut down under OSHA regulations.
2. **Serious.** These are conditions where there is a great probability that death or serious physical harm could result from the alleged violation. The company may be fined whether the employer knew of or, with reasonable diligence, should have known of the hazard.
3. **Willful and Repeated.** Violations are considered willful when the employer either intentionally or knowingly violates the OSHA standards or, although not consciously violating it, is aware of hazardous conditions without making an effort to eliminate them. Repeated violations are those for which OSHA has issued a second citation for the same act.

> **Figure 3-14. OSHA'S Five Categories of Violations**
>
> 1. Imminent Danger—Exposure to the hazard could be expected to cause immediate death or serious physical harm.
> 2. Serious—Likely that death or serious physical harm could result.
> 3. Willful and Repeated—Employer knows about violation. Employer keeps doing it.
> 4. Nonserious—A violation that is not considered serious but does have a direct impact on occupational safety and health.
> 5. De minimis—A minimal violation with no immediate or direct impact on safety and health of the employees.

4. **Nonserious.** A violation that is not serious but has a direct or immediate relationship to occupational safety and health.
5. **De minimis.** *De minimis* means a minimal violation that has no immediate or direct relationship to the safety and health of the employees (Figure 3-14.).

Accident Reporting

OSHA calls for specific recordkeeping of accidents that occur at the workplace or while performing work-related activities. As a supervisor, you might need to initiate or maintain these records. Employers have a legal obligation to maintain accurate, honest and clear records. Inaccurate recordkeeping is bad policy for everyone and can lead to significant fines and penalties.

OSHA-Required Training

Under OSHA regulations, employers are expected to train new employees and to have an ongoing training program on occupational safety and health. This training is most often carried out by supervisors. The National Safety Council also offers many of the required training programs.

Training should cover instruction and observance of safety regulations, routing and procedures for emergency evacuations, and accident and injury treatment (Figure 3-15). Training should also cover hazard communication (chemical exposure), occupational health and environmental controls, hazardous materials, use and care of personal protective equip-

Figure 3-15. Supervisor's Checklist:

Training Subjects on Occupational Safety and Health
- following safety regulations correctly
- routing for emergency exit
- treating accidents and injuries
- checking the occupational health and environmental controls
- handling hazardous materials
- proper use and fit of personal protective equipment (PPE)
- giving first aid
- handling medical emergencies
- protecting against fires
- safe materials handling and storage
- machine guarding
- welding, cutting and brazing

ment (PPE), medical and first aid, fire protection, materials handling and storage, machine guarding, and cutting and brazing for welding operations.

Employee Rights Under OSHA

OSHA provides employees with a "bill of rights," when it comes to maintaining occupational safety and health (Figure 3-16). Supervisors need to know these rights, since assertion of the rights by an employee will most often first be directed to you, as the supervisor.

Employees have a right to:
- request an OSHA inspection if they believe an imminent danger exists or that a violation of a standard exists that threatens physical harm.
- have a representative accompany an OSHA compliance officer during the inspection of a workplace.
- advise an OSHA compliance officer of any violation of the OSHAct that they believe exists in the workplace and privately question and be questioned by the compliance officer.
- have regulations posted by the employer to inform them of protection afforded by the Act.
- have locations monitored by the employer to measure exposures to toxic or radiation materials, have access to the records of such monitoring or measuring and have a record of their own personal exposures.
- have medical examinations or other tests to determine whether their

Figure 3-16. Employee Bill of Rights Under OSHA

Employees have a right to:
- request an OSHA inspection.
- have a representative accompany OSHA compliance officer.
- privately advise and question OSHA compliance officer.
- have OSHA regulations posted in workplace.
- have toxic or radiation materials exposure monitored.
- have access to the records of such monitoring.
- have a record of their own personal exposure to material.
- have medical examinations or tests to determine if health is affected by exposure. with results of tests furnished to their physicians.
- have posted on the premises any citations made to the organization by OSHA.

health is being affected by an exposure and have the results of such tests furnished to their physicians.
- have posted on the premises any citations made to the employer by OSHA.

As you see, this is a very extensive and clear-cut list of rights. No disciplinary action can be taken against an employee for asserting these rights. In fact, we strongly recommend that you and your employer insist on and maintain complete compliance with these OSHA standards for a safe and healthy workplace. They make sense. They are right. They improve productivity.

OSHA Self-Inspection Checklist

While the organization's safety officer probably has primary responsibility to ensure these OSHA standards are met, you as a supervisor are in charge of the day-to-day implementation and application of the standards. Therefore, you should regularly check your work area for these factors (Figure 3-17).

OSHA Visitations

If an OSHA compliance officer visits your facility, it is useful to know what they are likely to review. Compliance officers start by checking injury/illness records and required written programs. Based upon the records, they may look for the following hazardous conditions:
- eye irritation
- strong odors
- visible dust or fumes in the air
- excessive noise
- spilled or leaking chemicals
- use of substances known to be dangerous even when handled properly.

Figure 3-17. OSHA Self-Inspection Checklist.

1. Is the required OSHA workplace poster displayed in your place of business as required where all employees are likely to see it?
OK_____   Action Needed: _____.

2. Are you aware of the requirement to report all workplace fatalities and any serious accident (where 5 or more are hospitalized) to a federal or state OSHA office within 48 hours?
OK_____   Action Needed: _____.

3. Are workplace injury and illness records being kept as required by OSHA?
OK_____   Action Needed: _____.

4. Are you aware that the OSHA annual summary of workplace injuries and illnesses must be posted by February 1 and must remain posted until March 1?
OK_____   Action Needed: _____.

5. Are you aware that employers with 10 or fewer employees are exempt from the OSHA record keeping requirements? Unless they are part of an official Bureau of Labor Standards or state survey and have received specific instructions to keep records?
OK_____   Action Needed: _____.

6. Do all employees know what to do in emergencies?
OK_____   Action Needed: _____.

7. Are emergency telephone numbers posted?
OK_____   Action Needed: _____.

8. Are all electrical cords strung so they do not hang on pipes, nails, hooks, etc?
OK_____   Action Needed: _____.

9. Is there no evidence of fraying on any electrical cords?
OK_____   Action Needed: _____.

10. Are metallic cable and conduit systems properly grounded?
OK_____   Action Needed: _____.

11. Are portable electrical tools and appliances grounded or double insulated?
OK_____   Action Needed: _____.

12. Are switches mounted in clean, tightly closed boxes?
OK_____   Action Needed: _____.

13. Are all exits visible and unobstructed?
OK_____   Action Needed: _____.

14. Are all exits marked with a readily visible sign that is properly illuminated?
OK_____   Action Needed: _____.

15. Are there sufficient exits to ensure prompt escape in case of emergency?
OK_____   Action Needed: _____.

16. Are portable fire extinguishers provided in adequate number and type?
OK_____   Action Needed: _____.

17. Are fire extinguishers recharged regularly and properly noted on the inspection tag?
OK_____   Action Needed: _____.

18. Are fire extinguishers mounted in readily accessible locations?
OK_____   Action Needed: _____.

19. Are NO SMOKING signs prominently posted in areas containing combustibles and flammables?
OK_____   Action Needed: _____.

20. Are waste receptacles provided and are they emptied regularly?
OK_____   Action Needed: _____.

21. Are stairways in good condition with standard railing provided for every flight having four or more risers?
OK_____   Action Needed: _____.

22. Are portable work ladders and metal ladders adequate for their purpose, in good condition and provided with secure footing?
OK_____   Action Needed: _____.

23. Are all machines or operations that expose operators or other employees to rotating parts, pinch points, flying chips, particles or sparks adequately guarded?
OK_____   Action Needed: _____.

24. Are mechanical power transmission belts and pinch points guarded?
OK_____   Action Needed: _____.

25. Are hand tools and other equipment regularly inspected for safe condition?
OK_____   Action Needed: _____.

26. Are approved safety cans or other acceptable containers used for handling and dispensing flammable liquids?
OK_____   Action Needed: _____.

27. Are your first-aid supplies adequate for the type of potential injuries in your workplace?
OK_____   Action Needed: _____.

28. Are hard hats provided and worn where any danger of falling objects exists?
OK_____   Action Needed: _____.

29. Are protective goggles or glasses provided and worn where there is any danger of flying particles or splashing of corrosive materials?
OK_____   Action Needed: _____.

OSHA compliance officers also will check:
- changes in the physical work environment or work procedures made by the employer to reduce health hazards.
- effectiveness of personal protective gear.
- maintenance of protective gear.
- training in proper use of personal protective equipment.
- isolation of eating, washing and resting areas from work areas containing hazardous substances.

Hazard Communication

The OSHA Hazard Communication Standard now extends to all employers. This regulation expands the rights of employees and the obligation of employers under the OSHAct. In general, the Hazard Communication Standard would be enforced over any similar state OSHA statute.

Essentially, the standard has one purpose: that people have a right to know about hazardous chemicals they may be exposed to at work (Figure 3-18). The standard requires that the employer carries out the following steps to implement this very simple right:

Figure 3-18. OSHA Hazard Communication Standard

People have a right to know about hazardous chemicals they may be exposed to at work.

1. Develop a written communication program that explains the organization's approach to compliance with the standard.
2. Provide a system to ensure chemicals are properly labeled.
3. Conduct a chemical inventory in order to establish the possible chemicals that individually or in combination provide a potential hazard.
4. Obtain material safety data sheets (MSDSs) from chemical suppliers and make them available to employees.
5. Establish an employee training program that covers:

- physical health hazards of the chemicals
- methods and observations that may be used to detect the presence or release of hazardous chemicals in the work area
- protective measures available (i.e., equipment, work practices, etc.)
- retraining when a new hazard appears, that is, other chemicals, procedures, new techniques for processing, etc. (Figure 3-19).

Voluntary Guidelines

Standards and regulations, whether issued by OSHA, DOT, EPA or MSHA are the minimum requirements established by law for employers to reduce the number and severity of occupational injuries and illnesses in the workplace. Many employers, through industry trade associations, local safety groups or national organizations such as the National Safety Council seek to establish "*best safety practices*" for their establishment. These are often adopted as company policy or standard operating procedures for a given operation or industry. Although voluntary in nature, these best practices often take on a life of their own and often become the basis for new or modified standards or are driven by the demands of customers in the market.

OSHA, along with its enforcement activities, has gotten into the business of partnering with businesses and industries to develop some of these best practices, especially in areas where they have experienced difficulty establishing a standard or regulation. An example was a negotiated settlement with the meatpacking industry to develop guidelines to reduce the incidence of cumulative trauma disorders (CTDs), common in that industry. Even though there is no ergonomic standard, the

Figure 3-19. Employer Requirements of OSHA HazCom Standard

Employers must provide the following:
1. written communication plan
2. labels and warnings
3. chemical inventory
4. material safety data sheets
5. employee training

guidelines were established to assist the meatpacking industry with their specific problems and to provide general guidance to others outside the meatpacking industry.

International best practices or standards like ISO 9001 and 14001 are becoming common in most organizations that do business with other countries. ISO14001 is an environmental management standard and strongly related to occupational safety and health. ISO 9001 is a quality management standard and does not deal directly with safety and health issues, but carries some implications for the establishment of adequate safety management systems.

More and more companies are making the commitment to become ISO "compliant" or "certified." They may be owned by a foreign company, or because of a requirement established by their customers, or due to other market pressures. We are likely to see more influence of these standards on the safety efforts of companies, both in the United States and abroad.

Under the British system, a standard referred to as OHSAS 18001 was created from several existing standards to combine the efforts from a number of the world's leading national standards bodies, certification bodies and specialized consultancy groups.

OHSAS 18001 gives requirements for an occupational health and safety management system to enable an organization to control its occupational safety and health risks and improve its performance. It was developed to be compatible with both the ISO 9001 (quality) and ISO 14001 (environmental) management systems standards.

U.S. Fair Labor Standards Act of 1938 (FLSA)

The U.S. Fair Labor Standards Act of 1938 (FLSA) asserted the right of U.S. Congress to regulate the minimum standards for hours and wages of employees covered by the Act, child labor and overtime (Figure 3-20). Among other reasons, it came into being because workers were required to work long hours at low wages and were often so tired that they created major safety hazards for themselves and others. Today, the standards set under FLSA are the bedrock for most of our workplace law.

Minimum Wage

Most industries and employers are regulated under FLSA. Since minimum wage is set by U.S. Congressional Act, it doesn't change often. The longer the time between changes, the fewer people who actually benefit under the minimum provisions. For instance, before it was changed in 1989, the minimum wage was $3.35/hour and very few workers were receiving a wage that low. In certain industries, like hotels and restaurants, there are some exceptions to the minimum wage requirements.

> **Figure 3-20. Fair Labor Standards Act of 1938 (FLSA)**
>
> The Fair Labor Standards Act, 1938 (FLSA) regulates:
> - the minimum standards for hours and wages of employees covered by the Act.
> - child labor.
> - overtime.

Child Labor

The FLSA also regulates child labor. Currently, the law provides that:
- People 18 years and above can hold any job, hazardous or not with unlimited hours.
- Only children 16-17 years old can hold any nonhazardous job with unlimited hours.
- Children under the age of 16 have many restrictions, such as hours, conditions and parental approval.

Overtime

The FLSA also regulates overtime rates for employees who are nonexempt. *Nonexempt*, in a sort of logically reversed meaning of the word, means employees who are covered by special regulations of FLSA. Under these regulations, overtime is defined as more than 40 hours in a workweek. A workweek is 7 consecutive days. For example, these hours may not be averaged over a 2- or 3-week period. Overtime pay must be at least 1.5 times the regular rate. Regular rate is defined as the rate per hour actually paid the employee for the normal, nonovertime workweek. As a supervisor, you often have responsibility for filling out the timesheets, so this requirement must be applied for your nonexempt employees.

Exempt Employees

Exempt employees (those employees not covered by these special regulations) are defined as:
- administrative, executive and professional.
- commissioned salespersons of retail or service establishments.
- domestic service workers residing in the employer's residence.
- farm workers.
- railroad and airline workers.
- auto, truck, trailer, farm implement, boat or aircraft salespersons, parts persons and mechanics employed by non-manufacturing dealers.
- outside salespersons.
- retail-service establishment(laundry-dry-cleaning businesses not included).

However, the actual determination of exemption also depends upon one's duties, not just the job title. Generally, many supervisors are exempt employees. However; the distinction depends on the duties and responsibilities assigned. While the minimum wage and overtime regulations do not cover these employees, there is a requirement that those in managerial positions get paid on a *salary basis.* This means that they are to be paid for any week they work, regardless of hours or days worked. FLSA provides specific tests to find out which positions fall into which category (exempt or nonexempt).

The Equal Pay Act of 1963

The Equal Pay Act is an amendment to the FLSA. It prohibits unequal wages for women and men working in the same establishment, doing equal work that requires equal skill, effort and responsibility and that is performed under similar working conditions. The Act provides that the equal pay standard does not rely upon job classifications or titles, but depends on the actual job requirements and duties performed. It also provides that equal pay includes vacation and holiday pay, premium payments of any kind and fringe benefits.

There are three specific exceptions to this Act (Figure 3-21). Equal pay is not operable if the differential in pay is the result of a wage payment made (1) under a seniority system, (2) a merit system or (3) a system measuring earnings by quantity or quality of production.

Another, broader exception involves pay differential based on anything other than sex. It is important that you do not confuse equal pay for equal work with comparable pay for comparable work. Comparable pay for comparable work is a right that is being asserted but is not yet the law. The former is the law. Let's look at two examples to see the difference.

Figure 3-21. The Equal Pay Act of 1963

Equal Pay for Equal Work

Exceptions:
- seniority systems
- merit systems
- production/piecework systems

Example 1. Jim and Jill work at Compatible Computers. Jim is a Technician 1 and earns $16.50 per hour. Jill is a Technician 2 and earns $15.50 per hour. Both needed a college degree for the job. While their titles are different and their pay is different, an analysis of their duties shows that they perform substantially the same job. Jill, on that basis, is entitled to the higher rate of pay.

Example 2. Jane and John also work at Compatible Computers. Jane is a Technician 2 and earns $16.50 per hour. Jim is a Programmer and earns $22.75 per hour. Both needed a college degree for the job. Their titles are different and their pay is different, although they both had to have some of the same entry-level requirements (college degree, in this case). However, a technician's work is significantly different from a programmer's. Technicians primarily work on operating and maintaining existing equipment, while programmers are developing new systems and procedures. The latter requires a greater depth of knowledge and experience. Therefore, there may be comparability but the work is not equal. Jane has no claim under current case law.

U.S. National Labor Relations Act (NLRA)

The U.S. National Labor Relations Act (NLRA) is the basic labor law of the United States. In a nutshell, the NLRA establishes and protects the rights of employees to organize themselves into a labor union and to be represented by such a union to their employers. Representation usually comes about through a representation election conducted by the National Labor Relations Board (NLRB), the agency that administers the Act. The employer is not allowed to interfere in such organizing. Although entitled to express opinions about the organizing, the employer must do so without threat of intimidation or reprisal to the employees. After the union is certified by the NLRB, the union has the right to represent such employees for the purposes of negotiating with the employer over the terms and conditions of employment. These include wages, hours, benefits and conditions of work. The employer and the union must both bargain in good faith over these issues. They are not required to reach an agreement, although the thrust of the law is in that direction.

Bargaining Unit

Union elections involve only those employees included in a bargaining unit. The bargaining unit, generally, is a particular group of workers within a plant or facility who have a common interest. In an auto plant, this might be the production workers but might exclude the clerical workers. Supervisors are excluded from the election and the bargaining unit, except in the airline and railroad industries, which are covered by a different law (the Railway and Airline Labor Act).

Union Organizing Activity

If the facility where you work is nonunion and a union is trying to organize the workers, or if there is an existing union and a competing union is trying to take over, you, as a supervisor, will inevitably be involved in this process as a representative of the company. If a union campaign or election occurs in your workplace, you should familiarize yourself with the company's position. If that position is to resist the union, permitted activities include:
- representing your company in a positive manner.
- raising questions about employees' representation under a union contract.
- handing out employer literature.

Remember that as a supervisor, you represent management. Management interference is prohibited during a union election. Therefore, you must avoid:
- any actions that affect an employee's pay or job.
- arguments over questions of the union.
- threatening through a third party or dealing with any of the union's organizing officers without the advice of top management.

Specifically, you are not permitted to:

- promise rewards for not joining the union.
- make threats about what might happen if the union represents employees.
- pressure employees to commit themselves to the company.
- ask if they've signed a representation card.
- spy on employee/union activity.
- invite employees into your office to privately discuss the union.
- discriminate against employees due to their union views or activities. Discrimination is defined as any action, such as discharge, layoff, demotion or assignment to a more difficult or disagreeable job on account of the employee's union stance or membership (Figure 3-22).

> **Figure 3-22. The National Labor Relations Act and Union Organizing Activity**
>
> As a supervisor you can:
> - represent your company in a positive manner.
> - raise questions about employees' representation under union representation.
> - hand out employer literature.
>
> As a supervisor you cannot:
> - promise rewards for not joining the union.
> - make threats about what might happen if the union represents employees.
> - pressure employees to commit themselves to the company.
> - ask if they've signed a representation card.
> - spy on employee/union activity.
> - invite employees into your office to privately discuss the union.
> - discriminate against an employee for his/her union views or activities.

The Supervisor and the Union Contract

Supervisors have a very important role in administering a labor agreement (Figure 3-23). If your company already has a union contract, familiarize yourself with it and know the requirements regarding assignments, pay, hours of work, duties, the grievance procedure, etc.

Remember that the shop steward represents the employees on these issues, just as you represent the company. On many other aspects of work, you act in the role of agent for your employees, so it is sometimes difficult to keep things straight! In the context of the labor agreement and the items covered in it, you do not represent your employees. The shop steward does.

You should develop a good understanding between yourself and the committee person, steward or business agent, always recognizing the differences, but always seeking harmony as a goal. To avoid problems, keep them informed about what's going on. Ignorance and surprises cause problems. In a very real sense, you both share one common task: the fair and proper application of the terms of the labor agreement. Seek their cooperation, but remember that you're the boss and this is not a co-supervisory relationship.

It is also useful to recognize that the union can help you by supporting the company safety program. Union involvement in safety committees can only reinforce the idea that safety is of universal importance.

> **Figure 3-23. The Supervisor and the Union Contract**
>
> **Key Ideas:**
> - The shop steward represents the employees' labor agreement issues. As the supervisor, you represent the company.
> - Develop a good understanding between yourself and the steward or business agent.
> - Keep them informed about what's going on. Ignorance and surprises cause problems.
> - You both share one common task: the fair and proper application of the terms of the labor agreement.
> - Seek their cooperation, but remember that you're the boss and this is not a co-supervisory operation.

Conclusion

While there are dozens of federal laws impacting on employment and the workplace and literally hundreds of state and local laws, we covered those that are likely to most directly affect your work as a supervisor:

- Title VII of the Civil Rights Act, 1964
- Pregnancy Discrimination Act, 1978 (amendment to Title VII)
- Civil Rights Act, 1964 EEOC
- Age Discrimination in Employment Act, 1967 (ADEA)
- Rehabilitation Act, 1973

- Civil Rights Act of 1991
- Americans with Disabilities Act, 1990
- Family and Medical Leave Act, 1993
- State laws dealing with discrimination in the workplace
- OSHAct, 1970
- OSHA HazCom
- MSHA
- EPA
- DOT
- Fair Labor Standards Act, 1938 (FLSA)
- Equal Pay Act, 1963 (an amendment to the FLSA)
- National Labor Relations Act (NLRA)

Supervisors also must assure that:
- you comply with employment and workplace law.
- your employees comply with them.
- you send a consistent message that the law is the law and must be respected.

This chapter emphasized the following ideas:
1. The fundamental principles of employment and workplace law try to address the democratic rights of people and employees to fair, appropriate and safe treatment.
2. These laws evolve over time and are written in response to the needs of people and employees.
3. The laws not only must, but should, be enforced.
4. Part of your job is to see to it that this happens and that the people who work under your supervision understand why it is so.

Case Study

As a supervisor you either hire, or are asked to interview, prospective employees. During the interview you are chatting with the employee, just trying to get to know him or her. You ask the candidate if he or she has children, their ages, and the school they go to. You ask whether the candidate has any hobbies or activities they like to do. You ask if the candidate is married. You ask what kind of employment experience he/she has, and ask if he/she has ever been injured on the job.

How many violations of the federal antidiscrimination laws have just occurred?

Asking about spouses and children during the job interview phase can be a violation of Title VII. (You may be able to get this information after the candidate has accepted a job in order to enroll the candidate's family in a benefit plan, etc.) Asking about injuries on the job is a way of getting medical condition information, which is a violation of the ADA. Even asking someone about their hobbies can be a violation, since it may solicit information about physical abilities/conditions or other information which may provide a basis for discriminatory activity.

As you can see from this brief and innocent example, it is very easy to run afoul of the laws when you stray from work-related questions. *"Can the candidate do the job, with or without an accommodation?"* is the question to keep in mind.

Review Questions

1. As a supervisor, you should ask yourself: Do I have hiring responsibilities?

2. Do I have responsibility for awarding promotions and raises?

3. Do I have discipline or discharge responsibilities?

4. If I work in a unionized workplace, am I familiar with the collective bargaining agreement?

4 Partnering with Human Resources

by Meredith Onion
George Sanders

What Will I Learn in This Chapter?

- good reasons for developing a partnership with Human Resources (HR)
- how and when to partner with HR to meet organizational goals.

Overview

In an ideal organization, supervisors and Human Resources (HR) professional walk side by side to manage. They communicate openly to make the best use and development of the employee skills and training. They manage change through careful planning, and resolve conflict through integrated processes based on fairness and consistency. Ideally, HR is your business partner, and helps in organizational development, acts as an employee advocate, and a change agent. All of these activities contribute to the bottom line of the organization.

Today, though, HR is more actively involved in helping to recruit staff, advise on employee benefits and resolve conflicts. Whether you work in manufacturing facilities, an engineering laboratory, an e-commerce startup or in the aisles of a super discount department store, the relationship between supervisors and HR professionals tends to be far more pragmatic and focused on immediate or relatively short-term needs. These are driven by the desire to "get the job done," which is, after all, the reason you are in business.

Supervisors and HR need to blend the short-term needs of the operation with a well-conceived strategy that allows HR professionals to bring functional expertise to bear in supporting business goals and objectives.

Supervisor's Connection to Human Resources

Much of a supervisor's job is focused on the organization's *human resources*–in other words, your staff. Dealing with people daily and ensuring maximum productivity is the bottom line for most supervisors. In research conducted at the University of Chicago, "people issues" show up in at least 13 of the 16 essential management skills (Jones, 1993). The need for supervisors to have finely tuned "people" skills lies at the core of the relationship between supervisors and the HR function. The 13 people-related skills mentioned in the research data are shown in Figure 4-1. To be successful, supervisors must brush up on their people skills in these 13 critical areas. New supervisors should make these 13 skills the foundation of their professional development.

The role that HR plays in an organization depends on the:

- size of the organization.
- type of business being conducted.
- age of the organization—whether the business is old or new.
- the relative skill level of the HR professional
- basic business values and norms.

Despite the 1990s change in the roles that HR plays, most organizations still have a "typical" HR function. The roles describe HR functions that are important and need to be well executed to handle people-related issues. Often, typical HR roles ought to be handled by the supervisor. And sometimes HR roles are not perceived positively.

1. HR as Rule Maker

The most important HR rules are those related to professional, voluntary standards compliance and those required by law (see Chapter 3). Sometimes HR creates rules to approach common issues in

---

Figure 4-1.
16 Essential Managerial Skills

- Setting organizational objectives
- Financial planning and review
- Improving work procedures and practices
- Interdepartmental coordination
- Developing and implementing technical ideas
- Judgment and decision making
- Developing group cooperation and team work
- Coping with difficulties and emergencies
- Promoting safety attitudes and practices
- Communications
- Developing employee potential
- Supervisory practices
- Self-development and improvement
- Personnel practices
- Promoting community organization relations
- Handling outside contacts

Baehr, M.E. (1992). *Predicting success in higher-level positions.* Westport, CT: Quorum.

the exact same way. HR is the area that usually makes these rules because their staff has background and training in employment law and practices. But often the "rules" are developed with employee input and management approval. Rarely does HR make the rules without the input of others.

The rest of the rules, or *operational guidelines*, should come from the business as required by supervisors to get the job done. HR professionals can partner with the supervisor to make the guidelines fair, thoughtful and people friendly.

2. HR as Holder of "People Values"

HR is the operation that upholds the organization's "people values." If a conflict arises in which the company's people values are being challenged, HR can keep the balance between business requirements and doing what is right for employees. A supervisor can help in this situation by maintaining a balance in his or her views when faced with difficult decisions regarding people and business requirements.

3. HR as Disciplinarian

Employees often view HR as the disciplinary arm of the organization. It's true that HR is often where disciplinary issues are handled, because of the need for consistency and fairness.

"They're taking me to HR," laments an employee who has run into attendance or other problems. Once in HR, the employee receives a warning, or a write up, and hopefully some good advice on how to avoid issues in the future. But there is no reason why HR must handle all the discipline issues. Supervisors are equally capable of administering discipline fairly and consistently. However, there must be an overview of all discipline administered to ensure fairness and consistency at some level in the organization, and to make sure no laws are being broken.

4. HR as Bureaucrat

HR manages the day-to-day administration of the organization's staff. This usually includes payroll, benefits and other administrative activities. Supervisors help HR by making sure that timesheets and other data are correct and submitted on time; and that payroll and benefits are administered professionally.

5. HR as Fixer

In the workplace employees will come to HR to get something fixed that is broken. Usually, whatever is "broken" is the result of a business necessity that upsets the work environment and causes an unfavorable situation to occur. Typically it is a situation that has continued beyond the tolerance of the employee. Examples include:
- boxes stacked too high for too long (safety issue).
- inappropriate language that is not corrected (harassment issue).
- coworkers not doing their share (performance issue).

These examples of familiar "broken" situations are familiar to most HR professionals. In these cases, the most direct fix comes straight from you, the supervisor. If HR needs to "come to the rescue" of the employee in simple situations such as these, the supervisor will quickly lose credibility and authority. Regardless of the "culture" of the organization, a broken environment needs to be addressed quickly and permanently by supervisors. This is the best way to keep the situation from escalating to an HR issue.

But HR can be helpful if there is dissension between employees and their supervisor. HR can serve as a neutral sounding board, hearing both sides of the story and offering "win-win" solutions to whatever the problem seems to be.

6. HR as Complaint Department

HR often hears employee complaints. Many are familiar:
- *Why do we have to work overtime this weekend?*
- *Why does Bill get all the good assignments?*
- *We should get five free tickets to the picnic, not four.*
- *The coffee in the cafeteria is bad.*

Though HR professionals are trained to handle these and other familiar employee complaints, in most cases, the employee simply wants to vent his or her feelings. Employees often visit HR because the supervisor is or seems too busy focusing on operational concerns to deal with these types of issues.

Try to make the time to address these kinds of things at your level. Perhaps you could set aside a few minutes each week to meet with your crew to cover current organization news and listen to their concerns. However, note that some complaints are very serious (for example, sexual harassment, gender discrimination, etc.). Complaints of this kind need to be managed thoroughly and professionally; both you and HR should be involved.

7. HR as Last Resort

When nothing else works, even supervisors who normally don't rely on HR can end up talking with an HR manager. Desperation sometimes forces a partnership between supervisors and HR when best efforts in managing a situation fail. The downside to this scenario is that preventive action in a situation that has been festering for a while becomes an exercise in damage control. But even damage control activity is a chance to learn how to approach issues in the future.

8. HR as a Roadblock

Unfortunately, sometimes an acrimonious relationship can exist between

HR and supervisors. This can mean that supervisors perceive HR as a "roadblock" to getting things done. This negative relationship sometimes occurs when a well-meaning supervisor has a great idea, only to be told by HR that the idea can't be implemented for a number of reasons, usually related to consistency or the law. Sometimes the supervisor unknowingly opposes some existing organizational policy, and ends up in HR facing discipline of some kind. But sometimes the bad feelings are from inefficiencies in the HR department that have an impact on the business.

- Paperwork is processed slowly or incorrectly.
- Personal data is wrong.
- Benefits are applied incorrectly.
- The level of professionalism leaves something to be desired.

In this situation, the supervisor should lay out his or her expectations to HR, and create a mutual focus on the future with the customer in mind. Indicators in the way the supervisor speaks about HR sometimes expose a view that HR is holding up operations, See Figure 4-2.

Figure 4-2. Human Resources: The Roadblock

Human Resources Won't Let Us….
Human Resources Doesn't Know….
Human Resources Hasn't Done Anything….
Human Resources Said We Have To….
Another Human Resource Person Said….
Why Can't I Get This Data….
Why Isn't This Data Correct….

9. HR as Terminator

Separating an employee from the organization can be a stressful and complicated event. The process can be as simple as "*You're fired,*" or as elaborate as carefully crafted separation packages related to employment agreements or legal risks. In either case, the supervisor can minimize mistakes by partnering with HR to make the exit as painless and risk-free as possible. HR is a resource to ensure alignment with policies and procedures, and as a support for the supervisor who is faced with his or her most difficult role of all. Supervisors should avoid using HR as a substitute for personally taking responsibility for the separation. The more responsibility a supervisor takes, the more likely it is that the separation will be done with dignity and respect. (See Figure 4-3 and Chapter 10, Measuring Performance, for more information on disciplining and terminating employees.)

Figure 4-3. In the case of layoffs, what should I do? What should HR do?

Unfortunately, layoffs resulting from reorganization or a downturn in the economy are a fact of life in many organizations. In these kinds of situations, if HR can help, you will want to consult with them. Many organizations have a standard procedure for handling this type of a termination; HR will be able to guide you through the process. In some organizations, the supervisor may have to handle the entire situation, while in others HR can do it all. Another of layoff scenario is handled by both the supervisor and HR. Typically, the supervisor's responsibilities will involve the following steps:

- *Prepare for these meetings.* The better prepared you are for these meetings the better they will go. These are not easy situations to handle and the more you have thought about what you're going to say and how, the less chance you will have of saying the wrong thing.
- *Communicate the decision to the employee(s) affected.* This is usually done one on one, not in a group. If your company has you make this type of announcement to a group, then be sure to make yourself available if employees would like to speak to you individually. When delivering this news to your employees, get to the point quickly and firmly. You don't want to let them think there is room for negotiating the decision.
- *State the reasons for the layoff.* The supervisor needs to make sure the employee understands that the decision has nothing to do with their individual performance or personality. Remember, these are the steps to follow for a no-fault termination, so the employee shouldn't leave feeling like they've done something wrong that resulted in this decision.
- *Outline any severance agreement or continuation of benefits.* Some companies have very formal separation agreements while others won't have anything in writing. HR may also want this discussion to happen in HR, not with the supervisor. As always, check your company policy on this.

- *Discuss how the transition of work will occur.* In some situations, the termination is immediate. While in others, the employee will be expected to continue working for a few days or weeks. Be clear with the employee about what your expectations for continuation of work will be. Also discuss how you want the employee to announce his or her departure with clients, customers and/or co-workers.
- *Let the employee know what the next steps will be.* Often the employee will go right from the supervisor's office to HR. Reassure the employee again that this decision had nothing to do with his/her employee and offer to speak again with the employee if they have any additional questions.

Here are some additional tips to keep in mind when handling layoffs:

- *Conduct the meeting in privacy.*
- *Avoid holding this type of meeting on the employee's birthday, anniversary, etc.* Friday afternoons are also generally not a good time to hold the meeting because you want the employee to be able to come in the next day with any questions he or she may have—making them wait over the weekend isn't generally a good idea.
- *Avoid saying too much.* A succinct, well-thought out message is the best. And usually the less that is said the better. Don't conduct a performance appraisal, don't discuss your feelings, don't allow for bargaining and don't criticize the company regarding the decision.
- *Be prepared for any number of potential reactions in these situations.* Even though it's not the employee's fault they are being terminated, the fact is you are the one letting them know they no longer have a job. Some employees will be angry, others will be passive, and some will try to deny what is happening, while others will cry. The supervisor needs to be kind, but not over-react to any of these responses.
- *Have an action plan for the employees that are not being terminated.* Following the lay-off process, it is always a good idea to meet with those employees who are remaining with the organization. It's best for them to hear directly from you what is happening. Let them know:
    1. the reasons for the decision.
    2. who is leaving and when.
    3. what the implications may be for those employees still employed (will they have to work more hours? What are the options for overtime? Will they be next?).

(Adapted from: Lee RJ. A Manager's Guide To "No-Fault" Terminations: Participation, Preparation and Review. New Jersey: Lee Hecht Harrison, 1990.)

Partnering with Human Resources

When a supervisor chooses to partner with HR, the results are almost always positive. By creating a relationship with the HR department, the supervisor gains resources and expertise otherwise not available in his or her operation. HR can help the supervisor find the right side of his brain, assuming the left side is full of charts and graphs and dollars and cents. The right side of the brain is the people side of the brain, where emotion and caring occur. There is also the notion of organizational wellness, which is represented by the body, which is also important for the supervisor to consider in running a healthy operation. In this concept, consideration is given to the well being of the individual employee and the collective health of the organizational body (Hawley, 1993). And in this regard, HR can support the supervisor in numerous ways.

Some of the advantages in partnering with HR are listed below. You can leverage the competency of HR by determining which of the following attributes exist in your own HR department.

1. Functional and Technical Expertise

The HR professional brings a wealth of information to the handling of employee-related matters. Either through formal education, on-the-job experience, or professional certification, the HR specialist brings a knowledge base to the business that most supervisors don't possess. Most important is the knowledge of laws that govern the relationship between employee and employer.

In addition to knowing about laws and regulations and how they impact the workplace, the HR professional either knows or has connections to the key components of HR management: staffing, training, compensation, benefits, organizational development and compliance.

2. Knowledge of the Organization

Depending on the size and complexity of your business, the HR department may have a broader view of the total organization than the supervisor. This is especially true in larger companies, where one HR function might serve several operations. In these cases, the HR professional can bring the knowledge of best practices and creative solutions to bear in other areas of the business that otherwise would be unaware of those practices. In a global operation, HR often serves as "the glue" that holds the business together, providing a common baseline for geographically and culturally diverse operations.

If your company has a Values Statement, Mission Statement, and/or Statement of Ethics, HR can help explain the thought process that went into developing these statements. More importantly, HR can help you apply this information to make them relevant in your day-to-day work. HR may also have a plan for helping you communicate these types of statement with your employees to help them become meaningful to them as well.

3. HR Data and Metrics

HR can bring a wealth of important information to the organization, depending on the sophistication of the information systems in the business or HR organization. Supervisors can look to HR for statistics and trends in critical areas such as turnover, compensation, training, performance and compliance.

Figure 4-4 What Is HR's Role If There Is a Union Agreement?

Many HR groups will have a **Labor Relations Specialist** if there are union employees. This individual can serve as a great resource for the Supervisor. Often, this specialist has been involved in the negotiation of the contract and so they will have first hand knowledge of not only what is in the contract, but also how it came to be negotiated. The **Specialist** will also be able to assist you with carrying out the terms of the contract, making sure you are in compliance. HR can also help if your employees may be upset about something in the workplace that could lead to filing a grievance ñ any assistance to avoid the filing of formal grievances should be welcomed.

4. A Second Point of View

Just like bouncing an idea off a colleague, getting an opinion from HR can't hurt, and it's usually free. If you are not sure about a decision you need to make, or if you are looking for advice on how to optimize a creative idea, the HR department is a good place to go. Many HR professionals are trained in consulting skills, and will ask the right questions to get you thinking about your idea in a different way.

Getting the HR perspective can also help keep the supervisor out of trouble. Many well-meaning ideas can have an unforeseen impact beyond the immediate organization. For example, a supervisor may want to offer a special incentive to his or her team to get a project completed on time. The operation on the other side of the factory gets wind of the program, and wants to know why they can't have the same program. The HR professional will anticipate situations like this and offer advice on how to handle the issue. In this case, communicating up front with the other organization might be a good solution, explaining the rationale for the incentive, and letting them know that in another situation, they too may be eligible for an incentive. Or, it may be the case that the incentive is applicable to the other organization, and it is a simple matter to extend the incentive across the organization.

5. Digging in vs. a Win-Win

In some instances, digging in on an issue makes sense, especially if a request or employee action is clearly unacceptable. Occasionally, however, a supervisor will simply dig in his or her heels and refuse to budge on an issue for personal or other reasons. The problem with this approach is that the supervisor is relying on authority, as opposed to his or her skills and knowledge, to solve a problem. Unfortunately, the net result for the supervisor is to compromise his or her authority, because he or she loses the respect of his or her employees by acting arbitrarily. HR can help in this situation, primarily by helping the supervisor envision a solution to the problem that receives everyone's acceptance. For example, an employee who has marginal performance wants to take advantage of the company's flexible work hour policy. The supervisor, who wants to get more productivity out of the employee, refuses to approve a flexible schedule. HR advises the supervisor to let the employee try a flexible schedule on a trial basis. If it works and the employee's performance improves, everyone wins. If the employee's performance remains marginal or degrades, then the flexible schedule is withdrawn. What is avoided in this scenario is an ongoing rift between the employee and supervisor.

What HR Can Do For You

Consider HR as an extension of your existing team. While different HR departments offer differing skills and services, tap into the potential. The possibilities for supporting your business are plentiful.

First and foremost, the HR department offers functional expertise that is required to run a successful business. But beyond your basic expectations of functional knowledge and execution, HR can provide other services to make the supervisor's job easier and more rewarding.

1. Moral Support

Even the best supervisors get down on themselves or hit an emotional or physical wall, even in jobs they love. Going to the HR manager and asking, "*How am I doing*," will give you an opportunity to receive some positive feedback and put troubles into context. Sometimes all you need is a light at the end of the tunnel, and often the HR manager can provide a shot of optimism at the right time. If the troubles run deeper, and anxiety becomes chronic, the HR manager can put you in touch with professionals who are accustomed to assisting employees who might need support and counseling. Stress relief programs and even physical therapy in the workplace can be arranged through HR.

2. Motivation

Most HR professionals are aware of intrinsic and extrinsic methods of motivation. Tied to basic principles of human motivation, correctly applied motivational tactics can work wonders in the work place. And it's not always about money! Supervisors who have a natural ability to get employees charged up typically use intrinsic and personal motivational techniques ("*Do it for the Gipper!*"). Supervisors who are less effervescent and motivational sometimes rely on extrinsic and structured motivational tactics ("*If we perform well for the Gipper, each of you will receive a cafeteria voucher worth $25.*").

> **Figure 4-5. Employee Motivation**
>
> **Internal vs. External Motivation**—Internal motivation comes from **inside** the employee and represents satisfaction with the job itself. External motivation comes from **outside** the employee, usually from the business, and is applied as a tool to motivate employees.
>
> | Internal Motivation | External Motivation |
> |---|---|
> | • Job well done | • Merit increase |
> | • Personal pride | • Reward and recognition |
> | • Benefit to the group | • Incentive programs |
> | • Good for the customer | • Promotion |
> | • Better than yesterday | • Office space |
> | • Espirit de corps | • Stock options |
> | • Personal values | • Special assignments |
> | • Being the best | • Flexible work options |
> | • Personal goals | • Salary |
> | • Role model | • Prerequisites |

3. Workforce Planning

Trying to determine the right number and mix of employees relative to business demand is an ongoing challenge for supervisors. Getting the right level of staffing to support your requirements is critical. Workforce planning is a projection of your headcount needs against business forecasts. Not only can it help manage your specific business, it can help the total organization move people from one operation to another, thereby saving hiring and training costs to the business. Effective workforce planning requires discipline and solid strategy, but has enormous potential if used conscientiously.

4. Feedback

While feedback from your operations associates and direct manager is helpful and important, the HR manager may be able to give you nonthreatening and unbiased feedback that others are reluctant to give. Operations feedback tends to be goal oriented, and the HR feedback may be related more toward behavior or interpersonal issues. These might be subtle observations that can help the supervisor do a better job in certain situations. For example, a hint on body language or a certain idiosyncratic behavior may be helpful in developing the supervisor's leadership skills, but might not be mentioned by a boss.

5. Coaching and Mentoring

Coaching and mentoring can be found in almost all businesses. Sometimes it is informal and a part of the culture of the business. At other times, formal programs exist that partner employees for a specific period of time. As a supervisor, you are expected to lead by example. A good way to lead by example is to participate in a mentoring relationship. Most HR departments can help you develop coaching and mentoring skills that can have a big payoff to your business. HR may also be helpful in identifying a mentor for you as well.

Figure 4-6. Coaching and Mentoring

Coaching

Coaching is a process of **helping employees perform better at work**. The best analogy is that of a sports or fitness coach, whose primary role is to improve the performance of athletes. The coach does not need to be the direct supervisor, but should be a specialist and expert in the area of focus. A coach can also assess the potential of an employee, and make recommendations to management regarding an employees developmental needs. Coaching can be applied as needed, or in a structured manner.

Mentoring

Mentoring is a process in which a junior employee is given guidance and **advice from a more senior employee**. Mentoring gives employees a support network outside the employees' departmental structure. A mentor typically comes from a job or profession that is of interest to the employee. A mentor is typically chosen by the employee, and is mutually agreeable. A mentoring process can be informal, or it can be formalized, depending on the number of employees interested in having a mentor.

6. Avoiding Pitfalls

Experienced supervisors know that there are many pitfalls in managing a business, and most have figured out the best way to avoid people-related pitfalls is to partner with HR. Inexperienced supervisors, either new to the job or new to the company, won't know the ins and outs of the business and are the most likely to fall victim to organizational pitfalls.

Some common pitfalls include:
- Fixing one problem leads to others.

    Being able to predict the impact of a proposed solution beyond its intended purpose is a key skill, usually developed by experience and trial and error. If fixing one problem only leads to other problems, the supervisor probably did not consider all of the "stakeholders" in his or her plan. Part of the HR manager's responsibility is to put on the "big hat" and assess the impact of an idea or plan on the total organization. So, if you think raising the starting wage in your downtown operation will help you with recruitment, you better be thinking about the impact on the suburban site when they find out you've raised the starting wage 10 miles away. You either need a really good rationale for the change, or you need to rethink the plan.

- Good idea, but is it legal?

    In order to meet production requirements, a number of hourly employees volunteered to work for free over the weekend. The new supervisor, Jose Sanchez, jumped at the chance to please his new boss and worked his team straight through the weekend. Jose provides a great example of esprit de corps and using his resources to get the job done. Unfortunately, Jose overlooked a couple of important legal issues, one state and one federal. In the state where Jose works, the state requires one day of rest in seven unless you get permission from the state, and the federal government requires that you pay nonexempt employees for time worked. A one-time slip will probably not get Jose in too much trouble. Repeated violations of the law will surely bring much grief to the organization, and to Jose. A quick trip to the HR office would most likely avoid these kinds of potential pitfalls.

- Works for you... but it may not work for the rest of the organization.

    Though it works for you, what about the rest of the organization? You came up with a great performance management system that has the buy in and support of your employees and manager. You are sure that you will be able to give great performance feedback to your team with your new process. One slight problem: the corporation is moving toward a uniform approach to performance management, and your system doesn't quite match the corporation's system. In this case, partnering with HR might have given you advanced knowledge of the new system, and you could have spent your time more productively elsewhere, perhaps contributing to the new corporate-wide process.

- Are you too tough or too lenient?

    How do you establish a broadband of consistency in your approach to employees? Clearly, the best approach for an organization to take is to identify operating practices and ensure that all members of the organization are following the practices consistently. This approach applies to how closely the supervisor controls deviation from the practice as well. Supervisors who do not require strict compliance to the practices are usually labeled too lenient, and supervisors who live by the letter of the practices are labeled too tough. Because the HR professional can see how each supervisor adheres to the practices, he or she can also coach supervisors on the expectations of the corporation or business when it comes to following the rules. Setting individual goals is a good way to make it clear to the employee what the supervisor is

expecting, thus eliminating the concern over being too lenient or too tough.
- Avoid inconsistent performance management.

    Consistency is a matter of setting the right expectations to all employees. Expectations are often reflected in performance documentation and are usually developed within the context of the performance system within your business. You are likely to have a successful performance system if your business strategy is reflected in individual goals. You are likely to have a dysfunctional or chaotic performance system if individual goals are established outside the context of business strategy. In a nutshell, determine what your business goals are, and then make sure all of your employees' goals are supporting the business goal.
- Avoid playing favorites.

    Nothing strikes at the credibility of the supervisor more than perceptions of favoritism. Two levels of favoritism exist: favoring an employee in a group of employees, and favoring a personal friend, acquaintance, or relative. The first type of favoritism usually causes discord amongst your team, and ought to be avoided. The second type of favoritism should be avoided at all costs, as it reflects poorly on your judgment. Your HR manager can give you tips on how

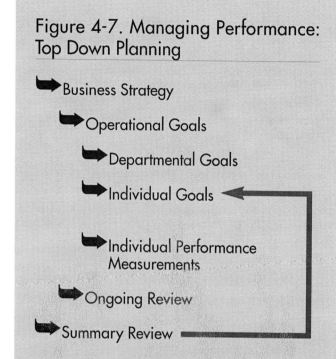

Figure 4-7. Managing Performance: Top Down Planning

➡ Business Strategy
    ➡ Operational Goals
        ➡ Departmental Goals
            ➡ Individual Goals ⬅
    ➡ Individual Performance Measurements
➡ Ongoing Review
➡ Summary Review

Practical Concept: Managing individual performance starts with a clear business strategy that can be translated into operational goals and departmental goals. Once departmental goals have been established, it is possible to create individual goals and measure those goals against specific performance measurements. Ongoing review (quarterly is good) leads to a summary review of performance that can then contribute to the next individual goal setting session.

> **Figure 4-8.**
> **Talking to Your Team: Basic Principles**
>
> **Always tell the truth.** Employees will know or figure out when you are not being straightforward and honest. Know what you are going to say. Have a point, and use information to support your point.
>
> **Listen.** Part of communicating effectively is listening effectively. Listening effectively allows you to respond with relevant information, and demonstrates your interest in your audiences perspective.
>
> **Don't guess at answers.** If you don't know the answer to a question, don't fudge. You'll dig a hole for yourself. Let the employee know that you will get back to them with an answer.
>
> **Summarize.** Summarizing, if done effectively, reinforces the main points of what you are trying to get across.

to manage perceptions of favoritism, including ways to share work and delegation of choice assignments that will minimize allegations of favoritism.

- Avoid unprofessional communication

Part of the leadership skill required of supervisors is communicating effectively with employees. HR professionals can help prepare communications that are well received by employees. In cases where the content has legal implications, engaging HR is vital to ensuring that the right information is communicated.

Communicating is a two-way street, and it is important to get feedback from employees on an ongoing basis. The HR department can help solicit feedback through employee surveys or formal feedback sessions. In either case, the key to a successful feedback process is getting back to the employees as quickly as possible with action plans and ideas for improvements.

- Master change in the organization.

Most pitfalls can be avoided through experience, by asking the right questions up front, and by understanding the nature of change. A supervisor who masters the principles of managing change will almost always deliver superior business results.

The HR department can help you think through the full scope of planned change, and avoid pitfalls that might surprise you. Figures 4-9 and 4-10 show you how to manage change:

- What's the difference between corporate hr vs. small and medium-sized HR departments?

A supervisor needs to know what kind of HR department he or she is partnering with. In most cases, a supervisor interacts with either a corporate HR department or a smaller autonomous department, usually reporting into the site business manager. In either case, knowing the nuances of the HR organization can help the supervisor be more effective. Take the time to learn what type of HR resources exist in your company, and to what extent your HR department can help assist you accomplish your business objectives.

Some companies may be so small that they don't even have a HR professional on staff. In that case, the supervisor needs to learn who carries out the functions of a typical HR department. For example, who handles payroll, benefits, vacation logs, etc? Also, who makes the rules and procedures and who should you talk to if you need to know what the rules are or if you want to change or make a rule. Find out who has to approve any of your decision, such as hiring or firing. Chances are, your immediate supervisor will take on many of these functions.

Figure 4-9. Defining Change

The Current Situation is not as simple to define as you might think. Process mapping is one way to define the Current Situation, although the procedure can be tedious. A quick way to assess the current situation is to ask the question, "What's the problem?"

Obstacles and Opportunities represent all the issues that either inhibit or accelerate your movement to the Desired Situation. An upfront brainstorming session will help you identify these issues early, and help you avoid unexpected obstacles.

The Desired Situation answers the question: "What do we want to accomplish," or "What do we want to look like?" Defining the Desired Situation requires a combination of vision and practicality. Start with vision, end with practicality as you define the desired situation.

Figure 4-10. Managing Change

Communicate Reason for Change
People react differently to change. Depending on circumstances, some will respond positively, and others will respond with more caution. The clearer your message on why you are instituting change, the better the reception from your employees.

Communicate Anticipated Change
You may not know every last detail of your plan, but you should at least know the milestones. The earlier you communicate, the more time you have to bring your team together around the change.

Address Concerns
While the rationale and plans may seem self evident or logical to you, the information is brand new to your employees. Be patient and clear as you present your information.

What's in it for Me?
As much as possible, address the benefits of the change to the employees. If the change is basically bad news, such as a plant closure, then be prepared to answer the question, "What will happen to me."

Customer Perspective
Think of change in terms of who is being impacted. Try to put yourself in the shoes of the employee, and think about what information would be important to you.

What's Next in the Partnership?

The role of the supervisor will change as business continues to change. HR can assist the supervisor in adapting to the change through timely training that keeps the supervisor abreast of current trends and ideas in management. Web-based information will proliferate, and the savvy supervisor will work with HR to extract the best information from the web.

As the demographics of the world change, so will the complexion of the workplace. A supervisor who is well equipped to handle the challenges of a diverse workforce will succeed in the future.

Managing a workforce that is flexible will require a better understanding of the dynamics involved in managing permanent vs. contract employees. And while life-long employment may be a smaller part of business culture in the future, treating employees with respect will always be rewarded in the long run.

Work and family balance will continue to be a central theme in American business, and will continue to be a major challenge to supervisors in every type of organization. Helping employees find the balance between work and personal time will at a minimum be appreciated by employees, and can have a positive impact on your goals and ultimately your customer.

Case Study

Based on the contents of this chapter, and your own knowledge, determine the contact points between you and HR in the following case study. How can your partnership with HR help drive the best possible outcome to the issues presented below?

On Thursday, Torrie Brunowski, the new first shift supervisor for a fast growing e-commerce call center, received instructions to accelerate the certification of his new call center employees in anticipation of a 100 percent increase in call volume for the next quarter.

With no open time on the departmental calendar, Torrie took an informal poll of his new call center employees to see how many would be willing to come in over the weekend to finish their certification. Because budgets were in the process of significant trimming, Torrie also asked if they would volunteer their time. Most of the eager new call center employees, all of whom were nonexempt hourly employees, agreed to come in on Saturday and Sunday. A few cited family obligations and requirements.

The training went very well over the weekend, although it was condensed from an 80-hour program to a 16-hour program. Only one person, the senior call center employee who actually did the training, entered the weekend hours on his time card. Torrie thanked the team for its efforts by closing the center an hour early the following Friday, giving each employee an excused absence without pay on the timecards.

Unfortunately, when the next quarter arrived, the documented call center metric for customer satisfaction dropped by 50 percent to an all-time low. Once again, Torrie began planning a weekend training session to improve his call center metrics. Any advice for Torrie?

Conclusion

To be a successful supervisor, you must find the balance between business results and the needs of employees. HR can help the supervisor manage the balance with timely and creative tools, ideas, and advice. Ideally, the roles of supervisor and HR blend to achieve great business results. Employees view the partnership in a positive light because it is consistent and fair in employee matters. The partnership allows HR to become more engaged in the business, and it gives the supervisor an opportunity to explore the people side of the business with more confidence and agility.

Developing a partnership with HR gives you an edge in meeting business goals. Whether you are a new or experienced supervisor, developing a positive relationship with HR will help you meet the challenge of managing your employees—your organization's human assets. Don't wait for HR to find you. Find HR, and start the partnership.

References

Baehr ME. *Predicting Success in Higher Level Positions*. Westport, CT: Quorom, 1992.

Hawley J. *Reawakening the Spirit in Work*. San Francisco: Berrett-Koehler, 1993, pp 12-14.

Jones JW. *High-Speed Management*. San Francisco: Jossey-Bass, 1993, pp 15-16.

Ulrich D (ed). *Delivering Results: A New Mandate for Human Resource Professionals*. Cambridge MA: Harvard Business Review Book, 1998, p 319.

Hawley, Jack. *Reawakening the Spirit in Work*. Berrett-Koehler Publishers, San Francisco, 1993, pp 12-14.

Review Questions

1. What is the basis for the partnership between supervisors and HR?

2. Who is responsible for the employees in your company, the supervisor or HR?

3. What areas of personal development would you work on with your organization's HR group?

4. If you were about to make a significant change in your operation, would you include HR in your process?

5 Supervising a Diverse Workforce

by Joy Colwell, JD

What Will I Learn in This Chapter?

In this chapter, we cover supervising today's changing workforce, focusing on the following:

- how the workforce (and workplace) is actually changing
- the growth of a multicultural workforce
- recognizing the importance of cultural differences and dealing with the foreign manager
- supervising the multicultural workforce
- how workforce diversity enhances the workplace.

Overview

Today's workforce is very different from yesterday's; and tomorrow's workforce will be different still. Workforce diversity was an outgrowth of the affirmative action movement, and is often thought of in terms of gender, race, age, disability status, and other protected classes. Today diversity is a much broader term and covers a workforce in which employers respect all the differences among workers. Each worker brings a unique mix of perspectives, skills, talents and influences to his or her job. A capable supervisor looks to bring out the best in everyone while respecting each worker's unique qualities.

Diversity in the workplace goes beyond the "protected class" status conferred by the federal antidiscrimination laws on the characteristics of race, gender, national origin, religion, color, age and disability status. Diversity includes all those and such things as personality type, sexual preference, experience, educational background, communication style and other socioeconomic characteristics (SHRM, 2002). Supervisors will want to create a respectful workplace in which everyone, regardless of his or her background and characteristics, will want to do the best possible job.

While cultivating diversity is the right thing to do, it also has a positive impact on the bottom line. The theories for the positive impact of cultivating diversity include:

- Increased worker satisfaction, leads to an increased competitive advantage.
- Organizations that cultivate diversity have the best reputations, and therefore attract the best personnel.
- Organizations with the most diverse workforce can attract the most diverse (and therefore widest) markets.

- Diversity in the workforce leads to creative thinking and better problem-solving, due to the range of thought patterns and discussions from a diverse workforce.
- Organizations that manage diversity have lower human resources costs, since they have lower turnover rates, lower rates of absenteeism, etc.

Regardless of which diversity theory you subscribe to, you will be supervising a diverse workforce today and into the future.

Fact or Fiction?

Here are some examples that supervisors might recognize. We will use them to illustrate common diversity issues.

Issue 1

Jennifer who is in her late 20s has been hired by EFG Company, and Steve is her supervisor. Jennifer has come to HR, with some concerns about Steve. Steve is in his middle 50s, and has been treating Jennifer in a way that makes her uncomfortable. When he introduced her to the department, he said, *"This is Jennifer: she'll go a long way to making things prettier around here."* When he introduced Justin, who was hired about the same time, Steve said, *"This is Justin: he comes highly recommended and I'm sure he'll do great things for the company."*

Steve calls Jennifer into his office regularly and asks her opinion on whether his tie matches his shirt, and what he should get his wife for a gift. He has even asked her which vacuum cleaner he should buy, because *"she's a girl and knows about things like that."* He has made several comments about Jennifer reminding him of his daughter, who is about the same age.

Jennifer tells HR that Steve treats her more like a family member than a professional.

Issue 2

Maria, who is Latina, has been hired by EFG Company, and Steve is her supervisor. Maria has come to HR, with some concerns about Steve. Steve is in his middle 50s, and has been treating her in a way which makes her uncomfortable. When he introduced her to the department, he said, *"This is Maria: she'll go a long way to making things more colorful around here."* When he introduced Justin, who was hired about the same time, Steve said, *"This is Justin: he comes highly recommended and I'm sure he'll do great things for the company."*

Steve calls Maria into his office regularly and asks her opinion on whether his tie matches his shirt, and what he should get his wife for a gift. He has even asked her which vacuum cleaner he should buy, because *"she knows about things like that."* Maria tells HR that Steve treats her unprofessionally, and that she's leaving the company.

Issue 3

One of your employees is of Middle Eastern descent. This employee comes to you and says that the others are making remarks about Islam and Arabs. One of the employees is saying that he must be a terrorist. He thinks the others are avoiding him, or are speaking to him less. What should you do?

Issue 4

Mark is a long-time employee, and recently joined a very strict fundamentalist Christian church. Some of your other employees have come to you to complain that Mark is using breaks and lunch hours to convince them to join his church. One of the young male employees has had Mark take him to task over his smoking, drinking, partying lifestyle. Another of your employees, a young single mother, has had Mark make remarks about her "bastard" child and life of sin.

Another employee, who is gay, has received strong statements from Mark, about going to hell for his lifestyle choice. Mark has asked this employee to go with him to church, because God *"hates the sin but loves the sinner."* Your employees have asked you to speak with Mark.

Issue 5

A new employee has been assigned to your area. The new employee uses a wheelchair. The other employees generally ignore the newcomer. In the past they have invited the new employees to share break or lunchtimes with them, they have failed to do so with this employee. The employees also routinely invite each other out after work to socialize, and make these plans during work time in the hearing of other employees, but have never invited the new employee. What should you do?

Issue 6

One of your employees, Chris, is extremely overweight. The others make remarks about this employee, calling him/her names and making comments about eating habits. Some of your employees have made comments like *"Is there anything left in the cafeteria?"* when Chris returns from lunch. If there is a cake or other food in the work area, the employees make remarks like *"better hide this before Chris sees it."* Comments are made about breaking chairs, etc. What should you do?

These situations cover a range of typical issues that can face a supervisor. This chapter provides information that will help you handle them.

Changing Nature of the Workforce

The United States has always taken great pride in the fact that it is made up of many different kinds of people. Today, however, the nature of our diversity is changing. Table 5-A shows some of those changes. The number of African Americans, Asians and Hispanics in our population has grown. The most recent census gives us some ideas about the numbers and the percentages.

The stereotypical image of a white, male, European-heritage workforce has disappeared (many would say it only existed in certain parts of the country for a very short period, anyway). The statistics show that those able and available for work (the labor pool) is actually shrinking because the U.S. population is aging. The World War II "Baby Boom" adults are passing through middle age, and there are fewer people to replace them in the workforce. In 1997, the Baby Boomers (who were age 32-50 on January 1 of that year), accounted for 29.5 percent of the total population. By 2005, workers age 55 and over will be nearly 20 percent of the workforce, and by 2010 a Hudson Institute study warns of a severe labor shortage as the Baby Boomers begin to retire (information from *Maturity Works* website).

As a result of all these changes, the workforce is changing to include more women, racial and ethnic minorities, immigrants and

Table 5-A. The Changing U.S. Population

	2000	%	2050	%
Total Population	281.4 million		394 million	
White	211.4 million	75%		53%
African American	34.6 million	12%		15%
Asian	10.2 million	3.6%		9%
Hispanic (of any race)	35.3 million	12.5%		24%
American Indian	3.53 million	.9%		1%

Source: The U.S. Census 2000 (and projections)

Figure 5-1. Tips for Supervisors

- Practice sound supervisory skills.
- Apply them universally, not according to gender.
- If your authority is being questioned or ignored:
  - Determine if other supervisors are having the same problem.
  - Confront the employee with your observations.
  - Outline your expectations for a change of behavior.
  - Explain the consequences if your expectations aren't met.

- If employees are going around you to your manager:
  - Go to your manager and seek support to ensure that your authority isn't being undermined.
  - If the problem still persists, take appropriate disciplinary action with the employee.

people with disabilities. In the rest of this chapter, we will be dealing with how supervisors can respond to this changing workforce.

Women in the Workforce

According to the U.S. Bureau of Labor Statistics, in 2001 women made up approximately 46.7 percent of the workforce. Listed below are a few guidelines that will help you think about working with women.

- **Treat all employees with respect.** Treat female employees as equal to male employees You should avoid sexual remarks and innuendo and enforce that policy with your employees. Language should be civil and businesslike at all times.
- Adopt and practice sound supervisory skills, and apply them universally, not according to gender. Good supervision is good supervision, regardless of gender.
- If you are a female supervisor, and you find your authority is being questioned or ignored, find out if other supervisors are having similar difficulties. Don't automatically assume that it is gender-related. It may be some other factor. Confront the individual(s) with your observations, just as you would with any other employee behavior problem. Outline expectations and the consequences if the expectations aren't met.
- If employees are going around you to your manager, go to your boss and seek support to ensure that your authority isn't being undermined.

If the problem persists, take the appropriate disciplinary action stated in the policy manual.

If we consider Jennifer, in Issue 1, we can see that some of the tension between her and her supervisor is based on gender issues. Steve, by consulting her about issues such as vacuum cleaners and gifts for his wife, is singling her out on the basis of gender to discuss non-work-related issues. While Steve may think that he is paying her compliments, and that she likes his remarks and attention, she obviously feels belittled. Steve should work to become aware of how his treatment of female employees may affect the working relationship.

Racial and Ethnic Diversity in the Workforce

As shown in Table 5-A, minorities are becoming a larger part of the workforce. It is predicted that by the year 2020, white non-Hispanic people will be 67 percent of the workforce, down from 76 percent. Hispanic people will comprise 14 percent of the workforce, up from 9 percent. Asians will be 6 percent of the workforce, up from 4 percent, and African Americans will remain about 11 percent of the workforce.

When dealing with racially and ethnically diverse workers, here are some tips:
- Be aware of any biases or stereotypes that you may have. If you have any biases or stereotypes, do not act on them. Fair treatment of all workers is your goal as a supervisor.
- Be sure you don't use any racial or ethnic slurs or jokes, and ensure that coworkers don't either. As an example: If you're Irish, you may enjoy Irish jokes, but they are not appropriate for the workplace. Using racial or ethnic slurs can provide the basis for a very expensive antidiscrimination complaint.

- Don't treat minorities differently, either positively or negatively, just because they are minorities. Don't show off your minority employees to try to prove you're not prejudiced.
- If a claim of harassment or discrimination is brought to you, try not to overreact to charges of mistreatment or discrimination. Remaining calm can help to defuse the situation while you seek a solution and conduct whatever investigation is required by your workplace.

If we look at Issues 2 and 3, we can see that race and ethnicity can present diversity issues (and potential discrimination issues). In Issue 2, if Steve treats Maria, who is a Latina, the way he treats Jennifer, it may be a gender issue that Steve has. If we look at Steve's particular remarks in Maria's case, it can be inferred that he is making comments about his doubts about Maria's suitability for the job: it sounds like he is implying that Maria might be better suited for other types of employment. Steve may lose a good employee in Maria for his insensitive or biased treatment of her as either a woman or a member of the Hispanic community.

In Issue 3, the supervisor must take steps to insure that harassment on the basis or race, ethnicity or national origin does not occur. Such harassment can expose the company to liability for discrimination under Title VII (see Chapter 3, Supervisors, Employment and Workplace Law. All employees have the same basic needs, one of which is to be treated equitably and *fairly*. Remember, good supervision means the same treatment for everyone who works in the modern workplace.

The Aging Workforce

The mix and range of ages in the workforce is changing very rapidly. Age 55 and over is the usual statistical breaking point used to define older workers. The U.S. Census Bureau estimates that by the year 2005, people 55 and over will have greatly increased, and by 2010 will be nearly 25 percent of the workforce. Baby Boomers now account for about 29.5 percent of the population. The average age of the population is rising, and by the year 2040 the average age will be 40.3 years. We are faced with an aging population, and the retirement of the Baby Boomers will have a large impact on the U.S. workforce. This is one reason why we have to learn how to supervise the changing workforce.

Generation X, generally refers to those born between 1961 and 1984. This younger generation may not respond to the same sort of motivational strategies that have worked in the past with Baby Boomers, and they may have different expectations of the workplace. Supervisors and older workers sometimes think that Generation Xers do not have appropriate behaviors at work, and may think them lacking in intelligence and/or ambition. Some flexibility and adjustment in at-work behaviors may be required on the part of both older and the younger workers.

In the 21st century, many workers will be encouraged to work to an older age. Because of the changes in Social Security and increased life expectancies, many will find they need (and want) to work well past age 65. Some people may retire from one company and start another career. People will return to work from retirement.

Today, you'll be supervising a lot of older workers, regardless of your age. If you're younger than many of those you supervise (and that's increasingly likely), you may feel there are special problems involved, for you and them. If you are an older worker and a supervisor, you may feel there is some difficulty in communicating across the age gaps, or in getting the right level of production out of your fellow employees. There are some differences between older workers and others in the workplace. Of course, as with everyone else, there are many who don't exhibit these differences. For the majority of people over age 55, however, there are some fairly common characteristics that will help us all to understand why they work and how they work (Figure 5-2). This understanding will help in determining how you can best supervise them.

> Figure 5-2. Key Issues when Supervising Older Workers
>
> - Recognize value differences.
> - Focus on job satisfaction.
> - Avoid stereotypes.
> - Appreciate experience.

- Recognize value differences. Older workers have values that are often quite different from those of younger or middle-aged workers. The older workers will be products of the post-depression and post-World War II, Korean and Viet Nam Conflict eras. They will probably have a strong work ethic, and will place a premium on job and financial security. They will probably be very loyal to the organization they work for.
- While certainly not true of all seniors, many at this stage in their careers may put more value on how satisfying their current work is, rather than salary increases or advancement. They may not desire or be motivated to advance any further, concentrating instead on job satisfaction.
- The older worker is probably not a "me first" type. Younger workers have grown up in the Me Generation. They may look for self-actualizing work and faster advancement, and that may mean skipping from one organization to the next. The older worker may have difficulty accepting these differences in values.
- Avoid stereotypes. If you dig into it, you'll find that the aging process has little to do with the core personality. Again, the principles of good supervision will serve you well. Don't assume that personality changes or characteristics are due to aging.

Appreciate older workers as the valuable resource that they are. Studies have repeatedly shown that older workers generally possess some characteristics very much prized in the workplace: loyalty, lower rates of turnover, lower rates of absenteeism among healthy workers and higher rates of job satisfaction. One major study even found that older workers surpassed younger workers in both speed and skill, indicating that experience rather than age determined performance. Overall, most of the studies show that there are no great measurable differences in productivity between age groups in the workplace, although older workers generally have fewer on-the-job accidents, especially in situations that require judgment based on experience. Extensive research has found no relationship between age and on-the-job performance (*MaturityWorks*).

If we go back to Jennifer in Issue 1, some of her issues with Steve may be due to generational differences. Steve may be treating her like a daughter, not a worker. Some of his behaviors may be a reflection on his perception of how it is proper to treat a young lady, and are not intended to be discriminatory or patronizing. A discussion with Steve may point out that an employee, even a young one, may not appreciate his efforts as they were intended, and he needs to modify his approach.

Disabled in the Workforce

More and more organizations have come to realize that persons with disabilities are an often overlooked but valuable human resource. Through a combination of state and federal government affirmative action programs on behalf of persons with disabilities, and the Americans with Disabilities Act, organizations have found effective and meaningful ways to employ these workers. Physically and mentally impaired people, identified under the legal definition of disability, are a large potential pool of very effective workers (see Chapter 3 for more information).

There are lots of resources to help employers and employees find accommodations, so that workers with disabilities can be employed. Workers with visual or hearing impairments or other disabilities often have access to technical devices that make it possible for them to perform a very wide range of work activities, or know where to find out information about such devices. Be as thorough when orienting and training disabled workers as you would with any other worker. Remember that the disability does not affect the willingness to work.

Aside from the particular worksite and job accommodations that might be imposed by the disability involved, don't treat the disabled worker any differently—better or worse—than any other worker. Issue 4 describes a common situation: other employees appear to be uncomfortable with a disabled worker, or treat the person differently. Educating your staff about the disability can help improve coworker relationships. In Issue 6, if Chris is clinically obese, his or her weight might arise to the level of a disability, which would be protected under the ADA. If not, Chris' supervisor should still make sure that employees treat everyone with respect, regardless of their entitlement to protection under federal laws. Remember that diversity is a broader concept than the antidiscrimination laws, so supervisors should be encouraging all employees to treat each other with respect.

A Multicultural Workforce

What is *culture*? It's all those things that make up a way of life and ways of doing things: language, customs, beliefs, feelings about work and play, methods of working, family life and so on (Figure 5-3).

Some Differences in the Workforce

According to the U.S. Department of Labor's *Workforce Two-Thousand One* report, immigrants are expected to represent the largest share of the increase in the workforce and population as a whole in the next few decades. International migration is projected to remain at about 820,000 people per year from now until the year 2050. The reports relate that the largest influx will be from those of Hispanic and Asian origins. This is clearly a change from the past when most immigrants came from countries and cultures of European origin. Several other cultures such as Afghani, Bahamian, Cambodian, Eritrean, Ethiopian, Filipino, Greek, Indian, Iranian, Iraqi, Pakistani, Thai, Turkish and Vietnamese are expected to increase over the next decade.

Understanding Cultural Differences in the Workplace

Today's workplace is made up of people from our previous groups of immigrants, such as African, Belgian, Dutch, English, French, German, Hungarian, Irish, Italian, Polish, Spanish, etc. Of course, this varies in different parts of the country, just as it always has. In manufacturing facilities, it is common to find employees from a variety of ethnic backgrounds. Many are first-generation immigrants. In high tech labs, one often finds immigrants who have specialized in computer technology. In previous eras, we find that entire industries were dominated by certain immigrant groups. All of these people, then and now, brought their cultures with them, practiced and often maintained those cultures while melting into that of the United States.

Figure 5-3. What Is Culture?

Culture is all of those things that make up a way of life and ways of doing things: language, customs, and beliefs, feelings about work and play and methods of working.

This multicultural workforce is made up of the people whom you will be supervising. If you don't understand some aspects of their cultures, you will have a difficult time doing your job.

Examples of Cultural Differences that Affect Work

When we talk about cultural characteristics, we talk in generalities (Figure 5-4). There will always be exceptions to the generality. Those we discuss here are generally recognized as common cultural traits, even though individual members of a given culture may not follow all of the practices. Thus, you can only use these descriptions as a guide to understanding behavior. Do not assume that they are true of all members of any group. Avoid turning useful concepts into stereotypes.

In the United States we are accustomed to the idea of *individual rights*, and we expect people to stand up for their rights. We are used to ideas of *individual importance, respect for rights, and equality*. But in many foreign cultures:

- The *group is more important than* the individual.
- Relationships *do not emphasize respect for individual rights*.
- There may be *more cultural respect for hierarchical relationships*, such as the supervisor-employee relationship.
- Some cultures have a *great respect for tradition*, and may be uncomfortable with change.

Figure 5-4. Examples of Cultural Differences

- Some foreign-born employees may be reluctant to demonstrate initiative.
- Many Asian cultures are sensitive to group harmony.
- Cambodians are team workers.
- In the Middle East, ones word is one's honor.
- To Mexicans, small talk before business is the way to do business.
- French workers may have difficulty believing working hard will improve ones position beyond what one is born into.
- To Japanese, group success rather than individual success is what counts.
- Japanese and Europeans feel that simply being hired by the company will motivate employees.

- Many cultures favor an *indirect communication style,* while U.S. citizens favor a direct approach to communication.

When dealing with persons of different cultures, some of these different attitudes may appear in the workplace.
- Some foreign-born employees may appear *reluctant to show initiative.* Their respect for authority can make them hesitant to do so.
- They may *pretend to understand directions* because they are afraid to ask questions.

East Indians, for example, expect decisions to be made by their superiors in the company and have a difficult time with participative supervision and management. Many people from Asian cultures are sensitive to group harmony. As a result, being singled out for praise may not be viewed as positive. Praise can actually be interpreted to mean something is actually wrong (the exact opposite of what you may have intended). Tangible rewards may be viewed as more satisfactory.

The Japanese, for example, typically focus on group or team effort, with a great respect for seniority when it comes to promotion. Singling out an individual for praise is unacceptable. Promoting a junior employee over others, regardless of ability, is unacceptable. To the Japanese, tasks that involve working alone are not going to be very satisfying.

Cambodians are team workers, and their usual team is an extended family unit (fathers, mothers, sons, daughters, aunts, uncles, cousins). Several food-processing plants have had the experience of hiring these teams (usually without understanding they were relatives). The Cambodian team has an apparent leader and that is the person with whom the supervisor must deal. (Usually the best English speaker acts as if he is the leader—it would never be a woman.) The actual leader, however, may be an older and less physically able team member who doesn't speak any English but commands great respect from the team. These teams are usually very productive, outperforming most other teams. At the same time, they often carry some very unproductive family members along with them, one of whom might even be the team leader. Supervisors who try to do something about the unproductive members will, quite simply, either lose the whole team or destroy its productivity and morale.

In the Middle East, one's word is one's honor. If an employee is instructed to improve a certain element of his or her work and then the conversation is summarized in a memo, the employee may take the putting of a commitment in writing as a symbol of mistrust. On the other hand, Americans often assume a commitment exists with a handshake or smile. Middle Easterners do not. They must specifically state, "*You have my word,*" or the clear equivalent.

In the Mexican culture, it is often common to engage in small talk before dealing with the business at hand. Informal conversation before giving directives is viewed as the proper way of working together. Supervisors who ignore small talk and come right to the point are seen as crude, rude and demeaning. Most Hispanic cultures reflect these same values, but there are great variations. For example, Argentineans and Cubans seem to get to business much more quickly than Mexicans or Puerto Ricans, who place greater value on developing a relationship. Many cultures value developing a relationship first, before doing business, and feel that jumping right in and getting to the point (a U.S. approach) is inappropriate or rude.

The French tend to be class conscious, and this carries over into the workforce. French workers may have difficulty accepting the American idea that working hard may improve one's position beyond the place in life one is born into. That place in life is usually seen as reaching back many generations.

Asians generally have a great deal of concern with face. Westerners often refer to this as saving or losing face, but the concept also includes gaining, maintaining and having face. For example, *Santosumi san has much face* means Mr. Santosumi is a person who has a sense of his oneness and place in life, but the phrase does not imply status or intelligence. If you treat Mr. Santosumi in a way that might embarrass him, for example, by singling him out for praise or chastisement, he will lose face, and so will you!

Both Japanese and Europeans feel that a key employee will be motivated by the mere fact the company has hired him or her. In Japan, particularly, this motivation through identification with the company may go on for a lifetime of very low wages. In the United States we may look more at monetary rewards as motivational or as a form of recognition.

When it comes to safety, take special care. Some cultures do not place the same emphasis and value on individual life as we do. Many do not place legal responsibility for safe procedures on the employer. Consequently, in many parts of the world, unsafe practices tend to be the rule rather than the exception. When you have an employee from one of these areas, you will have to watch his or her safety habits and probably do a good deal of retraining. Note: This information is not a complete list of cultural traits. It doesn't even touch the surface. It just shows the impact that cultural differences can have in the workplace.

While diversity may not be a concept familiar to other cultures, *respect and fairness seem* to be universal concepts. By stressing respect and fairness in relationships, and good intent, a supervisor can go a long way in bettering relationships in a diverse workforce.

Working with Foreign National Managers

Working for a foreign national manager has become more and more common for supervisors. The growth of foreign-owned or mixed-ownership companies in the United States is increasing rapidly. Most Americans do not understand that the same is true all over the world. The reality is that the world's economy has truly become global. There are few finished products made anywhere in the world that do not involve a significant number of parts made in other countries.

Generally, U.S. antidiscrimination laws apply to U.S.-owned and controlled companies located in foreign countries, and to foreign companies with workplaces located in the United States. This can create issues for foreign managers here, or for U.S. managers in foreign countries, who may be dealing with very different ideas about workplace rights and appropriate treatment of workers.

Many managers coming to the United States from foreign countries may not be used to dealing with the diverse workforce that is common here. Because of wide-ranging antidiscrimination laws, Americans are accustomed to seeing and dealing with all kinds of people in the workforce on a daily basis. This is not true in other countries. Relatively few countries have the kind of antidiscrimination laws which we take for granted. For a foreign manager, dealing with our diverse workers may be even more of a challenge.

Moving Managers

One of the natural results of the growth of global companies is that the home-country headquarters of a company frequently sends trusted managers to newer operations. As these companies become truly global, they ship their managers anywhere they're needed. Many truly global companies require their managers to take assignment outside the manager's home country if they wish to be promoted to higher levels in the company. Thus, it would be relatively common to find a U.S.-based multinational company sending one of its British managers to work in North Africa, or even in the United States. So the odds continue to increase that someday you will be working for a foreign national manager.

Special Problems for Supervisors

Managing a company in a country other than your own is a difficult business. It is very similar to supervising a multicultural workforce, only this time you, the supervisor, are on the receiving end (Figure 5-5). The problem for you is twofold:
1. The foreign manager may not really understand the American culture and may inadvertently create communication problems.
2. What you can do about the misunderstanding so the manager's expectations can be met, or if they cannot, the reasons will be understood.

While the manager may have received some training about the language and culture of the country, it was probably quite limited, and may have lasted only a few days. Essentially, many managers sent abroad (and this also applies to those who come here) get a "crash course" in language, culture and customs on the job.

To illustrate the special task you have, let's look at an example.

Figure 5-5. The Supervisor and the Foreign National Manager

The supervisor should assume that the foreign manager:
- knows what he is doing but may not know how it will work with U.S. citizens.
- regards his request as reasonable so your job is to suggest better ways to achieve the goal.
- is trying to adapt to the U.S. business style just as you are trying to adapt to his.

Case Study: Foreign National Managers

Seiji Sakamoto is from Japan. He has been a manager for 12 years in Japan and Southeast Asia for the Nihon Manufacture and Export Consortium (NMEC). This is his first assignment in the United States. NMEC bought out your company and has introduced all kinds of new human resource management techniques. They have introduced common employee uniforms for everybody, including the managers. There is a common cafeteria where everyone eats together, officers and employees. Teams and quality circles have been formed, and top management has set a goal of increasing production by 20 percent in the next 12 months. They advise you that this will still leave the U.S. plant production 16 mpercent behind a comparable NMEC facility in Osaka, Japan.

Your team has not been achieving the production goal. Mr. Sakamoto advises you to introduce group criticism sessions as a way to identify problems and improve production. He insists on attending them with you at the beginning in order to get things off to a good start.
At the first session, Mr. Sakamoto asks you and your employees to stand up and describe what they are doing wrong, what mistakes they have made in the past week, and then let the group address how these mistakes and errors should be corrected. Nobody bites.

What's going on here? There is a major problem of cultural misfit. In the Japanese culture, self-criticism is a way of life. If you say to a Japanese woman, Your husband is a very smart man, I am impressed by how well he does his job, she will likely respond, Oh no, you must be mistaken; my husband is not so bright and only does what is necessary. This is the sort of thing that goes on throughout Japanese life. In the Japanese culture, praise can only be responded to with self-

Case Study

criticism, and the self-criticism is sincere. Thus, in a typical Japanese employee self-criticism session, workers will stand and recite their individual mistakes and ask for suggestions. The basic assumption is that you are prone to mistakes and have many shortcomings as an individual.

It would take a lot of conditioning before that could become routine in a U.S. factory, and we doubt if it ever really could. This is not to say that U.S. workers can't find ways to improve things. They can, but they prefer to do things in a positive way. How can we improve the process? What else can be done to make things better? That is the way we do things in our culture. The basic assumption is that we are doing things well, but will try to improve.

So what do you do in these circumstances? You probably didn't know about the self-criticism part of the Japanese culture, but you would know that Mr. Sakamoto's approach was not going to be successful. Therefore, you try to head it off with some explanations about how you think things could be improved with your work team.

Essentially, you should assume that the foreign manager:
- knows what he (99 percent of the time, since gender equity is not alive and well outside the United States) is doing, but may not know how it will work with Americans.
- regards his request as reasonable, so your job is to suggest better ways to achieve the goal.
- is trying to adapt to the U.S. business style just as you are trying to adapt to his.

In the next section, we deal with some tips on supervising the mixed-culture workforce. Many of these tips can be applied upward to your foreign manager.

Supervising the Mixed-Culture Workforce

So how do you put it all together? The cardinal rule is: *be aware of cultural differences and the fact that your style of supervision can be misinterpreted due to cultural differences.* Don't assume that just because your workers are in the United States now, they understand all of the U.S. ways or customary practices (Figure 5-6). The following tips will help you supervise employees of other cultures:

- Be aware of any of your own biases and remember that it is *your responsibility to treat all employees fairly and with respect*. Fairness and respect are concepts that can cross most cultures.
- Simplify your communication.
- When giving spoken instructions, use clear and simple words.
- If possible, show pictures or slides to illustrate what you mean. Use universal symbols and drawings or photographs.
- Be specific and explain if words or phrases are misunderstood.
- Emphasize safety. Explain the safety rules and instructions for all processes and activities for the employees.

Figure 5-6. Tips on Supervising a Workforce from Different Cultures

- Be aware of any of your biases.
- Treat all employees fairly. Fairness is a concept that crosses most cultures.
- Simplify your communication—and insist on feedback on what you've said or written.
- Be specific and explain if words or phrases are misunderstood.
- Avoid using slang or jargon.
- Avoid jokes or sarcasm.
- Get feedback.
- Strongly encourage interaction.
- Look at the employees' nonverbal cues (facial expressions, body language, etc.).
- Explain any miscommunications or misunderstandings.
- Do not talk down to employees.
- Show some interest in their culture, language and traditions.

- Insist on feedback to assure that you are understood. If they cannot speak English, always use an interpreter and get the feedback through the interpreter.
- Strongly encourage interaction so you can check to be sure that you are being understood.
- Avoid using slang or jargon that could be misinterpreted or not understood.
- Avoid jokes or sarcasm. Some humor does translate from one language/culture to another. Much does not. Worse yet, some humor translates in exactly the opposite meaning.
- Look at the employee's nonverbal cues and body language to check understanding. If he/she looks confused or blank, someone missed the mark.
- Use clear and precise writing and instructions. Use universal symbols and drawings or photographs, when possible.
- Never talk down to the foreign-born employee.
- Where possible show interest in their culture, language and traditions.

Conflicts Between Coworkers

Supervisor must be aware of any conflict among your staff, and you should try to resolve it. As we have already emphasized, you can't just ignore conflict. You must confront it and resolve it. Cross-cultural conflicts between employees can flare up and become very hot, often resulting in racial or ethnic slurs and leaving bitter memories. There are some straightforward techniques you can use to correct these situations:

- Avoid taking sides, regardless of your own prejudices or preferences, and *stress similarities rather than differences.*
- Maintain an unemotional stance. Don't overreact by offering ultimatums. Transferring or firing an employee is usually not an effective

solution. *Remaining levelheaded helps to defuse otherwise emotionally charged situations.*
- Give the employees an opportunity to resolve their differences, *with you as a neutral, objective, third party.* In this *mediator role,* use the active listening process to identify the facts and attempt to move everyone toward a solution.
- If necessary, refer the employees for further coaching or training, usually to the employee assistance program (EAP) or employee relations area in your organization.
- Remember, supervisors are not counselors—leave it to the professionals to give employees lots of in-depth coaching and training.

Importance of ISO Standards in Your Workplace

ISO stands for the *International Organization for Standardization.* The mission of ISO is to promote the development of standardization to facilitate the worldwide exchange of goods and services. It originally created standards to ensure consistency in manufacturing through quality management systems. The ISO 9000:2000 standards propose a process model that can be applied to any type of business, not just manufacturing, to produce consistent quality.

One of the eight Quality Management Principles of ISO 9000:2000 concerns involvement of people. Principle 3 states: "*People at all levels are the essence of an organization, and their full involvement enables their abilities to be used for the organization's benefit.*" The key benefits of this provision are:
- motivation and commitment of the workforce
- innovation and creativity
- accountability and participation in continuous improvement.

While this quality management principle does not specify diversity in the workforce, it does embrace a sense of empowerment and respect for workers' abilities. Note that by the end of 1999, ISO had issued 343,643 ISO 9000 certifications for quality management, worldwide.

Conclusion

We reviewed aspects of the diverse U.S. workplace of today and the immediate future. Some may not be comfortable with the vision, but all are going to have to live with it. In reality, the U.S. has gained from each person in it. We need the talents, skills and abilities of everyone to make the United States the best in the global marketplace.

The workplace of today and tomorrow will be made up of more minorities, more women, older workers, workers with disabilities—and new citizens from other countries who, by their presence, affirm their belief that the United States of America is still the best place to live and work. Supervisors will need to be sensitive to all these changes, and to know the different ways to deal with all these people from different cultures who make up the workforce. At the same time, supervisors must recognize the need to maintain control and to supervise. Good supervision and fairness are the keys to success with the diverse workforce.

Reference

Society for Human Resource Management White Paper. *How Should My Organization Define Diversity?* Alexandria, VA: SHRM, Oct. 9, 2002.
Maturity Works website: http://www.maturityworks

Review Questions

1. How do I treat employees who are much younger or older than I am? Who are of a different race, religion, ethnicity or gender?

2. Am I aware of how coworkers are treating each other? What do I do to create an atmosphere in which all employees feel included?

3. What can I do to create an environment of respect for everyone?

6 Communication

by Meredith Onion
Alicia J. O'Brien

What Will I Learn in This Chapter?

In this chapter, we will be dealing with five key aspects of effective communication between supervisors and their employees. These are:

- looking at current skills
- the three kinds of communication
- active listening
- communicating one-on-one with those you supervise
- communicating with groups.

Overview

Although in today's fast-paced business environment, there are many more means of communication (including teleconferencing, video-conferencing, e-mail, voicemail, page messages, fax messages, etc.), this also means there are that many more ways to miscommunicate. In addition to the many new means of communication, in today's global workplace, supervisors are working with a more culturally diverse workforce. You may also be supervising, or at least dealing with, people across the country or somewhere else in the world. Now more than ever, it is important for supervisors to improve their communication skills.

Looking at Current Skills

More than anything else, being a supervisor means working with people. To work with people, you must be able to communicate. Therefore, being an effective supervisor means being an effective communicator. If you have ever seen or worked with, a supervisor who didn't give clear, concise instructions, or who mumbled a few words to you that you didn't understand, or who used jargon that was unfamiliar to you, you learned a little about ineffective communication. In this chapter, we will be dealing with the skills needed for effective communication with your employees.

There are three types of communication:
- verbal (talking)
- nonverbal (body language)
- written.

Clear and to-the-point communication leaves the impression that you are knowledgeable. Vague communication leaves the impression that you don't know what you're doing. If you want your team to respect you as a supervisor, learn and practice good communication skills.

Don't assume good communication happens naturally. Just like being a good leader, good communication is an acquired skill, and good communication skills are a result of thinking and practicing. Try to remember one or two work situations when you felt you had successfully communicated with others. These could be verbal, nonverbal (body language, gestures, eye contact) or written communications. For example, you delegated an assignment to one of your employees and it was completed just as you expected and right on time. This is good communication. Write down one or two examples.

Now think of one or two work situations when you didn't successfully communicate verbally, nonverbally or through written communication. For example, you were in a hurry to get to your next meeting and as you passed your assistant in the hall, you told him to "handle that safety situation." Without giving him time to ask questions, you were off to your meeting. When you returned, you found "the situation" hadn't been handled, but the assistant had requisitioned all new, top-of-the line safety glasses for your entire staff. You meant for him to have the spill on the shop floor cleaned up. Write down one or two examples of when you have poorly communicated.

Look over your examples and ask yourself:
- How could I have improved my instructions in the cases where things didn't work out?
- Was the problem mine or was it with the employees?
- Did I anticipate problems and communicate accordingly?
- Did I listen to what they were saying?
- Did I know what they could or couldn't do?

- Did any cultural or language differences contribute to the miscommunication?

Listening to Feedback

When you are a supervisor, you must be attentive to feedback from employees and those above you. What kind of feedback have you received from your subordinates, peers, or boss?

Do people often have to ask you to speak more loudly or clearly during a conversation? Then you have a communication problem and maybe a hearing problem as well.

Has someone had to ask, *"Are you listening to me?"* Has someone called and said, *"I'm a little confused by this memo you sent me."* Or, have you tried to have a serious, important conversation with one of your employees while you were on your cell phone on your way into work. When you do finally get to see the employee face-to-face, they mention that they missed half of what you said because you kept breaking up? These are examples of feedback that indicates there is a communication problem. You should listen to this feedback and act on it.

You should seek out feedback. Ask for feedback from a trusted colleague, boss or friend who will give you honest, constructive input regarding your communication skills. It can hurt a little to receive some criticism, but it's the only way you have to eliminate communication problems.

You can also ask yourself what things you're doing that you really don't intend to do. What nonverbal clues are you sending to those you supervise? Do you give instructions like a drill sergeant? Do you walk around with a frown? Do you stand with your arms crossed and folded in front of you? These can all be taken as signals of anger. Maybe you don't intend to convey anger, but that is how the nonverbal message is received. In today's very diverse workforce, the supervisor must be conscious of the signal intended and the signal received. (More on this in Chapter 5, Supervising a Diverse Workforce)

Try having your written correspondence read by a friend, a spouse, a parent or older child, and ask for interpretation of the meaning to see if the message that is received is the same one that is intended.

Finally, think about those people you know who appear to have good communication skills. How do they do it? Think about the techniques they use.

Three Kinds of Communication: Verbal, Nonverbal and Written

Good communication involves three aspects: talking, using body language and writing. To be an effective communicator, you must master all three of these ways of communicating.

Verbal Communications

We may all know how to talk, but how well we can communicate with others in the workplace is a different matter. There are some fairly simple steps you can take to improve your verbal communication as a supervisor.

Plan Your Message

You should plan what you intend to communicate. Off-the-cuff instructions seldom produce the intended results. Your employees are not mindreaders; so don't expect them to be good at reading your intentions from a few casual remarks. Decide what you want done and convey the message clearly. To do that, you have to plan your message. Ask yourself what the objective of the communication is. Then clarify your ideas so that the point of the communication is not clouded by miscellaneous chitchat. This doesn't mean being abrupt or unfriendly. It does mean thinking about what you want accomplished by the communication.

Consider the Receiver

Just who is receiving the message you are sending? Ask the following questions about the receiver:

- What type of communication does he/she respond to best? (Jose always responds better if you talk to him alone. My boss prefers e-mail messages to phone messages.)
- When and where will the receiver be able to listen to you without any undue distractions? (Mid-shift at the construction site may be too noisy.)
- Does the receiver have any biases or strong feelings about the message you plan to communicate? (Martina will have a very long, cumbersome commute to the new site you are assigning her to.)
- Does the receiver have any disabilities that you need to be sensitive to (hearing loss, impaired vision, etc.)?
- How can you communicate to help the receiver keep an open mind regarding your message? (*"Martina, I know this new location will make for a longer commute, but it is a promotional opportunity for you and maybe we can discuss a flexible work schedule so you won't have to commute at the height of rush-hour."*)

Consider How You Sound

Have you ever listened to yourself on a tape recorder and noticed that your voice sounds different from what you hear in your head? In a similar way, what other people hear when you speak is different from what's in your head. They must interpret your tone and attitude without all the thoughts in your mind. There are some key things you can do to improve the sound of your communications.

- *Tone and volume of your voice.* Is your tone of voice communicating anger, impatience, or lack of interest? Does your tone change, or is it monotone? Do you speak loudly enough for the receiver to hear you? Do you speak so loudly that everyone in the room can hear you?
- *Rate of speech.* A very fast pace, or a very slow pace of speaking can be distracting. Speaking fast causes people to miss words. Speaking too slowly causes boredom and inattention to what you are saying. Listen to those around you. If they sound slower or faster than you, you will improve communication if you try to follow their pace. Rate of speech will also vary in different parts of the country and around the world. For example, a New Yorker recently placed a phone call to a colleague in the South. After a few minutes, the colleague in the South stopped the conversation and said, "*Honey, you just need to slow down.*"
- *Clarity of language.* Articulation and choice of words is important. Articulation means getting the whole word out without swallowing huge parts of it like "*ya'll come!*" Or "*Whadaya mean?*" Or "*Dintchya unnerstan me?*" To articulate, you must speak clearly so the receiver can understand you. Avoid leaving off the end of word, such as "goin'" instead of "going" and avoid "um" or "uh."
- *Word choice.* Choose the most appropriate word for the message and the receiver. Avoid words with double meanings or words or phrases that can offend or be misinterpreted by the receiver. A simple rule of thumb when giving instructions is to keep the message short and simple.

- *Jargon.* Using jargon is only effective if all the people you are dealing with understand it. If they don't (which is probably the case), they feel ignorant or you sound arrogant. Computer buffs that talk in terms of bits, bytes, RAM and k's and they can understand each other. The person trying to learn how to use a computer doesn't have a prayer of understanding. If there is standard jargon used in your department and you're sure everyone understands what you're talking about, it's probably fine. But be careful when communicating to others outside the department.

Ask Questions

Do you ask questions to clarify understanding when you have issued some instructions or assignments? If you don't, you're depriving yourself of feedback necessary to make sure things are done right. That means you're setting yourself up for a fall. Start asking those questions to check on the delivery of your communication to the receiver, to see if he or she has interpreted your message as you intended.

Ask open-ended questions to elicit a response. For example ask, *"What do you think we can do to improve on this approach?"* Instead of *"Do you understand?"* An open-ended question has to have an answer other than *"Yes"* or *"No."* Asking open-ended questions means you'll get the feedback you're looking for.

Nonverbal Communication

Nonverbal communication covers a lot of behavior. For example, think about the supervisor who walks by a nurse who is distributing medications to patients, but doesn't stop to lock the drug cart when she goes into their room. The supervisor turns his back and walks away. He has communicated with his eyes and his body. The communication is clear, *I don't care if you violate the rules.* That may not have been his intended message, but it certainly was the received message. And all that happened without a word being spoken. Approximately 75 to 80 percent of what you communicate is done through nonverbal means. That seems like a startling amount, but just look at what constitutes nonverbal communication.

Eye Messages

Eye contact expresses interest in what you are communicating and your interest in the receiver(s). Lack of eye contact indicates that you are not interested in what you are communicating or the receiver. Think about it. What is your reaction to people who won't look you in the eye, or who always shift their eyes away from you when they give an answer. They're sending messages. How do you interpret these messages? Looking at someone when they are talking to you also means you will be able to pick up on the nonverbal cues that they are sending you.

Strong eye contact is the American way. With all communication, keep in mind that there will be differences in cultural norms. In some cultures, eye contact is not a good thing. Be aware of these potential differences and preferences in your diverse workforce.

Posture Messages

What does your posture say? Turning your back to someone during a conversation will likely send a message of dislike, disrespect or lack of importance of the subject. Good posture, on the other hand, will generally send a message of self-confidence and authority. A slouching, laid-back posture sends a slouching, laid-back message.

Hand Messages

Hand gestures send a lot of messages. There are some everyday hand gestures that can send messages that are negative, even when unintended. When a supervisor points a finger at an employee it will almost always be interpreted as accusatory or reprimanding or condescending. If you've ever had it done to you, you understand this. So why do it to others? Holding your hand up like a traffic officer indicating "Stop" can cut of all lines of open communication, even if you were only looking for a pause. On the other hand, a good firm handshake demonstrates self-confidence and a sincere message of "*It's nice to meet you,*" or "*Thank you for doing a good job.*"

Body Messages

Body language is a popular phrase that refers to all the nonverbal messages your body sends out even when you don't know it. We discussed the anger example earlier: frowning face, tightly crossed arms, spread-leg stance. In contrast to this, uncrossed arms and legs often communicate that you are open to the ideas being communicated as well as open to the communicator.

Sometimes even the distance between the communicating individuals sends a message. As you move across the United States, you find that people in different areas of the country stand at different distances from each other when they are talking. Easterners tends to stand 12 to18 inches apart (a closeness that makes Westerners very uncomfortable). Midwesterners stand 20 to 30 inches apart; Westerners 36 to 40 inches, and West Coast residents stand 20 to 24 inches apart. That is what is called the social distance. When you move too far into or away from the regional customary social distance space, people get uncomfortable.

Supervisors who get transferred from one area of the country to another, or who deal with people from different areas of the United States or even different countries should be aware of these regional differences in speaking distance and the body messages being sent. Ethnic and cultural differences complicate this even more: Mediterranean people tend to stand closer together and touch each other: Germans stand apart with little direct contact: Japanese stand quite far apart and are very formal, and so on. All of these, of course, are generalizations and there will be exceptions to each. The main point is to be aware of these differences and try to be sensitive to the preferences for personal space of the individual you are communicating with.

Dress Messages

With the movement to a more casual workplace, knowing how to dress for work has gotten a little more complex. But it holds true in most workplaces that how you dress for your job does make a difference in most supervisory positions. Is the way you dress for work consistent with your supervisory position? Look around you and make note of how your boss dresses. It's always a good rule of thumb to dress more like the boss, than your employees.

In almost every work situation, supervisors do dress somewhat differently from those they supervise. We've been told that the Japanese don't do things this way, but that's because our cultural eyes are not trained for seeing their distinctions in dress. Japanese supervisors may appear to be wearing the same coverall uniform worn by the workers, but a careful eye will note subtle distinctions in rank, such as stripes or marks similar to those on military uniforms or simply the quality of materials and tailoring.

Of course, how you dress will also depend on your industry. The formal business suit is still the dress for supervisors in many organizations. In others, shirts and ties, casual shirts and khakis, or lab smocks over jeans are acceptable. Whatever your industry norms are, dress neatly and professionally.

Case Study

Mike is a supervisor in a mid-sized manufacturing company. Mike's company recently acquired a smaller firm, with employees from Asian and Latin American countries. Fifteen of these new employees became part of Mike's team. Mike met with Human Resources to review the files of his new employees. In his review, he discovered that Julianna, one of his new employees, had a verbal warning regarding her performance and had not improved. Consequently, Mike had to address the issue. To prepare, Mike reviewed company policy on performance issues and laid out his plan to HR. With their approval, Mike proceeded to the next step.

Abiding by company policy, Mike set up a meeting with Julianna. Because Mike had not met Julianna in a one-on-one setting, Mike made every effort to make Julianna comfortable before he approached the subject of Julianna's performance. To do this, Mike shook hands with Julianna, welcomed her to his team, and gave a brief overview of his expectation of employees. However, Mike noticed that from the moment he shook Julianna's hand, Julianna did not make eye contact. Mike found this puzzling.

As the conversation continued, Mike approached the issue of Julianna's performance in a non-threatening and open manner. However, Mike felt that Julianna did not fully comprehend Mike because Julianna continued to avoid eye contact. Mike began to perceive this lack of eye contact as a lax attitude about the gravity of the problem and also as a lack of respect for Mike as a supervisor. As Mike's frustration grew, he spoke more rapidly and finally ended the conversation by asking Julianna if she understood the problem and the ramifications of her poor performance. Julianna assured Mike she did understand and

Case Study

would make every effort to correct the problem but still avoided looking at Mike. The meeting then came to an end.

What factors were at play in this exchange of communication? Did Mike prepare for the meeting and consider his verbal and nonverbal methods of communication? In this case, Mike did follow established procedures by meeting with HR and reviewing Julianna's file. Mike did prepare and also took appropriate steps to craft his message, deliver it in an appropriate setting, and correctly used face-to-face communication as his mode. So what went wrong?

Well, despite his best efforts, Mike missed a critical piece of information. Had Mike taken the time to consider the element of cultural diversity, he would have realized that in Julianna's culture, it is considered a sign of disrespect to look someone of authority in the eye. Also, had Mike done a personal inventory of his own bias, he would have realized that eye contact was a critical factor for him in one-on-one communication and recognized that all employees are not comfortable making eye contact.

Written Communication

Written communication is probably the most overused form of communication in today's workplace. Between e-mail messages, computer faxes, page messages, cell phone text messages and high-speed copy machines, our ability to generate tons of written communication have been on a steep upward increase. There was hope that with electronic enhancements, our workplace could become "virtually paperless". While the paper being generated may be less, the number of on-screen messages has increased. Of course there are numerous advantages to these electronic devices. However, in our rush to send these "fast" messages, there are more and more opportunities, once again, to mis-communicate.

So, if there is a first rule in written communication for supervisors, it is only use it when absolutely necessary. It's a much better rule of thumb to deliver a message in person so that you can allow for input, feedback, nonverbal communication and personalization.

Advantages

There are, of course, some advantages to written communications in a supervisory situation. We suggest these generally come as a follow-up to verbal communication. In that context, the advantage of written communication is that it:

- reiterates something said verbally.
- provides a record of the message delivered.
- may be taken more seriously if put in writing.

Short messages that won't leave room for misnterpretation are appropriate to put in writing in an e-mail or other text message. For example, e-mail is a quick effective way to notify the whole team that the time for the staff meeting has changed. If the agenda for the meeting is to discuss pending layoffs, putting that in an e-mail 3 days before the meeting is a good way for anxiety to take over and for production to come to a screeching halt for 3 days.

Potential Pitfalls

There are three major pitfalls to written communication. Written communication does not always offer the opportunity to check if the intended message was the message received. Also, written messages are usually impersonal and don't build rapport as verbal communication can. Finally, written communications tend to freeze flexibility. You wrote it, and now you have to live with it.

Guidelines for Effective Written Communication

Go back and review the guidelines for verbal communication because the same rules apply.
- Plan your correspondence with an objective in mind.
- Keep the receiver in mind.
- Choose words carefully to avoid jargon, slang or words that could be misinterpreted.
- Keep sentences and paragraphs short. Get to the point, keep it brief and keep it as simple as possible.

Report Writing

As a supervisor, you will at some time in your career be called upon to write a report. Reports are used for many purposes. For example, you may need to write a summary of an accident that occurred with one of your employees. In addition to reporting the facts, you may be asked to evaluate how the accident happened and to make recommendations for improvements so that this type of accident won't happen again. Another example might be to

Case Study

Theodore is a supervisor in a mid-sized bank. As part of an expansion, the bank acquires 10 new branches in satellite locations. Because of his tenure with the company and excellent performance levels, Theodore is promoted to director of the customer service units at the new branch locations. Theodore immediately sets up staff meetings with his new employees at each satellite location. Theodore also asks the HR department to provide him any available employee files, etc. for his new staff.

As Theodore proceeded to meet with the staff of each branch office, he was struck by the casual dress of many of his new employees. At the bank's corporate headquarters, there was a strict policy regarding employee attire. Among other things, this policy required male employees to wear a shirt and tie, prohibited female employees from wearing slacks of any type and also prohibited blue jeans. Theodore felt that it was important for all employees to dress professionally and abide by the same dress code.

As a result, after his meeting with all branch employees, Theodore decided to communicate the bank's dress code policy to each branch. Theodore determined the most efficient and expedient way to do this was via a group e-mail. Theodore simply crafted a short e-mail, which stated that effective immediately, the dress policy in place at the bank's corporate headquarters was applicable to branch employees. Theodore included the policy in his e-mail. In his opinion, he was simply communicating a standard company policy in the most effective mode possible.

Within a few days, Theodore received several e-mails from branch office supervisors regarding the dress code policy. Theodore was sur-

Case Study

prised that the issue caused such controversy. Questions from supervisors raised issues Theodore had not considered. For example:

- Did this policy pose a financial hardship for those female employees whose wardrobes consisted mainly of slacks or for male employees whose wardrobes did not contain sufficient shirts and ties?
- Was there any flexibility for the many part-time students that the branch office employed? Many of the student employees came to work immediately after school and formal business attire was not always practical at school.
- Were denim dresses, shirts, and skirts acceptable?
- Did the rules apply to mailroom and delivery personnel?

As you can see from these examples, Theodore's e-mail had caused a problem. In addition to the questions he received, Theodore's communication had also left branch employees with a poor impression of their new director. They felt he had not carefully thought out the immediate nature of the dress policy or the differences in between the corporate and branch work environments. All in all, Theodore had delivered what was perceived as a negative message and done so in a less-than-ideal way.

1. Did Theodore consider the full impact of his communication?
2. Do you think e-mail is the best way to communicate changes in company policy?
3. How would you handle a situation like this?

write a report to justify your request for allowing your staff to have the flexibility to work from home. Whatever the situation, here are a few guidelines for writing reports:

- *Know the purpose.* Most reports that you write will be at the request of your boss. If this is the first time you have written a report for your boss, schedule a meeting with him/her to fully understand the purpose and expectations of the report. If you are voluntarily writing a report, be sure you have a clear purpose in your own mind about why you are writing a report.
- *Know the expectations for the format.* There are numerous formats for report writing. Again, find out from your boss what he/she expects. Find out if the company has an accepted format for reports. For example, some companies will have forms to complete for a safety violation report. Other companies want proposals that are only one page long, short on text and high on bulleted, to-the-point information, with visual graphics to support your point. Other organizations, such as in university or research settings, like reports that are long and cover the topic in great detail. Don't waste time guessing what is expected. If you can get copies of past reports as examples to follow, all the better.
- *Consider delivery of the report.* Know who your intended audience is for the report and know what their preference is for how the report will be delivered. Does your boss expect a printed, bound copy of the report? Or is there a short deadline that requires the report being sent via e-mail to recipients across the globe? In addition to your written report, will you be expected to make a verbal presentation with Power Point visuals as well? Are there others in the organization that need to be copied?
- *Prepare an outline.* Even if it's a brief report, prepare an outline. An outline allows you to focus and organize your thoughts. It's a huge time

saver to plan your report in an outline instead of just typing away with no guidelines in mind.

- *Do the research.* If the purpose of your communication is to report the facts of a situation, be sure to have the facts correctly. For a safety report, this will mean interviewing the people that were involved or observed the situation. Don't rely on hearsay. If your report is to be persuasive, research sound business reasons for your proposal. Proposing flexible work arrangements because it seems like a nice thing to do for your employees probably won't fly. Are there cost savings that can be realized? Are you losing great employees to your competitor down the street because they offer this type of arrangement? Support your argument with accurate, persuasive facts.

- *Proofread, proofread, proofread.* Nothing can affect the credibility of your report more quickly than a sloppy, poorly written document. Spelling and grammatical errors just aren't acceptable. Don't rely solely on the spell/grammar check on your computer though. It won't catch everything, and it won't check the flow and readability of your report. **Always**, have at least one other person read the report before you submit it. Let the reader know what the intended purpose of the report is to see if they think you have made your point. How reader friendly is it? Did they find any spelling or grammatical errors? Be open to suggestions—even the best writers have editors!

- *Follow up.* Once you have submitted your report, follow up with your audience to be sure that the report met their expectations, to see if they need any additional information or if they have any questions.

- *It gets easier.* Your first few written reports are usually the toughest to write. But the more you practice, the more you get to know the boss's and organizations expectations for report writing, the easier they will become. Writing comes more naturally to some than others, so be patient with yourself if writing isn't your strong suit. Like most supervisory skills, the more you apply them, the easier they become.

Active Listening

Active listening is one of the most useful skills a supervisor can gain for dealing with people. It doesn't take much extra effort, just some practice.

Listening

Since we all listen, we think we know all about it. You just sit back and let the ears work. But listening is not a passive activity. It takes effort, concentration and practice. In everyday life and in your job as a supervisor, how well you listen sends a message. How well you listen also influences how much you hear and how effective you will be. Effective listening means *actively* listening. It takes practice. If you become an active listener, you will have acquired one of the most useful supervisory skills available to you.

Tips for Becoming an Active Listener

There are many different ways you can improve your active listening capacity. The following tips will help you become a better listener.

- **Have a positive attitude.** Wanting to listen is half the battle.
- **Practice.** We often aren't accustomed to really listening to others. Try it out with friends, your children, or your spouse, in all sorts of places outside of work.
- **Avoid distractions.** Turn off the radio. Find a quiet place to converse if the hospital floor you work on is noisy. Turn on the "do not disturb" button on your phone. Close your door. Clear off your desk. Avoid too

much note taking so you can concentrate on what's being said. Don't doodle.
- **Schedule the discussion.** When you schedule time for important conversations, you can plan ahead to avoid distractions or interruptions.
- **Postpone if distracted.** Postpone conversations if you are distracted and can't change that situation at the moment. Maybe you're angry, tense or nervous, or just in the middle of finishing a report with a tight deadline, and you need to listen at a later time when you're not preoccupied. But do set a time.
- **Be aware of your biases.** Don't jump to conclusions. Concentrate on what's being said, not how it's being said or by whom. Try to be open to new ideas and concepts.
- **Be empathetic.** Try to take the speaker's point of view or frame of reference when you are listening.
- **Listen to the whole message.** Really wait for the whole message to be put forth, and don't filter out facts along the way. You may miss the whole concept by selectively listening to only certain facts.
- **Watch for nonverbal clues.** What message is the sender's body language, hand motions, and/or eyes sending?
- **Avoid quick answers.** Don't formulate an answer or response before the speaker has finished. S.I. Hayakawa, a noted linguist, stated:

Listening doesn't mean simply maintaining a polite silence while you wait for a conversational opening. Nor does it mean noting the flaws in the other person's argument so you can show him up.

- **If you can't hear, ask.** Don't let people mumble along and miss half the message they are trying to give you. Politely ask the person to speak up.

- **Listen to and be sensitive of feelings, emotions and unspoken needs or concerns.** Respond with concern, but carefully, remembering you are not a counselor.
- **Be patient.** Patience and keeping your anger or annoyance to yourself while someone else is communicating with you is important.
- **Ask clarifying questions.** But don't cross-examine. Always keep in mind that your primary purpose is to listen.
- **Send interest messages.** Use nonverbal clues that show active listening, such as eye contact, open body positioning and posture.
- **Sum up.** Summarize and paraphrase what has been said to insure that you understood and interpreted correctly.

If you practice these techniques, you will find that active listening not only leads to clearer communications but also sends a positive and motivating message to your employees. It fosters open communication between yourself and those you supervise. It will even improve your communication with your boss and peers as well.

Communicating One-on-One with Your Employees

It seems obvious, but your employees need to be talked with as individuals. Sometimes it's hard to talk to some people, but you have to try. You must encourage open lines of communication with your employees. They need to know they can come to you with a problem or concern. You must send consistent messages and listen actively to develop their trust in you and the fact that you really are interested in them. The bottom line is, if you are to have an effective team, you must reserve time for one-on-one communication with your employees.

Addressing problems with individual employees must also be addressed to that individual employee. Many a supervisor has tried to address a problem with one or two employees by bringing the problem up in a staff or group meeting. It seems easier to address the group and not name names than to confront the problem directly with the employee(s) with the problem. For example, if one or two of your employees are turning in their monthly reports late, call each of them into your office individually and clearly let them know that you have noticed their reports are late and that you expect them to be on time from now on. If you address the group, the individuals turning them in on time will resent the implication that they're not; and the ones who aren't turning them in on time, probably won't even hear your message. Individual performance issues, however big or small, need to be addressed individually. And by all means, address them. Problems seldom disappear, but overlooking or neglecting them is a very effective way to make sure they get worse.

Example

Question: I have one employee who is very difficult for me to communicate with. She doesn't listen very well and is constantly interrupting me when I am trying to give her directions. I find myself avoiding her instead of trying to communicate with her. Do you have any suggestions?

Answer: *Some people are just easier to be around than others. Sometimes the more difficult ones will end up on your staff. It is part of your job however, to try to treat all your employees as equitably as possible. Make a special point to schedule a meeting with her when you are at your best. This will help you be more patient with her.*

Preface what you have to say to her with an opening statement that will let her know that you need her to listen to your entire message before she has the opportunity to ask questions or comments, such as "Natalie, I need you to listen carefully to what I have to say. When I'm done, you will have a chance to ask questions or make comments." When/if she starts to interrupt you, tactfully and patiently, stop her immediately and ask her again to wait until you are finished. If she continues to interrupt you, you need to let her know that this behavior is affecting her performance because she's not able to fully understand her work assignments. Hopefully, you can coach her and guide her toward improved listening skills, without it having to become a documented performance issue. When she does improve, be sure to compliment and reinforce her improved behavior.

Communicating with Groups

Supervisors are frequently called upon to deal with groups, from a small team meeting, to a presentation to a group of teams, or even to an occasional presentation to management. Communicating with groups is different from communicating with friends and individuals. The principles of good communication, however, continue to apply.

Calling a Meeting

Rule 1. Don't call a meeting without a purpose. Respect your staff by not wasting their time in a meeting with no purpose.

Rule 2. Don't call a meeting if the problem can be handled with one or two people and doesn't involve the whole group.

Both of these rules can be followed by asking yourself: What is the purpose of the meeting and is this purpose appropriate for a group setting?

Leading a Meeting

Once you've established the purpose, invite only those that need to be there. Now consider the following steps:

- Consider the number of attendees and effectiveness of the size of the group. If the purpose is only to disseminate information, it can be a fairly large group. If you want to have a meaningful discussion, the group shouldn't be much larger than 10 to 12 people.
- Prepare and distribute an agenda. Follow the agenda and keep to the time frames established. It is usually helpful if everyone knows the purpose in advance and, ideally, has a copy of the agenda in advance. This allows everyone to prepare for the meeting.
- Open the meeting by stating the purpose. This provides focus and direction.
- If the purpose of the meeting is merely to disseminate information, make that clear so the meeting doesn't become a debate.
- If the meeting is to solve a problem, state the problem and any background information.
- Spend most of your time directing the conversation by actively listening, paraphrasing to clarify understanding and asking open-ended questions to gain information and suggestions from participants.
- Guide the conversation to keep the discussion focused on the agenda or purpose. If other pertinent topics come up, make note of them for discussion at another time.
- Sum up issues, suggestions and any conclusions.
- Prepare minutes of the meeting, outline decisions reached, responsibility assigned and expected time frames.
- Distribute minutes as soon after the meeting as possible.

Difficult Group Members

There are always those who make it a little hard to run meetings. Some are earnest; they just want a lot more detail and background. Some are people who like to show off their knowledge. Some really want to please you and keep asking friendly questions that nonetheless divert you. Some are just plain troublemakers. The most common ways of handling these problems in meetings are:

- Restate the purpose of the meeting or topic if people start to get off the track.
- Ask for input from participants who haven't had a chance to offer their input either because they are shy or someone else is trying to dominate.
- No matter what, don't belittle a participant in front of the group.
- Remember that it is your place to run the meeting.
- If someone on your staff habitually is disruptive or inappropriate in meetings, talk with them privately and point out your observations regarding their behavior and state your expectations for their behavior in future meetings.

Virtual Meetings

As global companies continue to flatten their organizational structures, supervisors may find themselves responsible for staff at another location across the country or across the globe. Flying staff in for meetings or flying you to their locations may be prohibitive due to cost considerations. Teleconferencing and/or video conferencing may be necessary from time to time. Although certainly not ideal ways to communicate (face-to-face is always the best), these electronic meetings are becoming more and more common. Keep in mind the following tips:

- Try to get to know the members of your global team in person first. Trying to get to know staff via the phone or a video is not ideal.
- Get to know the differences in cultures and languages that you may be dealing with.
- Respect how global diversity strengthens the effectiveness of your team.
- Consider time differences when scheduling the meeting.
- Typically in these types of meetings, it is especially important for only one person to speak at a time. Be sure to let the meeting participants know this as well.
- When teleconferencing, have each person identify themselves before speaking so everyone knows who is saying what.
- Recognize that participants may be nervous about being "video'd"–the more you use this medium, the more you and your staff will become comfortable with it.

Conclusion

This chapter has covered communication, a very important aspect of becoming an excellent supervisor. Effective communication, whether verbal, nonverbal or written, is critical to your success. Here are a few more important considerations for all means of communication:

Respect

Respect your audience. Whether meeting with a group or one-on-one, be on time and be as brief as your communication allows. Be considerate of your audience. It may help to put yourself in their shoes. Remember, never belittle an employee, whether in an e-mail, one-on-one or especially in a group setting.

Honesty

Above all, be honest with your employees. Once you are perceived as being dishonest or insincere, your credibility with your employees is lost. If you lose credibility, your communications with them will always be circumspect. Honesty, even when delivering the most sensitive of messages, is still the best policy.

Confidentialty

Some of your communication with your staff must be kept confidential. For example, all performance reviews, whether extraordinarily positive or those leading to disciplinary action, are between you and the individual employee and should **never** be disclosed to other members of the team. This type of sensitive information should only be shared on an absolute need to know basis (i.e., the employee, HR, your boss). Employees may also from time to time, share very sensitive, personal information with you. For example, an employee may be experiencing personal problems that are causing them to be distracted at work. If your employees trust you enough with their personal information, don't abuse this trust by breaching their confidentiality. Be sure you have a place in your office where you can securely lock sensitive and confidential information. Be careful about sending e-mails that contain confidential information. It doesn't take much for electronic messages to get into the wrong or inappropriate hands.

Two-Way Street

Last, but not least, keep in mind that communication, in any country, in any language, and in every workplace, should be a two-way street. Your manner of communication must welcome feedback. Consequently, your communication should invite feedback. Embracing and acting on feedback builds team morale and shows that you are a good listener.

Review Questions

1. What are the three key methods to consider in effective employee communication?

2. When preparing communication, why is it important to consider your audience?

3. What role does your team's diversity play in how you communicate?

4. Is communication always a two way street?

5. When is it appropriate/inappropriate to choose one-on-one as your mode of communication?

6. What are the positives and pitfalls of electronic communication?

7. When is it appropriate to belittle an employee?

8. What steps can you take to ensure your communication is as smooth as possible?

7 Attracting and Keeping Employees

by Meredith Onion

What Will I Learn in This Chapter?

In this chapter, we will learn to:

- focus on why it is important to become a skilled recruiter and the skills necessary for a supervisor to become a successful recruiter and interviewer.
- present the recruitment process, including interview techniques and guidelines, and how to help keep good employees once they've been hired.

Overview

At first glance, "*recruiting*" may sound like something only the HR department does. Supervisors may think of themselves as "interviewers", but not recruiters. A manager with good recruitment skills impacts the workplace in several ways. The better the interview, the better the person hired; the better the person hired, the better the productivity and safety; the better the productivity and safety, the better the organization.

Much has been written and discussed about the labor market. There are periods when it is very hard to attract good employees; then there are times when there's a surplus of available, talented employees. Being able to attract and keep employees for your team is a critical skill. From organization CEOs on through all staff levels, time planning and strategizing about how to attract, develop and keep employees is time well spent.

Being a good recruiter is what gives companies their competitive edge. Not being able to fill vacant positions can be costly in terms of reduced productivity. It may also negatively impact the morale of co-workers if they have to pick up the work for the vacant position. Filling the position with the "wrong" employee can also cost the company in terms of poor productivity, turnover, training and recruitment costs. Supervisors and managers are often held very accountable by their bosses on their ability to attract and keep employees. A supervisor's ability to effectively recruit is a reflection on their ability to be a good manager.

Today's global market and workplace, also demands a diverse workforce. A supervisor must be able to recruit a diverse team as well as know how to keep a diverse team.

The Process

Recruitment is a multi-step process. It involves much more than just an interview. The company's HR department can be a huge resource, but also keep in mind that hiring employees is ultimately the responsibility of the supervisor, not HR.

Getting Ready

There are several steps to take and a lot of information to consider and review before you ever interview anyone for a job. Here are some guidelines:

1. Become familiar with your organization's hiring policies. Your HR Department may have very specific guidelines to follow for filling a vacancy. A systematic and consistent approach to filling jobs is the only really reliable approach.
2. Take advantage of any training offered by your company regarding your organization's hiring process.
3. Identify the skill gaps in your work group and what you need to fill that gap. Don't assume you should fill a vacancy with the exact same type of skill set. For example, if your secretary resigns, this is a good time to review what skills you could really use to help the team. In addition to someone that is good at answering phones, you may really need someone with good financial analysis skills to help with the budgeting process.
4. Identify the position for which you are hiring and the qualifications necessary to succeed in the position. Complete the following steps:
   - Locate the appropriate job description or write a new one. Review it for accuracy and up-to-date information.
   - Determine the actual skills, experience and education necessary for the job, and rank their importance in relation to each other. For example,

if experience is more important than years of education, say so.
- Avoid adding qualifications that are not absolutely necessary for the position.
- Identify and rank characteristics that are necessary for the job, such as initiative, attention to detail, and/or ability to get along with others.
- Identify elements of work environment for the job, such as numerous deadlines, tight time frames, safety considerations, split shift work or overtime.

5. Consider the diversity of your current team. Does everyone look and think the same? Take a long hard look at how your work group reflects your customer base. Is everyone on your team strong strategically but you're having a hard time implementing. Recruiting is a great opportunity to diversify, in terms of race, culture and gender, but also in terms of diversity of thought and skills.

> **Figure 7-1.**
> **Where can I find potential candidates?**
>
> - your internal job posting system—this may be a bulletin board or an electronic posting on the organization's Intranet
> - your company's website
> - web-based applicant pools or advertisements
> - professional associations
> - ads in newspapers, schools, colleges/universities, etc.
> - local labor halls (this may be required if you're a union shop)
> - government resources such as the unemployment office
> - employee referrals
> - employment agencies or other search firms.

Finding Applicants

Finding good applicants is critical to the process (Figure 7-1). Most HR departments keep responsibility for soliciting applicants and you may not have to conduct this step in the hiring process. If this is the case, it is still wise to share with HR your ideas regarding possible sources for candidates.

How Does the Organization Find Employees From Other Countries?

The first place to start is with your company's HR department to find out your company policy on recruiting international employees. There are several immigration, legal and cost considerations that need to be addressed in these types of situations and it is a good idea to check your company's philosophy and practices before recruiting on your own.

If you do need or want to look for job candidates outside of the United States, there are several ways to do so. First, if your company has overseas locations, check with your colleagues or HR in those locations for possibly transferring employees from your own company. If it's not possible to transfer employees, these satellite offices will be good resources for knowing how to recruit employees from that region of the world. There are also retained and contingency search companies that have expertise in international recruitment.

International professional associations may also publish job bulletins for their members across the globe and you could post your opening in their newsletter, often for free or a nominal fee.

There are numerous potential sources for candidates. Job postings can most likely be placed on your company's web-site. Ask your HR liaison if the company uses other web-based applicant pools or sources. Advertisements can be placed with local/national/international newspapers, community organizations, schools, colleges/universities, and affirmative action networks and trade associations. Some of these are free resources while others can be costly. Be sure to check what your budget will allow for these types of expenses.

If you are in a union environment, check local labor union resources. In some instances, hiring from the union hall may be required under the terms of the labor agreement between the union and the company. This is particularly true of the skilled trades and the construction industry. In other cases, the relationship between management and the union is positive and the union may frequently refer potential applicants. In any event, be sure to check your organization's policies on this.

Seek out government resources. State employment services maintain current rosters of available workers. Equal Employment Opportunity networks often provide referral services. Most companies require you to post your notices with these agencies. Some companies are obligated under affirmative action orders to use these programs extensively.

Seek employee referrals. Many organizations use incentives for these types of referrals while others actually discourage referrals. Again, know the policy of your organization.

Contingency and/or retained search firms are also a possibility. A *contingency firm* only changes you if you hire one of their contingency firm only changes you if you hire one of their referrals. A *retained firm* is paid a retainer and is usually reserved to conduct mid- to senior-level searches.

Check other professional associations. Most associations have a newsletter or web-site that includes a section for employers to post job openings. Some associations even have a candidate match service where an employer can send a job description and the association searches their data-base for potential candidates. Sometimes these services are free; sometimes there's a fee. Professional associations are also a good way to recruit diverse employees–See Figure 7-2 for a small sampling of such associations.

Screening Applicants

Screening is a process that most companies keep in HR, but the trend is to involve supervisors in this early process. Before you can do any screening you need to be familiar and comfortable with company policy and government regulations regarding minorities, affirmative action, persons with disabilities and other protected classes. The legal part of this was covered in

Figure 7-2. A Sample List of Associations/Websites Useful in Recruiting Diverse employees

- Financial Women International — www.fwi.org
- Black Data Processing Associates — www.bdpa.org
- Society of Women Engineers — www.swe.org
- Women in Technology International — www.witi.com
- Executive Leadership Council (African-American) — www.elcinfo.com
- National Black MBA Association, Inc. — www.nbmbaa.com
- National Association of Black Accountants — www.nabainc.org
- National Association of Asian American Professionals — www.naaap.org
- Society for Hispanic Professionals — www.nshp.org
- HireDiversity JobSeekers Resources — www.hirediversity.com

Chapter 3, Supervisors, Employment and Workplace Law. Company policy is probably printed in your organization's *policy manual.* Having reviewed that, you move on to screening. Since interviewing is time consuming, the first thing you need to do is screen. Sort on a preliminary basis, to see which people you will interview. Take a good hard look at all of the resumes. Ask yourself these questions to help you select which applicant you may want to interview:

- Is the application/resume complete? Note any employment gaps or omissions.
- Is the overall appearance of the resume legible and organized?
- Does the applicant possess most of the credentials necessary for the job?
- Note any special training the applicant has had.
- Review for any overlaps that don't make sense. Attending school and

working at the same time is quite possible, but notice if the school and work are in the same city, for instance. Note volunteer work that may explain gaps, and that also may have transferable skills. For example, volunteer typing and office work for a church society may well show the ability to type, compose letters, handle mailings etc.
- Look for any inconsistencies. For example, do the credentials suggest that the applicant is overqualified for the positions they have held? Is the salary history consistent with the positions held?
- Check for the frequency with which the applicant has changed jobs. There may be legitimate reasons for frequent changes due to the nature of the industry involved, or it may reflect that the person has difficulty holding a job.
- Note the reasons the person has listed for leaving previous employment. Generally, keep notes on a separate sheet of paper, possibly attached to the application with a staple.
- Based on all of the above, determine who looks like the most qualified and create a pool of those you would like to interview.

Testing

HR typically conducts pre-employment testing, when it is used at all. Many companies rely entirely on the interview assessment process instead of testing. Testing has always been subject to close scrutiny by Equal Employment agencies, since it can result in adverse impact on hiring from protected classes. But some companies do test. Some companies share testing data outside the HR department. Most do not.

If your company does test, it must be justified in terms of the actual needs of the job and must be applied to each and every applicant for that job. Even police and fire departments are eliminating many of the excessive physical test requirements they have had, with no apparent adverse impact on the quality of people being hired. If you use skill tests, do so only with the full approval of HR.

Some companies can require applicants to take a medical examination after an offer has been made but prior to hiring. Such examinations often include drug screening.

Do not, under any circumstances, develop your own test, written or physical, for screening potential new hires. It is the job of HR to put tests in place.

Interview Methods

Interviewing, unfortunately, is not an exact science and there are many opportunities for the process to fail. However, the more planning that is done and the more continuity that is applied, the more the process will be beneficial and successful.

Before you interview an employee, you should have some idea of what you want to know and how you will find it out. But, you say, I have always just talked with them. Maybe you learned what you needed to know, and maybe not. There are some methods that will make it a lot easier for you to find out what you need to know about a job applicant. So, the first step is to determine the type of interview technique you will be using. There are three types of interviews: structured, semi-structured and unstructured.

Structured Interview

In the *structured interview*, the interviewer knows exactly what is to be found out and how it will be solicited. You come to the interview with a prepared list of questions that are asked, in full, of each and every candidate. This method is the most valid and reliable because you will be comparing answers to the same questions: apples and apples, not apples and oranges. The structured interview technique may be an easier method if you do not interview frequently because with this method you know ahead of time how the course of the interview will go. It brings out the information you need. The structured interview is rigid in format, although the way people respond to the questions will vary widely. It also virtually eliminates biased questions from inexperienced interviewers and is, therefore, particularly popular when there have been problems with interviewers giving the wrong impression about company policy, affirmative action and so on.

Semi-Structured Interview

The *semi-structured interview* technique calls for some prepared questions to be used for all applicants and other impromptu questions that are developed by the interviewer as the interview progresses. This method allows for more flexibility to pursue, for example, a particular expertise of the applicant. It may be less reliable for making a hiring decision if the impromptu questions are not asked of all candidates. The impromptu questions can also lead to diversions in the interview that cause it to drag on, sometimes to the extent that you do not get all of the information you need.

Unstructured Interview

Often referred to as the *fly-by-the-seat-of-your-pants* method, this is probably what you have been doing if you haven't had some direction or training. No questions are prepared ahead of time. The interviewer asks questions based, at least, on a review of the application. This is the least reliable type of interview technique because the same questions are not consistently asked of each applicant, the interviews tend to wander and the interviewer tends to do all the talking.

As a suggestion, a good beginning would be to try structured interviews for the first time you recruit. After that, you might try a semi-structured interview format for the next position. The more you practice using these two types of interviews, the more natural they will seem. Experienced interviewers can make these interview come across like a natural conversation, rather than an uncomfortable stiff interview. So start practicing. *We do not recommend the unstructured interview under any circumstances.*

Planning and Conducting Interviews

The detailed planning stage must occur before the interview takes place. Be clear about your objectives and company policy on hiring, firing, performance and discipline. Here are some major guidelines you should follow:

- DO prepare and plan for the interview. Review, once again, the key or critical qualifications you are looking for in an applicant.
- DO prepare questions ahead of time for use in the structured or semi-structured technique. (DON'T use the unstructured technique.)
- DO prepare questions that are job-related and will bring out information regarding the key qualifications you have identified.
- DO develop questions that will elicit examples of past job performance.
- DO prepare questions around hypothetical situations for which the applicant must find a solution... *What would you do if there were an accident on the plant floor?*
- DO prepare open-ended questions and not just questions that can be answered with a yes or no response. For example, *When you worked for XYZ, Inc. what did you do about...? How did you...? Why did you...? Tell me about...*
- DO prepare questions that touch upon various areas of experience, such as education, work experience, career goals/ambitions, assessment of one's own strengths and limitations and upon attitudes toward current job, safety regulations, equipment, company and industry.

- **DO** ask questions that solicit answers that will help you understand the person's temperament and assess their fit within the culture. For example, if you have a very progressive, fast-paced culture, ask questions about how they handle tight deadlines and time pressures. On the other hand, if you have a very conservative culture, ask questions about how they deal with bureaucracy, etc. You may find a great candidate with the perfect set of skills, but if their personal style won't match the culture, you will both be frustrated quickly once the person is on board.
- **DO** prepare probing questions. Probing questions are the only way you can get most people to open up and tell you about themselves. After all, people are tense when it comes to an employment interview, and who can blame them? But it is your job to find out about them and make an assessment as to their suitability for the job and compatibility with the rest of the team (Figure 7-3).

Interview Tips

Now that you've done all of this planning, you'll be ready to actually conduct an interview. If you're uncomfortable interviewing an actual candidate, you can always role-play an interview with a willing colleague, friend or spouse. A good dry run may make the real interview much easier.

Here are a few more tips for conducting a successful interview:

- **DO** make the applicant as comfortable as possible in the interview. Develop rapport with the candidate. Be friendly and welcoming. Free yourself from any distraction by closing the office door, forwarding your phone calls and turning off your cell phone/beeper and letting others know that you are not to be disturbed. Arrange comfortable seating. Concentrate on the applicant by having good eye contact.
- **DO** allow enough time to complete the interview at a relaxed pace.

Figure 7-3. Sample Interview Questions

These following examples of behavioral questions may help you solicit the type of information you will need to assess a person's ability, as well as their fit in the position and your corporate culture.

1. "Now that I've told you a little bit about this position and our company, tell me about your background and how you see your skills transferring to this position?"
2. "What do you find most attractive about this opportunity? What do you find least attractive?"
3. "What do you look for in a job? An organization?"
4. "What experiences do you think you have carried from your education and applied in your work experience?"
5. "Do you prefer to have a job in which you have well laid-out tasks and responsibilities, or one in which your work changes on a frequent basis?"
6. "What types of responsibilities would you like to avoid in your next job?"
7. "What previous job have you held that was the most satisfying? the least satisfying? And why?"
8. "What types of experiences have you had dealing with difficult customers?" (Be sure to elicit specific examples and how they dealt with the situation?)
9. "Describe a difficult co-worker you've had to deal with and how did you manage the situation?"
10. "What kinds of people do you like to work with?"
11. "Describe a situation when your boss had to return work to you because it didn't meet his/her expectations?"
12. "Tell me about an objective in your last position that you failed to meet and why?"
13. "Describe a skill area that you've been told you need to develop more? What have you done to develop it?"
14. "Tell me what your boss would tell me about you? Your subordinates? Your peers?"
15. "What have you done that is innovative?"
16. "In what ways do you think you can make a contribution in this job? Give a specific example."
17. "Describe how you schedule your time on an unusually hectic day?"

18. "Describe some situations in which you worked under pressure or tight deadlines?"
19. "What would you do if someone asked you to do something unethical?"
20. "Tell me about the leader that you most admire, their characteristics and why you admire them?"
21. "Describe your leadership skills?"
22. "Tell me about a time when one of your staff turned in a project that didn't meet your expectations? How did you handle the situation?"
23. "As a manager, have you ever had to fire anyone? If so, what were the circumstances, and how did you handle it?"
24. "If you were able to bring two or three people with you to this company, who would you bring and why?"
25. "How are you best led?"
26. "What hurdles have you overcome in your career?"
27. "Tell me the three accomplishments in your life that you are most proud of?"
28. "Why should we hire you?"
29. "What questions do you have for me?"

Rushing is very apparent to all and will cause the applicant to wonder why you even bothered to hold the interview.

- DO keep in mind that you are representing the organization. Project a favorable, professional, friendly image and understand that in the applicant's eyes you are the company.
- DO have an introduction at the opening of the interview. This introduction should describe the interview process and, briefly, the position the individual is applying for. It should also describe the organization and your particular department within the organization.
- DO ask the questions that you have prepared ahead of time. Ask the easier questions first and progress to the more difficult questions. This helps to put the applicant more at ease. Don't divert yourself or allow

the applicant to divert you. Stick with your interview outline.
- DO allow time for the applicant to respond. Remember that the purpose of the interview is to listen to the applicant.
- DO allow for pauses or silences; the applicant may offer additional information. Pauses are sometimes difficult for some interviewers, and they tend to fill in the void with their own talk. That is a mistake. A well-timed silence or pause will often cause the applicant to offer you more information of value.
- DO listen more than you talk.
- DO probe for further information if the applicant doesn't initially answer the question as completely as you'd like. Probe further if the applicant seems hesitant or nervous about a particular situation. If you don't probe at these points, you may overlook some very critical information.
- DO restate responses from time to time to make sure you understand the applicant's answers to the questions. For example, *"If I understand correctly, Juan, you left your previous job because the tension was too great, and you prefer a more relaxed atmosphere?"* Or, *"I'm still not certain, Danita, about where you were working between December 2002, and March 2003. Would you go over that again, please?"*
- DO restate questions if the applicant doesn't understand them the first time.
- DO take cursory notes. Unless your memory is phenomenal, you'll need them.
- DO keep in mind cultural differences when communicating during an interview. Many interviewers turn down well-qualified people because they have a little difficulty understanding them or think language is critical when it really isn't for the job at hand.
- DO have a conclusion to your interview. Ask the applicant if he or she has any questions.

- DO take this opportunity to review the highlights of the position and the company that you think will help attract the person to this position and company. Remember that you sometimes have to sell the candidate on the job, as much as they have to convince you that they are right for the job.
- DO explain the next step(s) in the hiring process. Be sure to thank the applicant for his/her time.
- DO evaluate the information you have gathered and make a hiring decision. Exchange and compare notes with anyone else who interviewed the candidates. Have additional interviews or interviewers if additional information is needed. Focus decision-making on the critical requirements for the job that you identified initially. Don't start redefining jobs to fit a particular individual.
- DO make reference checks before extending an employment offer. People do occasionally lie when they apply for a job. Remember that employer reference checks are usually very guarded, with current practice generally limiting responses to dates of employment and title.
- DO follow-up with all candidates. You never know when you may want to hire them in the future. Or they may be potential customers. Even if a person is not hired for a position, you want to them to feel that they were treated with respect.

Interview Pitfalls

Here are a few more tips on how to avoid common pitfalls in the interview process:

- DON'T hold an interview if you are unprepared, don't have enough time or are too distracted to give the applicant your undivided attention.
- DON'T ask illegal or irrelevant questions. Hiring decisions cannot be

based on one's sex, race, color, religion, age or disability. Therefore, don't ask questions like:
- Where were you born?
- How old are you?
- Do you have any illnesses we should know about?
- What church do you go to?
- Are you married?
- Do you have children? What are your childcare arrangements?
- How can you travel when you have children?
- Do you smoke?
- What political party do you belong to?

- DON'T ask questions that have no relevance to the position requirements. For example, don't ask questions about how many pounds a person can lift if lifting is not a requirement of the job.
- DON'T exaggerate the job responsibilities, career opportunities or salary information. Be honest about the organization's culture and work environment. If a suit and tie are still the norm, don't suggest that a polo shirt and khakis are acceptable daily dress.
- DON'T talk more than you listen and DON'T interrupt the candidate while he/she is talking.
- DON'T jump to conclusions or give in to your prejudices or biases. DON'T make a decision prematurely. First impressions play a role but should not exclude additional factors. There are a lot of talented, creative professionals out there with funky hairdos and earrings in interesting places. How important is what someone looks like in relation to their ability to successfully perform the responsibilities of the job.
- DON'T hire someone just because he/she was referred by someone you

like, and DON'T dislike someone just because someone you don't like referred him/her.
- DON'T make a decision based on your own values, standards and beliefs, either positively or negatively. For instance, someone who graduated from the same high school you did should not be a shoe-in for the job.
- DON'T concentrate more on reading the application and resume or taking notes than on listening to the candidate. In most cases, the applicant expects that you have already read the application. If you haven't, you should have.
- DON'T telegraph—that is, don't give information or ask questions in such a way that the applicant can readily determine the responses you want to hear. For example, a question like, *"You can handle stressful situations can't you?"* will produce a *"Yes, of course!"* People will try very hard to give you what they think you want to hear.

Checking References

As with hiring interviews, the question of who conducts reference checks is usually spelled out in your organization's policy manual. HR often carries it out. It sometimes will be the responsibility of the supervisor.

Checking references is a key component to the recruitment process. On a very basic level, it is important to verify the individuals work history, including salary history, and any and all professional credentials that the individual claims to have. Unfortunately, it is not all that uncommon for people to lie on their resumes. Personal references can also be insightful, by gathering additional information regarding the person's skill set and what types of work environments the person seems to have thrived in (Figure 7-4).

Figure 7-4. How Do I Check References?

Assuming it's the organization's policy for the supervisor to check references, what procedures should you follow?

Here are some basic steps and procedures that should prove helpful:

- Secure a signed release of information that allows you to check references, past employers, education, etc.
- Remind the applicant that a firm offer of employment cannot be given until a reference check is successfully completed. If the applicant doesn't want you to complete a thorough reference check, it is a red flag. The exception of course, is not checking with the candidate's current job, so as not to jeopardize that employment until a firm offer of employment has been made and accepted.
- Ask the applicant to provide a 360° list of references — a former boss, a peer, a subordinate, and a customer/client. Current and previous supervisors are often the best sources. As you know, a supervisor knows the individual's performance and capabilities. But peers, subordinates, and client/customers are also very important, especially as more and more companies are recognizing they need to focus on their customers first.
- The HR department of the organizations that the applicant has worked for will be able to verify dates of employment, salary and title information. Beyond that, however, they probably won't be able to give you specific information on the applicant's performance.
- Prepare questions that you will want to ask references. Many of the questions you used in the interview with the candidate can be adapted for reference checking interviews. You should target questions that address technical skills, work attitudes, interpersonal skills, communication skills, past accomplishments, future potential and character.
- Begin with positive questions so the reference person you are interviewing is not put on the defensive. Most people want to spread good news about a fellow or former employee. Give them that opportunity before you move on to the more difficult or sensitive questions.
- Keep your questions direct and concise. Be aware of the references own time constraints and schedule a phone appointment if the person doesn't have time to talk to you the first time you call.
- If you don't get a clear answer, rephrase the question and try again. Sometimes you may have to push a bit, and sometimes you simply will not get an answer. Most often, the latter means potential trouble. However, many companies now have policies that forbid Supervisors to give references on past or current employees. You may want to ask if that is the case if the reference seems reluctant to provide much information.
- Always identify yourself, the organization you represent and the individual you are seeking information about. Let the reference know that you have the applicant's written consent to do

> - the reference check. You may have to fax this consent form before they will talk to you.
> - Be professional and courteous at all times as you ask the questions that you have prepared.
> - Keep in mind the nature of the source. For instance, the most recent employer may still be resentful of the individual for leaving and thus may not be very complimentary. (That is why it is so important to ask specific questions about performance, so you get more than just opinions.)
> - Document the reference checks. Note the names of the references checked, the date and the questions and response.

Keeping Employees

Making a good hire is no longer enough. Michael Dell, CEO, Dell Computers has stated that his number one priority is, "*talent: finding it and keeping it.*"

People are motivated and driven to succeed by a variety of things. As a supervisor, it should be one of your top priorities to find out from each of your employees what will keep them happy and motivate them to stay with your organization. Customize your efforts to your employees and for your organization.

The following are steps you can take to help keep good employees in your workgroup.

Orientation

Some experts feel that orientation should begin before the employee even starts. And keeping employees really begins with the interview and recruitment process. Perspective employees should be given realistic and accurate information about the job expectations and the organization's culture. Opportunities to develop employee skills should be discussed during the recruitment process. The best person to deliver this type of information is their supervisor. No one wants to be surprised that the job they've accepted isn't the job that was described in the interview.

If appropriate, some soon-to-be employees like to receive material before they start. When you are hiring college students upon their graduation, there is often a several month delay between the time you offer the position and when the person actually graduates and starts work. Some companies that hire employees right from college, keep in touch with their candidates through an e-mail newsletter. Maybe there is an employee handbook or a benefits brochure that the employee can review before they begin. The important thing is to start making the employee feel welcome the minute they walk through your door for the interview.

Chapter 11, Developing Employee Skills and Careers covers orientation of the employee once they are on board. Refer to this important information as it relates to keeping and training your employees.

Ongoing Efforts

Probably the best retention tool is to be a good leader. (See Chapter 8, Leadership.) One of the best ways to be a good boss, of course, is to stay in tune with your employees and what they are looking for personally and professionally. Here is a great list of 10 questions to ask employees to stay in tune with what they're looking for:

1. *Why do you stay at the organization?*
2. *What would make you leave?*
3. *What is your next professional career move?*
4. *What motivates you to excel?*
5. *What three things is the company doing to keep you?*
6. *What three things should the company stop doing to keep you here?*
7. *What three things should the company start doing to ensure you will stay?*

8. *What really ticks you off about working here?*
9. *What one benefit do we need to change and why?*
10. *What new benefit offering should the company offer to keep you?*
    (Parus, 2001)

Don't just ask them once, but keep asking questions and developing your employees and you are bound to have higher retention rates. And it may sound very simple, but when was the last time you said "thank you" for doing a good job? We're human and we all enjoy positive feedback and recognition for our time, energy and talents. Recognizing your employee's contributions goes a long way to keeping your team satisfied.

Keeping Diverse Employees

If you are a man, think for a moment how you would feel attending a women's book club discussion of *The Divine Secrets of the Ya-Ya Sisterhood*. If you are a woman, think how you would feel attending a male-only golf club. If you are white, how comfortable are you visiting a jazz club patronized primarily by blacks? While it is easy to say our society has come a long way with equal rights, we still have a long way to go in being completely comfortable and free of biases in diverse situations. As a supervisor, it is your place to make sure that all of your employees are assimilated into the workplace. If you hire the first woman to work in an otherwise all-male organization, you will need to consider special steps to make this new employee feel welcome, comfortable and valuable. Consider these tips in keeping diverse employees:

- Create an assimilation plan (your HR department may be able to help) before your employee even starts.
- Consider any cultural or language differences that need to be considered and/or accommodated.

- Sensitize your team and head off any biases that you may be aware of. (i.e., "A construction site is no place for a woman.")
- Identify a mentor with the same cultural background for the new employee. This can be someone from another department and their jobs don't have to be the same or even similar.
- Find out if your company has any internal diversity organizations. Many large company's have internal networks for various diverse employees.

Remember that recruiting diverse employees is just the first step. A good supervisor also knows how to keep a diverse workforce.

Exit Interviews

In spite of all that you do to keep good employees, some are bound to leave you for a variety of reasons. *Exit interviews* are done when employees leave the company to determine the employee's reasons for leaving and to gather impressions of the responsibilities, the supervisor and the organization in general. Depending on the circumstances of the employee's departure, the exit interview can bring out some very candid and often valuable information.

As with other types of interviews, supervisors should check first to see what the organization's policy on exit interviews is. Most often, exit interviews are the responsibility of HR. The exit interview is most effective when done by an objective third party, such as someone in HR. However, even if you don't do the interview yourself, you may want to share your ideas with HR about what you would like to find out through the interview.

Exit interviews can be a very important and insightful exercise. As we have discussed, retention of great employees is an important part of every supervisor's job. Johnson & Johnson completed a whole study called "*Regrettable Losses*" in which they interviewed "star employees" that voluntarily left the organization. Their findings from this study have helped address some of the factors causing key employees to go elsewhere.

Here are a few tips in conducting an exit interview, just in case your HR group doesn't handle this process:

- It is not a good idea to do exit interviews in the circumstances of lay-offs or a plant closing. This may only add insult to injury and will usually yield very little helpful information.
- Conduct the exit interview a day or two before the employee leaves. The day of departure is usually too emotional, and once the employee leaves she/he will not be likely to come back for an exit interview.
- As with other interviews, conduct the exit interview in a private, relaxed location.
- Develop a standard list of questions that will be used for all exit interviews. By always asking the same exit questions, you may start to see trends regarding why people are leaving.
- Areas you may want to explore in the exit interview include: the reason for departure, the new job and salary, advantages of the new position, rating of the present job, supervision, working conditions, safety of the environment, equipment, co-workers, morale within the department and company, advancement opportunities, orientation, training, pay, benefits, etc. Would the employee ever return? Could the departure have been prevented? What did the employee like best/least about the job? Are there any suggestions for improvement? General comments.
- Document the exit interview and keep the information in a confidential location. This information should not become part of the employee's personnel file, however.

Case Study

Shawn McKenna was very excited about the employment offer he had received from the ProMaster Company. Not only did the job responsibilities sound challenging, but he also felt there was good chemistry between he and his new boss and the culture of the organization. He happily accepted the offer. He was informed by his new supervisor that he would still have to have a physical examination and they would have to complete the reference checking. Assuming all went well, he could start in 3 weeks. Shawn signed the release for his reference check and scheduled his physical for the very next day. Then 2 ½ weeks went by and he didn't hear anything from anyone at the ProMaster Company. As time went by, he began to worry that there was some sort of problem with the references or his physical exam. He had heard about false-positives with drug screening and he started to imagine the worst. Or maybe they had changed their mind and didn't want to hire him after all. The day before he was to start, he received a call from an HR person he hadn't even met, reminding him to bring in various documents on his first day, since he'd have a lot of paperwork to fill out on his first morning with the company. Instead of being excited about his first day, Shawn began to wonder if he had made a mistake...

1. If you were Shawn's new boss, what should you have done to stay in touch with him between the **time** he was offered the position and the time he actually started?
2. How should you coordinate with your HR Department to make sure Shawn starts off on the right foot with the organization?

Conclusion

Attracting and keeping talented employees in your organization is probably one of the most important, if not *the* most important, job of every supervisor. Candice Carpenter, Founder and ex-CEO of iVillage.com reported that recruiting and keeping stars was one of the most critical factors in her company's success. She used numerous innovative methods for attracting, developing and keeping employees.

Preparation and practice are the keys to effective interviewing. Keep in mind the factors involved in effective communication and apply them in all of your interview situations, from recruitment, to reference checks, to a regrettable exit interview. Keep your biases/prejudices in check and be open and sensitive to cultural and/or generational differences. Recruiting is a great opportunity to diversify your team both in terms of traditional diversity, (i.e., race, gender, etc...) and also diversity of thought. Once you bring in strong employees, be sure to do all that you can to keep them.

Reference

Parus B. Igniting passion in employees. *WorkSpan, The Magazine of World at Work*, February 2001, pp 34 – 37.

Review Questions

1. Think about some of your experiences being interviewed and recruited. What went well? Where was there room for improvement?

2. As someone coming into an organization for an interview, how do you like to be treated? What type of follow-up is important to you?

3. How do you define diversity? How diverse is your current team? How comfortable are you in dealing with cultural differences? What biases might you have that you need to be aware of?

4. Why is it so important in your role as a supervisor to attract and keep top employees?

5. What are some of the most important factors in attracting and keeping employees? How are you doing keeping diverse employees?

6. What information would you like to gather from employees that choose to leave the organization?

8 Leadership

by Yang Shao, PhD

What Will I Learn in This Chapter?

This chapter covers how to supervise and help employees adapt to change, working with teams and collaborative work: Some specific items covered include:

- constant change in the workplace.
- adapting to change.
- teams and collaborative work.
- leadership defined & key elements of leadership.
- sharing vision & setting goals.
- motivating employees.
- effective leadership behavior.
- leadership styles.
- adjusting supervisory style to the needs of a diverse/global workforce.

Overview

In today's fast changing and increasingly competitive environment, leadership capability is becoming more and more critical to the success of any business. As a supervisor, identifying and developing leadership skills can help you manage your team and achieve organizational objectives more effectively. We cover the changing roles of the leader in today's workplace environment; describe the key elements of effective leadership and leadership styles. We will also discuss how to be an effective leader in the increasingly diverse and global work environment.

Leadership

The last 10 years of the 20th century can be characterized as a decade of unprecedented changes in all facets of our life. The following spells out some of the major changes in the 1990s:
- On the political front: end of the communist system—the fall of the Berlin Wall, the collapse of the Soviet Union, dramatic political and economic reforms in China;
- On the technology front: the ever increasing speed of computing—today's palm-held computer has more power than a state of the art computer at the beginning of the 1990s. The Internet revolution has fundamentally changed the way people communicate and relate to each other and the way business is transacted.
- On the economic front: the increasing trend of globalization has opened up new markets and new supply sources for organizations and

also made the once relatively self-contained national economies more inter-dependent of one another. As we have witnessed, the economic crisis in Asia or the collapse of the Russian stock market, can have a significant impact on the markets elsewhere in the world.

- On the demographics front: as revealed in the latest U.S. census, one of the most significant changes is the increasing diversity of our population—many cities and regions have witnessed double digit population growth among the minority groups—African Americans, Hispanics and Asians. For the first time in history, less than half of the population in New York City is white. The aging of the population—more and more baby boomers going into retirement age, people are living longer and healthier lives and they are not just retiring into inactivity.

- On the work front: the increasing transition of employees toward knowledge workers, the need for technology and professional know how is at an unprecedented level. The changing work style—telecommuting, flexible work arrangement, job sharing. The changing mindset about careers—people are more proactively managing their careers by building work experience in different functions, organizations and industries. Very few people will stay in one company for their entire professional life as they used to do in the 1980s.

All of these changes have significantly impacted the way we live, think and work. Of course, it also impacted the way organizations are run and managed. The old, hierarchical way of managing and controlling might still be effective in certain situations, but overall it is rendered ineffective in today's constantly changing, dynamic, diverse and global environment. To be successful in the 21st century, business leaders need to create an organization that is nimble, focused and creates true value for all of its constituents—its employees, customers, suppliers, partners and shareholders. To do that, they need to adopt leadership styles that foster creativity, build knowledge, value diversity and can bring out the best in employees and create superior organizational results.

Supervising, Adapting to Change, Teams and Collaborative Work

As the saying goes: "*In life, the only constant is change.*" Change is becoming a way of life in today's business environment. But it is not change for change's sake. Organizations are changing because that is the only way to survive and succeed. These changes are happening in every aspect of business:

- Companies are changing the way they organize—going from stogy, hierarchical organizations to fluid, flatter and team-based organizations.
- Companies are changing the way that they produce and market their products—they are focusing on developing and delivering new products faster to market, they are focusing on quality and on building a strong brand and sending the marketing message directly to their end users.
- Organizations are changing the way they recruit, motivate and develop their employees—competency and skill sets are becoming more and more critical in the human resources management processes.
- Organizations identify what core competencies or skill sets are needed for their success and are actively recruiting for these qualities in their new hires, aggressively developing these qualities in their employees and managing and measuring employees against these standards.

What do these changes mean to you as a supervisor? How should you manage and lead your team effectively in these changing times?

In this chapter, we will address some of these issues and explain the different leadership styles that you can use and leadership factors that you should consider in leading your team to maximize performance.

Adapting to Change

As the famous management author Peter Drucker pointed out:

> *"The goal of most organizations is not just to deliver services, but also to foster change and improve lives. In a time of rapid change, the opportunities for improving, for getting results, are also changing rapidly."*
> (Drucker, 1999).

In order to adapt to change, you should first understand why things are changing, become aware of the kind of changes that are occurring around you and then identify and take effective actions to adapt to and initiate change. Peter Drucker described three imperatives for successful innovation and managing change (Drucker, 1999):

- Focus on the mission.
- Define the results we are after.
- Assess what we are doing and how we are doing it.

Focusing on the organizational mission can help you understand the fundamental reasons for change. If you work for a telecommunications company and its mission is to help people and businesses stay connected, you will understand why it should change to adapt to the rapid technology developments in Internet and wireless technologies. If you work for an automobile company, its mission is to produce safe and reliable vehicles; you will understand why it is changing to produce higher quality cars.

Understanding the "why" of change is very important. **Because only when you understand the reason for change, will you be able to adapt to it.** But you should also know the "how" of change–that is how things are changing and how you should change to adapt to it.

To understand how things are changing, we should examine what the key internal and external forces are changing the way business is done. Externally there have been some major changes in the 1990s that have deeply changed the way people live and organizations transact their business:

- The revolutionary change in information technology and the increasing computing power has created many new ways for organizations to develop, market and deliver their products. The use of computer-aided design to develop and test new products in many manufacturing organizations has significantly reduced the product development cycle and improved product quality; the use of information and internet technology to provide 24/7 customer support is becoming more and more prevalent; the adoption of internet based eCommerce exchanges has fundamentally changed how businesses source and market their products.
- Increased globalization has expanded the market place for both goods and labor to beyond the national borders, and allowed organizations to source materials, manufacture products and service customers at places that makes the most economic sense–whether a manufacturing plant in China, a customer call center in India or a software development operation in Israel.
- The changing demographics of the world's population has created many emerging customer segments with significant purchasing power and is shaping the way companies organize to capture these markets–the emerging Latin population in the United States has resulted in the creation of many new Latin TV channels and magazines; the emergence of the Generation X has led to many marketing programs that

209

are specifically tailored at marketing to this young audience.

As a supervisor in these changing times, you need to identify these changes and understand their organizational impact and effects on employees. Do technology changes provide opportunities for the company to be more productive and serve its customers better? What kind of skills do employees need to have to adopt these new technologies? Does globalization present new ways and markets for your products and services? How can your organization become prepared to serve its new customer segments?

Some people might think these are big questions that only senior executives of a company should be concerned about, however, that is not the case. To be truly effective at your job and adapting to the changing environment, asking these questions can help you understand the big picture and align your change efforts with that of the organization.

Once you understand why things are changing and how things are changing, it is time to plan your own actions to adapt to change. You need to plan ways to explain and implement the changes and involve employees in the change process.

Dr. John Kotter, Professor of Leadership at Harvard Business School and a frequent speaker at top management meetings around the world, has outlined eight key steps to ensure successful change efforts in organizational transformation (Kotter, 1998):

1. *Establish a sense of urgency.*
   - *Examine market and competitive realities.*
   - *Identify and discuss crises, potential crises, or major opportunities.*
2. *Form a powerful guiding coalition.*
   - *Assemble a group with enough power to lead the change effort.*
   - *Encourage the group to work as a team.*
3. *Create a vision.*

- *Create a vision to help direct the change effort.*
- *Develop strategies for achieving that vision.*
4. *Communicate the vision.*
   - *Use every vehicle possible to communicate the new vision and strategies.*
   - *Teach new behaviors by the example of the guiding coalition.*
5. *Empower others to act on the vision.*
   - *Get rid of obstacles to change.*
   - *Change systems or structures that seriously undermine the vision.*
   - *Encourage risk taking and nontraditional ideas, activities and actions.*
6. *Plan for and create short-term wins.*
   - *Plan for visible performance improvements.*
   - *Implement those improvements.*
   - *Recognize and empower employees involved in the improvements.*
7. *Consolidate improvements and produce still more change.*
   - *Use increased credibility to change systems, structures and policies that don't fit the vision.*
   - *Hire, promote, and develop employees who can implement the vision.*
   - *Reinvigorate the process with new projects, themes, and change agents.*
8. *Institutionalize new approaches.*
   - *Articulate the connections between the new behaviors and organizational success.*
   - *Develop the means to ensure leadership development and succession.*

As a supervisor, your focus is more than adapting to change by yourself. You need to lead and employ others to act on the vision of change. Producing change is about 80 percent leadership—establishing direction, aligning, motivating, and inspiring people—and about 20 percent management—planning, budgeting, organizing, and problem-solving. That is why developing leadership skills is very important for you as a supervisor.

Effective leadership is required in all kinds of organizations, but nowhere is the need greater than in the organization that is seeking to transform itself. And what company isn't or should be, transforming itself.

Teams and Collaborative Work

In the increasingly competitive and complex business environment, organizations need to rely on the collective efforts and talent of their employees to succeed. Few great accomplishments are ever the work of a single individual.

Management studies and company experiences proved that teams significantly outperform individuals. That is not surprising given the teams bring more resources to work on a task at hand than could any single performer. But an effective team is not a given. Simply putting individuals together in a team does not guarantee that this will be a functioning, effective and results producing unit. Creating and launching teams requires everyone in the team to:

- contribute and communicate effectively.
- feel valued and capable in their jobs.
- build collaboration, personal initiative and trust.
- understand their role in the big picture (Figure 8-1).

> ### Figure 8-1. Question
>
> As a supervisor leading a team, what key actions should I take to ensure team success?
>
> - Plan effectively when organizing a new team or when restructuring an existing team.
> - Explain the team's purpose and impact on the organization.
> - Describe the results and standards the team is expected to achieve.
> - Discuss and agree on the roles and responsibilities of each team member.
> - Identify procedures and resources for getting the work done.
> - Encourage team members to figure out and agree on ways to help one another.
> - Summarize and establish a specific follow-up plan.
> - Work with team members to figure out how to meet the team's goals.
> - Coordinate team members' activities and diagnose team problems.

Even when you are leading a team, you are also a team member. By taking a collaborative approach in working with other team members and supporting each other, you will help build a lasting positive working relationship and ensure team and organizational success.

Leadership Styles

Our notion of what leadership is and who leaders are has undergone a radical transformation in recent history. Before, when people talked about leaders, they tended to think about CEOs or senior executives of the company. Today, leadership is viewed as a much broader phenomenon and leaders exist at all levels of an organization. Compared with senior executives, as a supervisor, you might be accountable for less territory, your vision for the business may sound more basic, the number of people to motivate may be fewer, but you perform the same leadership role as your more senior counterparts.

Key Elements

There are many definitions of leadership. From a theoretical perspective, *leadership* is defined as "*a process in which a person* (leader) *influences others* (followers) *to achieve a mission or objective.*" Judging from this definition, leadership occurs at all levels of an organization. Every individual can be an effective leader regardless of the kind of title he/she holds. As Peter Drucker pointed out: "*Leadership is not rank, privileges, titles or money. It is responsibility.*" (Drucker, 1999).

The leadership process has several key components:
- **Purpose**—Leadership involves a purpose. Leaders should have a very clear picture of the organization's mission and goals and should be able to clearly communicate that mission to the followers and mobilize

them to achieve pre-defined objectives that will enable the accomplishment of the organizational mission. They should have a very strong sense of purpose and focus on organizational results.
- **Qualities**–Leaders should have certain qualities that will enable them to be effective leaders. This includes their beliefs, values, ethics, functional knowledge, skills and competencies. People are not born with these qualities. Instead, they can be accumulated through work and life experiences and can be acquired through training and development activities. People can choose to become leaders by consciously developing these skills and qualities.
- **Influence**–Leadership is an influence process. Leaders should motivate and enable followers to work together at achieving the organizational objective. Leaders need to understand their followers–their needs, desires and skill levels in order to select the most effective leadership approaches. Leaders should have the trust and respect of their followers.
- **Action**–Leadership is an action process. An effective leader is not someone who is automatically admired. He or she is someone who takes actions and sets examples and whose followers do the right things.

Sharing a Vision and Setting Objectives

As we discussed earlier, one of the key components of effective leadership is *providing purpose*. Effective leaders bring passion, perspective, and significance to the process of defining and communicating organizational purpose.

Good organizations convey a strong vision of where they will be in the future. To be an effective leader, you need to have a deep understanding and strong identification with the company's vision. As a supervisor, you will mainly be concerned with the employee group that you are managing, and set a vision for your unit that is consistent with the overall vision for the company. The vision for your unit should be a picture of where you want your department to be at a future date. For example, try to picture what your department would look like if it was perfect, or what the most efficient way to produce your product would look like, or perhaps if your budget was reduced by 10 percent, how you could still achieve the same quality product.

Setting and sharing the vision is a critical role of the leader. That is what distinguishes leaders from managers. Dr. Warren Bennis, founding chairman of the Leadership Institute at the University of Southern California has summed it up the best: "*Managers are people who do things right, while leaders are people who do the right thing.*" Leaders constantly ask "what are the organization's mission and goals? What constitutes performance and results in this organization?" Leaders are strategic; they understand how the task at hand fits in which the big picture and the overall objective, while managers are tactic. They focus on getting the job done (Bennis, 1994).

At their extremes, leading often means being out in front, pointing the way, and setting a good example for others to follow. Managing, on the other hand, means delegating responsibility, assigning tasks and waiting to see what happens. Both approaches are needed in running an organization. A good supervisor should learn to mix the function of leading and managing.

In order for the vision to be realized, employees need to know what specific actions they can take to make the vision a reality. As a leader, it is your responsibility to bring that vision down to meaningful and actionable objectives and link individual performance to organizational goals and values.

Goal setting is one of the critical components of a leader's job. Psychologists have found that performance goals are among the most robust motivational factors with a direct impact on performance. For a goal to be effective, it needs to be a SMART goal (Figure 8-2).

> ## Figure 8-2. Elements of An Effective Goal — SMART Goals
>
> **S—Specific:** A goal should be very concrete and specific. For example, the goal of "increase daily production of widgets by 100" is much more effective than a vague goal of "do your best to improve productivity."
>
> **M—Measurable:** A goal needs to be measurable. In management, people often say "what gets measured gets done". Measurement against goal achievement allows people to understand where they are against the set goal and make appropriate adjustments to their efforts or strategy to address that gap. For example, telling employees to improve customer satisfaction is a lot less useful than telling them to reduce customer wait time from 20 minutes to 10 minutes.
>
> **A—Actionable:** People should be able to take actions to influence the progress of the goal. A goal should be able to be translated into actionable and concrete tasks that people can accomplish. It is the completion of the series of tasks that makes the goal attainable.
>
> **R—Realistic:** This should not be confused with goal difficulty. A goal can be difficult, yet still achievable. If a goal is not realistic, people will simply give up and stop trying. While a vision can be a big stretch from where things are currently, the secret is to break that gap into a series of goals and objectives that are achievable through the combined efforts of your team.
>
> **T—Timeline:** A deadline for completion can mobilize employees to organize and allocate resources accordingly to achieve goals in a timely fashion.

When setting goals, please also keep in mind that goal-setting does not stop at the setting of goals, it should be coupled with ongoing performance feedback to keep employees informed about where they are and direct their future behavior and efforts on the right target.

Motivating Employees

Motivating others to achieve organizational objectives is a critical part of the leader's job. You need to interact with followers, peers, seniors, and other people whose support your need to accomplish your objectives. To gain their support, you must understand their needs and use that knowledge to help motivate them. Human needs are important drivers of human behavior and are powerful motivators. There are several psychological theories about motivation that can help you understand how human needs drive human behavior.

Maslow's Hierarchy of Needs

Maslow classified human needs into two major groups: *basic needs and meta needs*. These needs formed a Needs Hierarchy; the satisfaction of lower level needs will lead to the desire to fulfill higher level needs (Maslow, 1968). According to him, there are eight levels of needs:

1. physiological–food, water, shelter, sex
2. safety–feel free from immediate danger
3. sense of belonging and love–belong to a group, close friends to confide with
4. esteem–feeling of moving up in world, recognition, and few doubts about self
5. cognitive–learning for learning alone, contribute knowledge
6. aesthetic–at peace, more curious about inner workings of all
7. self-actualization–know exactly who you are, where you are going, and what you want to accomplish–state of well-being.
8. self-transcendence–a trans-egoic level that emphasizes visionary intuition, altruism and unity consciousness.

The first four levels are *basic needs*. They are also called "deficiency needs" because if they are not met, the individual will strive to make up the deficiency. The rest of the needs are called meta needs or growth needs. Because basic needs are more immediate and urgent, they are more powerful and often take precedence over meta needs. People whose basic needs are not met usually cannot focus on meeting higher level needs. A need higher in the hierarchy will become a motivator of behavior as long as the needs below it have been satisfied.

Understanding where a person is in the need hierarchy can help in determining an effective way to motivate the individual. When someone's basic needs are met, it is more effective to focus on the person's meta needs. But if someone were still trying to meet the basic physiological or safety needs, it would be far more effective to focus on meeting those needs. One of the goals for leaders is to help people obtain the skills and knowledge that will push up their position in the need hierarchy. People who have their basic needs met become much better workers.

> ### Table 8-A. Motivational Factors Theory
>
> **Demotivators**
> - salary & benefits
> - job security
> - working conditions/workplace safety
> - policies and administrative practices
> - fellow workers
>
> **Motivators**
> - recognition
> - achievement
> - growth
> - responsibility
> - job challenge
> - participation
> - autonomy

They are able to concentrate on fulfilling the vision of the organization, instead of constantly worrying about how to make ends meet.

Herzberg's Motivational Factors Theory

Herzberg differentiated between factors that motivate people (*Motivators*) and those that de-motivate people (*Demotivators*) (Herzberg et al, 1959).

Demotivators are those factors whose absence will make you feel dissatisfied but whose presence will not necessarily make you satisfied. A demotivator is something that will not necessarily make someone work harder, but its absence can cause someone to perform less or at a lower quality level. For example, if safety at the workplace is a concern, you will feel dissatisfied, but you will not necessarily feel satisfied at work just because the workplace is safe. Factors in the demotivator list must be present in your work environment to prevent employees from feeling dissatisfied. But having these factors in place are not enough. For employees to feel energized and motivated about performing their best, other motivating factors must be present. Motivators are those factors whose presence will make you feel satisfy and continue to motivate you to expand more efforts and achieve greater results. Such factors include recognition, a sense of achievement, opportunity for growth and challenge (Table 8-A).

What do we conclude? Money or workplace safety are not motivators, but the absence of a decent salary or lack of workplace safety are certainly demotivating factors. It is easy to see that both motivators and demotivators affect employee behavior, thus motivation. Look at each of the items in the two lists and think them through: why are some motivators and others demotivators? What factors are currently affecting each of your employees right now? How do you best leverage your knowledge of these factors to motivate your team to achieve organizational goals?

You also have to remember that motivating factors like people, are not static. They change with the time and the situation. What motivates an employee one day may not motivate him or her the next. It's the old "*what have you done for me lately?*" routine. Not only do you have to get to know your employees and what motivates them, you also have to be aware of changes.

Effective Leadership Behavior

AchieveGlobal, a leading global training and development organization, recently conducted a formal study of leadership behavior in 450 organizations across the United States. and Canada and took close to 2000 snapshots of what people at all organization levels think leadership is today (Bergmann et al, 1999). As a result of this research, they identified five critical leadership success strategies and seventeen core leadership competencies that are associated with leadership at all levels of the organization. These strategies and core competencies are listed in Table 8-B.

Leadership is about action and achieving results. Focusing on the competencies listed above can help you develop effective leadership skills that are valued by all levels of the organization.

Leadership Styles

Now that we have looked at some of the key tasks involved in leadership—sharing a vision, setting objectives, motivating others, let's look at some of the leadership styles that can be used to lead employees. There are many different combinations of supervisory leadership styles, but there are four major leadership styles that people often refer to:

- authoritarian supervisory leadership.
- democratic supervisory leadership.
- hands-off supervisory leadership.
- flexible supervisory leadership.

Authoritarian Supervisory Leadership

Authoritarian leadership style is often characterized as old-fashioned. In many circumstances, it is out-of-date and ineffective. Authoritarian leaders are very much task-oriented and are hard on their workers. They are autocratic with little or no allowance for cooperation or collaboration. Authoritarian leadership involves giving orders, and leaving little or no room for input or questioning by employees. The authoritarian supervisor usually:

- sets specific time-frames by which things are to be completed.
- lays out all work expectations.
- goes over all the how-to's and makes sure they are understood.

Table 8-B. Leadership Competencies and Strategies

Competencies	Strategies (CLIMB)
• setting or sharing a vision	Create a compelling future
• managing change • focusing on the customer	Let the customer drive the organization
• dealing with individuals • supporting teams and groups • sharing information • solving problems, making decisions	Involve every mind
• managing business processes • managing projects • displaying technical skills • managing time and resources	Manage work horizontally
• taking responsibility • handling emotions • displaying professional ethics • showing compassion • making credible presentations • taking initiative beyond job requirements	Build personal credibility

- expects people to do what they are told without question or debate.
- retains control by checking on the employee frequently to assure the expected outcome.
- is intolerant of what they see as dissent, so it is difficult for subordinates to contribute or develop.

Authoritarian leadership may be appropriate with some employees, such as: newly hired employees until they have learned their job responsibilities and company procedures; employees placed in positions they are not really trained or prepared to handle; employees handling new and unfamiliar equipment; employees who don't want to have to think but only to follow orders, and/or unskilled or untrained employees hired on a temporary basis or temporary employees in general. While it may be old-fashioned in many parts of the workplace, authoritarian supervisory leadership still fits in these circumstances.

For example, if you are short-handed and are sent an employee who is supposed to handle an expensive and dangerous piece of equipment, you had better use an authoritarian approach—set specific time frames for each task, lay out all work expectations, go over all of the how-to's regarding the equipment, safety rules and the job, make sure they are understood and check frequently to assure the expected outcome.

Authoritarian leadership is usually not appropriate with employees who are highly skilled or educated, long-term employees, creative or innovative employees. It tends to upset them and destroy their creativity and productivity. Even with these people, however, it may have to be used in emergency situations if time does not allow for input from others. If a fire starts, you don't debate it, you don't form a committee to discuss fire control. You give clear, precise and authoritarian orders to put out the fire.

Having established that authoritarian behavior is sometimes necessary, it is important to stress that it is not necessary most of the time and is usually counterproductive for the reasons already stated. Unfortunately, authoritarian behavior is often what supervisors fall back on when they feel insecure or threatened. In today's knowledge economy, where intellectual capital and employee creativity and contribution are key to success, use of authoritarian leadership style should really be cautioned.

Democratic Supervisory Leadership

Democratic or nondirective, participative supervisory leadership in all its various forms have a common theme of high focus on task and also high focus on relationship and employee participation. Under this leadership approach, employees provide input into how the task or project is to be completed. This style of leader leads by positive example and tries to foster a team environment in which all members can participate in the decision making process and reach their highest potential.

Democratic leaders often delegate his/her authority to the employee to do the job, assigns responsibility to the employee to make the decisions involved, while always retaining overall responsibility. Responsibility, in this way, is actually "shared".

The level of control by the supervisor in this process can vary. Some supervisors can allow the employee or employee group to make decisions:

- Totally on their own
- With some input by the supervisor, or
- Within input from the employees but the final decision is retained by the supervisor

In any event, while supervisors delegate responsibility to employees in varying degrees, they still retain full responsibility for the results of the employee efforts.

Characteristics of the democratic supervisor include: security; confidence in the staff's ability and competence; recognition of the need for staff development; and, willingness to share the control. Characteristics of employees who respond well to this style are: familiarity with the job, required skills and organizational rules and procedures; a willingness to participate in the decision making; and a higher level of experience, skills or seniority. Just as there are problems with an authoritarian style of supervision, there are also problems with the democratic style. Some possible pitfalls include:

- Many employees don't want to participate in the decision-making process (you don't pay me to do that. It's not in my job description.)
- Many supervisors really only give the process lip service, letting employees give input but ultimately implementing the supervisor's original plans anyway.
- Many problems do not need or lend themselves to group decision-making.

Hands-off Supervisory Leadership

The *hands-off supervisor* assumes employees have the skills and resources to perform their job and provides no direction or feedback in the process. A laid-back type, the hands-off leader is often seen as the answer to a workforce focused on finding job satisfaction.

The hands-off leader adopts a *delegate and disappear* style. However, the reality is that both authority and responsibility for tasks are being delegated, and the hands-off supervisor is trying to walk away from responsibility. That simply doesn't work. Supervisors cannot walk away from ultimate responsibility. Any delegation of responsibility or authorization to an employee to carry out a specific job remains a shared responsibility with the supervisor, and the supervisor is ultimately responsible to the organization.

The supervisor can delegate to an employee by giving him/her specific responsibility for doing part of the supervisor's job. This delegation conveys the "authority" to carry out specific tasks or functions, and the "responsibility" to make the decisions involved as agreed to. In this way, new responsibility is created for the employee involved, but the supervisor retains ultimate responsibility for what is or is not accomplished. It is a shared responsibility situation. Both the supervisor and the employee share the risk (and responsibility), although the supervisor holds ultimate responsibility and accountability in the eyes of the organization. Nonetheless, if you expect the employee to do a job, you must be prepared for such risks.

Another problem is that this style doesn't work in most cases and can as easily be described as the lassie-fair leadership style. There are, of course, some employees who are motivated by feeling they are trusted and respected to perform without much, if any, intervention. Presumably, they would be responsive to this style. We suspect they are few, since most would still feel some frustration about a supervisor who did little, if any, work or supervision.

The primary drawbacks of this style are pretty apparent. The hands-off supervisor never gives employees any positive reinforcement (everyone needs a pat on the back from time to time), and mistakes are usually not corrected until there is a crisis. Many supervisors of this type see themselves as a resource person whom employees will come to when there is a need. That, of course, assumes the employee will realize that there is a need.

Flexible Supervisory Leadership

The fourth style, *flexible supervisory leadership,* is a combination approach. It is often described as the "*situational leadership*" style. Many writers had described this style, most thoroughly by Kenneth Blanchard and Paul Hershey in several books.

Flexible supervision means choosing the style that fits both the particular situation and the employees you are working with in that situation. This means the supervisor must be flexible in the style to be used at a particular time and place and with particular employees.

Since most supervisors have a style they are most comfortable with, they must first become aware of what their own usual style is before they can become aware of how to use other styles. Look back over the characteristics of the styles we have described. You will probably find yourself somewhere between two of these.

Now comes the hard part: you can bet that one style is not appropriate for all situations. There are work situations where you simply must be authoritarian: enforcement of safety procedures, maintaining firm rules on substance abuse, and so on. Blanchard and Hersey call this style directing. They see a variety of styles ranging from directive to delegating (what we have called authoritarian to democratic). Figure 8–4 shows the wide range of styles within the authoritarian to democratic field. The flexible supervisory leadership style can utilize all of these styles, depending on the particular situation and the employees involved.

You must face up to the fact that while you try to keep teamwork going, a team is always made up of different individuals with many different abilities, motivations and needs. Getting to know your employees' individual needs and skill levels will help you determine which employees respond best to which leadership style. For example, by taking a hands-off approach, you allow your team to gain self-reliance. Being an authoritarian leader can instill a sense of discipline in an unmotivated worker. Being flexible enough to recognize that Jim is a fast learner, has the basic skills and is able to handle responsibility very well means that you can delegate a great deal to him—almost becoming a hands-off supervisor, but certainly a delegating type. Carol, however, doesn't learn as quickly, is a bit afraid of moving on to new projects, but does have some skills. You are going to have to coach her a lot,

Figure 8-4.
Assessing Your Own Leadership Style.

Understanding your own style can help you find ways to improve your leadership effectiveness. There are several sources you can use to assess your own style:

1. **Ask Yourself**—check the different attributes listed in Figure 8-.3 and identify which style best describes you. Try to think of different leadership situations when assessing yourself—how did you lead in routine situations, in emergency situations, with experienced employees, with new employees.
2. **Feedback from Your Peers**—identify a peer that you are relatively close to, who has the opportunity to observe you in your daily work. Ask him/her to tell you objectively what he/she thinks your style most often use with your subordinates.
3. **Feedback from Your Subordinates**—identify your subordinates who represent different experience/ability level, using informal questions to ask them assess your leadership style.
4. **Feedback from Your Supervisor**—use informal opportunities or formal performance or development review opportunities to ask your supervisor evaluate your leadership style. Seek his/her feedback on how you can be more effective in managing your team.

in a very supportive yet democratic manner. Reggie, on the other hand, waits for orders. "*Tell me what to do, and I'll do it.*" He may know how to do it, may possess the necessary skills, but he's one of those "*You don't pay me to think*" types, and the only way to handle him is with very authoritarian instructions.

There is no way to learn this, except practice. Practicing different styles with your employees in different situations will help you as a supervisor to reach a balance. That's flexible leadership (Figure 8-5).

Adjusting Supervisory Style to the Needs of a Diverse and Global Workforce

At the beginning of this chapter, we identified that the increasing diversity of the population and globalization are two major trends that are shaping the workplace today. The profile of the workforce today is a lot different from the way it was in the 1980s—women constitute about 50 percent of the workforce and 29 percent of the workforce is non-white. Increasingly, we are working with colleagues outside national borders—global task teams composed of people from all continents of the world working together on a project is becoming a common

Figure 8-5. Comparison of Leadership Styles

Leadership Styles

	Authoritarian	Democratic	Hands Off	Flexible
Characteristics	• Leader sets specific time frames for project completion. • Lays out all work expectations. • Gives orders. No employee input	• Seeks employee input • Encourages employees to participate in decision making • Employees sometimes on their own • Employees sometimes work with input from leader.	• Assumes employees can do the job alone. • Assumes skills are there • Provides no direction or feedback • Feels employees will be motivated if trusted and left alone	• Observes motivation and skill level of employees • Assigns tasks according to ability • Provides level of supervision adjusted to individual employee and task • Uses style appropriate to situation and/or employee
Type of Leader	• Unsure of others. Often insecure. • Inflexible. • Gives appearance of self-confidence	• Self-confident. • Secure • Believes in staff capabilities • Believes in collective decision making	• Laid back or lazy? • Feels employees must be responsible for their own work • Job satisfaction dominant	• Same as democratic except believes employee skills, nature of situation will determine style
Advantage	• Works well when you need to send the troops charging over the hill, or in a short-term emergency.	• Encourages participation. • Increases self-satisfaction and commitment to team goals.	• Great for self-starting, creative types who need no direction and have time for mistakes.	• Allows Supervisor to use style appropriate to situation and employee. Very effective in developing employees.
Disadvantage	• Demeaning to most employees. • Ineffective with bright, creative people. • Does not develop staff.	• Some people don't want to make decisions. • Some situations are not suited to collective decisions.	• Bad for everyone else.	• Requires Supervisor willing to learn and work smarter.

occurrence at many multinational organizations.

People are a vital resource in any organization. Every employee brings a unique combination of background, heritage, gender, religion, education and experiences to the workplace. Effective leaders know how to tap into this rich source of new ideas and intellectual vitality. When diverse groups fail to interact effectively, productivity suffers. Even worse, it can lead to lawsuits, high turnover, low morale, and loss of talent to competitors. When the global workforce fails to work together as an integrated business, organizations become less competitive, miss important expansion opportunities, lost market share and alienate global employees and customers.

Effective management of the diverse and global workforce requires the supervisor to be sensitive to the background and unique perspective of the employee and truly rely on leading rather than monitoring/controlling to achieve organizational objectives.

1. You should understand that diversity and globalization are not nice to dos or just another human resource program. They are becoming a way of life and are business imperatives for any company to succeed in the new market environment. As in any leadership situation, understanding the needs of those you are leading is very important. It is even more important in the case of leading a diverse/global workforce.

    In managing a diverse group, you need to take a look at the profiles of the people that you are leading and understand their unique background and perspectives:

- What are the special concerns of the female employees—family, child support, and women's wellness issues.
- What are the minority employees' perspectives—career advancement opportunities, do they feel that their opinions and background are valued, do they have a channel to share their concerns/issues.

- The aging population—concerns regarding their own careers, caring for their children and their parents, financial concerns and health concerns.
2. When working with a global group, there are three critical factors to successful global cooperation:
- knowledge of the cultures involved
- an attitude that respects the differences and says, *"your culture is as 'right' as mine."*
- interpersonal communication skills that lead to constructive relationships.

Understanding the Cultures Involved

There are many stories of business failures due to the lack of understanding of the other cultures and assuming that other cultures are just the same as ours. For example, a major U.S. automobile company has been trying very hard to export its cars to Japan without much success. It took them a long time to realize that in Japan, the driver's seat is on the right side of the car rather than on the left as is the case in the United States. When Coca-Cola first introduced its soda to the mainland China market, it did not do very well, because the name of Coca-Cola was translated as "Thirsty Mouth, Bitter Taste". Who would want to drink that?! When the Chevy Nova car was introduced in Latin America, nobody paid much attention to the name of the car. It turns out that in Spanish, it means "Chevy No Go". While these seem to be very obvious mistakes that can be easily avoided, it did reflect an attitude of taking for granted that everyone is the same, and that is a very dangerous attitude in international business.

Cultures evolve through many years of social-economical, political and technical influences. They are powerful factors that shape the way people think, act and relate to each other in both social and work settings. To understand other cultures requires some homework and an open and honest attitude to learn from others. As it relates to work, there are several key dimensions that you need to know.

Collectivism vs. Individualism

In western society, the focus is on individualism—personal achievement and independence are highly valued. In oriental society, the focus is more on collectivism—groups and society advancement, conformity and harmony are highly valued. An interesting contrast in the proverbs reflects this difference:

The U.S. proverb says: "*The early bird catches the worm*".

The Chinese proverb says: "*The first in the flock is the first to be shot*".

This difference has important implications for the way you manage and motivate employees from different cultures. For example, in the collectivism culture, group identity is very important and people are more comfortable being rewarded together with a team rather than becoming the single hero in the unit. They do want recognition for their efforts, but sometimes they might not feel at ease when they are singled out. Because Asian employees value conformity and harmony, they tend to avoid direct confrontation and the way they voice their disagreement or concerns may be indirect. By the same token, when you are dealing with employees of those cultures, you need to be aware of your own style, be sensitive, and avoid irritating them by adopting a too aggressive or confrontational style.

Communication Styles

Psychological research has found that there are two kinds of cultures when it comes to communication styles. There is the *Low Context Culture*, where explicit communication styles are most often used and people derive meaning from what is directly communicated. U.S. and most western cultures are Low Context Cultures–what you say is what you mean. Then, there is the *High Context Culture,* where communication is implicit and people derive meaning from direct communications as well as the context of the communication. Asian and some middle-eastern cultures are high-context cultures. In order to get the true meaning of the message, you need to hear between the lines and read the environment and many other cues.

A U.S. executive was puzzled as to why his Japanese employees did not deliver on what they had agreed to. It turned out when they nodded at him when he asked them to agree on a certain task, simply meant that they were acknowledging that they had heard him, but not necessarily that they were agreeing with him! As a result, in his subsequent discussions, he learned to probe more and get concrete agreement on actions. Because of the focus on harmony, in many Asian cultures, people will avoid saying "no" directly to you. Instead, they will use other means to communicate that message: e.g., *"I need to further study this, I am very busy at this point and can not attend to it."* To be effective, you need to be aware of this difference and be able to read the true meanings.

When managing a global team, you should try to use simple and easy to understand communication messages and try to ask for the same from your team.

Social & Business Etiquette/Protocol

- sense of time–In Japan and Germany, tardiness is viewed as disrespectful and should be avoided with great effort. In Latin America, the sense of time is more relaxed.
- work schedule–The Muslims shut down in the month of Ramadan in the spring. In Spain, Portugal and certain Latin countries, people tend to take long lunch breaks.

- humor—Can be dangerous if used inappropriately. Sports stories should be used very carefully. Football is the most popular sport in the United States. But outside the United States when people talk about football, they mean soccer.
- gift-giving—In Japan and the Chinese-language-speaking countries of China, Taiwan, Hong Kong giving some one a clock is considered bad luck, because the word "*Giving Clock*" has the same pronunciation as the word "*give someone a funeral*".

The attitude of acceptance and appreciation is very important. Attitudes that lead to positive results in cross-cultural relationships include: curiosity, openness, patience, personal respect, respect for history and flexibility.

At the end of the day, despite our differences, we are all human beings with common basic needs. To be an effective leader of diverse groups of people, you need to focus on these basics: respect for others, sharing a vision, making people feel part of the team and striving for results.

Conclusion

The world is changing at an ever-increasing pace and the need for leadership at all levels of the organization has never been greater. Leaders today need to recognize that managing change, working collaboratively and relying on teams are important aspects of every successful organization. To do that, you need to have a clear vision of the future, communicate that future and mobilize employees to work together toward the vision. There are different leadership styles and behaviors that you can use to achieve these results. To be effective, you need to tailor your styles and behaviors to the employees that you are leading, especially in today's diverse and global environment. Leadership can be developed and truly effective leaders are life-long learners who continuously develop themselves through their work experiences and learning.

References

Bennis W. On becoming a leader. *Perseus*, August 1994.

Bergmann H, Hurson K, Russ-Eft D. *Everyone A Leader: A Grass Roots Model For The New Workplace (Based on Achieve Global Leadership Competency Study)*. New York: Wiley, 1999.

Drucker P. Leader to leader: Enduring insights on leadership. *Leader to Leader Journal.* Jossey-Bass, March 1999.

Herzberg F, Mausner B., Snyderman BB. *The Motivation to Work*, 2nd ed. New York: Wiley, 1959.

Kotter JP. Winning at change. *Leader to Leader Journal No. 10.* Drucker Foundation and Jossey-Bass, Fall 1998.

Maslow A. *Toward a Psychology of Being*. New York: Van Nostrand, 1968.

Review Questions

1. What is your organization's mission and vision? Does your group or department have a mission? How much do your employees know about your company's/groups mission?

2. What type of change is your organization going through? What have you done or what can you do to help implement the needed change? What have you told your employees about the changes and do they feel like they are part of the process?

3. Think about the best boss you have ever worked for. What type of leadership style did he/she possess? How have you tried to emulate that style?

4. How much do you know about your employees and the type of leadership style they respond to?

5. How diverse is your group and how sensitive are you to team members' differences?

9 Supervising in a Union Environment

by Carl Jenks, PhD
John Lucas, PhD

What Will I Learn in This Chapter?

In this chapter, we will discuss:

- who is involved in the collective agreement.
- contents of a collective agreement.
- legal considerations for the supervisor in administering an agreement.
- an organization's policy-procedure manual, which usually occur when there is no collective agreement.

Overview

Supervising a unionized workforce has special implications for all managers especially supervisors. Supervisors must be familiar with an array of workplace rules, policies and, procedures, in addition to the *National Labor Relations Act (NRLA)*. They must also enforce workplace laws such as the Equal Employment Opportunity Act, American With Disabilities Act, Age Discrimination In Employment Act, just to name a few. See Chapter 3 for more information on these laws. In a union environment, however, supervisors must also adhere to the common law of workplace, which is usually referenced in the past practices and the collective bargaining agreement.

When referring to a labor agreement, we will use various terms: *collective agreement*, *collective bargaining agreement*, or simply *agreement*. The words collective agreement are used because they emphasize the fact that the agreement was mutually negotiated and agreed to by labor and management.

The Collective Agreement

Parties to the Agreement

One of the easiest things for a supervisor to forget is that the collective agreement is the result of collective bargaining. The parties to that bargaining, and to the collective agreement that results from it, are the union and the organization. It is a contract between these two, and one that both have agreed to uphold and enforce (Figure 9-1). In that sense, the collective agreement is no different from any

> Figure 9–1. It Takes a Union and a Company to Sign
>
> Agreement Between International Brotherhood of Widget Makers and the International Widget and Conductors Company, Inc.

other contract the organization makes. It was entered into by both parties in good faith, and both are obligated to live up to its terms. Thus, if supervisors feel frustrated by the terms of a collective agreement, it should be remembered that the organization signed and agreed to those terms.

Management in smaller companies often feel as if they had little choice in bargaining or accepting the collective agreement, since they often are involved in pattern bargaining or standby agreements. In *pattern bargaining*, all the various companies in a particular industry follow a collective agreement pattern. In *standby agreements*, the organization agrees to accept whatever comes out of negotiations between the union and the industry. However, the organization did sign the standby agreement, and thus agreed to sign the product of those negotiations. Nevertheless it is imperative that management introduce contractual language dealing with local issues. If consideration is not given to local issues, the efficiency of the organization will be degraded by constant disputes.

The National Labor Relations Act, the Railway Labor Act, and the laws of virtually all states (Figure 9-2) guarantee employees the right to be represented by a union. Those laws also provide that the organization and the union have a legal obligation to bargain in good faith over wages, hours and conditions of employment. If a majority of the employees truly want to be represented by a union, the organization is prevented by law from interfering with this process. For an organization to thwart the union's organizing efforts in any way would be the basis for an *unfair labor practice (ULP)* charge. Go back and review Chapter 3, Supervisors, Employment and Workplace Laws, if you have any questions on this issue.

Agreement

Generally, a collective agreement spells out the rights of the unionized employees, specifically those related to wages, hours, and conditions of employment. It also establishes a framework for the relationship between management (the supervisor and those above the supervisor) and the bargaining unit employees (those who are covered under the collective agreement). The question of who is in the bargaining unit is determined by the National Labor Relations Board (NRLB) in a "directed" election, wherein the NLRB decides the appropriate unit. In a "consent" election, the parties themselves make the determination as to which employees will be in a unionized bargaining unit. Most people in management are automatically *exempt*, that is, not eligible to be protected by labor laws. This exemption includes all levels of management including the supervisory level. In addition, the organization and the union may agree to exclude certain employees from coverage usually because they have some kind of specialized job that somehow relates to management activities. Sometimes this happens because they were not included in the unit involved in the union representation election, but sometimes they were simply excluded by mutual agreement between the organization and union.

Virtually all collective agreements cover the same range of topics. How they deal with the topics varies significantly from industry to industry, organization to organization, and even department to department. Typical topics are discussed in the following sections:

- Parties to the agreement–This agreement is by and between AMALGAMATED MAINTENANCE, INC. and the INTERNATIONAL BROTHERHOOD OF COLLATORS, SCRIVENERS AND MAINTENANCE WORKERS OF AMERICA, AFL-CIO, CLC.
- A statement of purpose–The purpose of this agreement is to improve and maintain the wages, benefits and working conditions of the employees of AMALGAMATED MAINTENANCE, INC.
- Recognition clause–The Organization recognized the Union as the sole and exclusive bargaining agent for employees. This means that the

organization will not deal with any other union for this specific group of employees until such time as a different union is selected by the employees. It also means that the union is obligated to represent all bargaining unit employees covered by the agreement even if they are not union members. The union has a legal duty to represent members and non-members equally in satisfying its fair representation requirement under federal labor laws.

- Coverage or scope—This clause usually spells out exactly which jobs and which locations are covered by the agreement, sometimes giving long lists of job titles, duties, pay schedules.
- Union shop. Union shop rules are a form of union security that require bargaining unit employees to become members within a stated period of time after they are hired (usually 60 to 90 days). There are 21 right-to-work states, which prohibit such a clause. Other union security agreements such as "Agency Shop" or "Fair Share" provide that those who object to membership may pay only dues or a maintenance fee in lieu of dues. Most unions view the union shop form of security agreement as a critical element to survival.
- Hiring hall. This is most commonly found in craft-type unions such as those found in the construction and maritime industry. The organization agrees to hire employees from a union-operated hiring hall on a temporary basis. The Federal Labor Laws prohibit closed shops such as exists in an *Industrial Union*. However, craft-type unions are generally closed shops because they do not have permanent employment relationships.
- Check-off —A check-off plan provides that union dues and fees will be automatically deducted from the employee's wages and paid to the union. However, the union must win this right through negotiations with the organization. Unions will normally make concessions to

management to obtain this security agreement.
- Discrimination—This clause prohibits discrimination against union members and against individuals on the basis of age, race, creed, color, sex or religion. Both, of course, are covered under federal law, so the rule tends to be in the nature of an organization proclaiming that it is an equal opportunity employer. Most agreements have similar language, such as that shown in Figure 9-2: The Organization will not interfere with, restrain or coerce the employees covered by this Agreement because of membership in, or activity on behalf of, the Union.

> **Figure 9-2**
> **The National Labor Relations Act**
>
> The Company will not interfere with, restrain or coerce the employees covered by this Agreement because of membership in, or activity on behalf of, the Union.

- Hours of work—Assigned hours, hours per week, shift times, lunch hours and break times are among the subjects covered here. Usually, prep time and clean-up time are spelled out specifically.
- Overtime—This clause spells out when there is extra pay for working hours other than those regularly assigned. The Fair Labor Standards Act requires overtime for time worked over 40 hours. The rate of pay for overtime may change for the day worked such as double time for working a holiday, but most overtime is paid at time and one-half.
- Shift premium—Many agreements provide an extra payment or premium for working swing or midnight shifts. Twenty-four-hour-per-day operations such as railroads and airlines often do not provide such premiums.
- Holidays—This clause usually spells out the precise paid holidays allowed, determines eligibility, and provides for extra premium pay if the employee is required to work on the holiday. The most frequent

241

disputes over holiday pay occur because there is not a clear understanding about working the day before and the day after a holiday.
- Call-in and reporting time—Call/report rules provide for how employees will be called in for special assignments, when they must report for duty, and how they must report absences. Management would generally prefer to work the employees on overtime, whereas unions would generally prefer to hire more additional employees to cover emergencies.
- Vacation—Vacation rules spell out the precise vacation entitlement, usually based on length of service and actual days worked in the previous year. They determine eligibility and provide for an extra premium pay if the employee is required to work in lieu of taking an earned vacation.
- Leave of absence—This covers the circumstances under which an employee is entitled to a leave of absence. These situations usually include health, child bearing, military service and union duties.
- Seniority—Competitive seniority rules establish the principle that most job assignments shall be based on the employee's length of service with the organization. This principle is usually modified by some reference to qualifications and restricted to job classes or departments. Thus, it will often read: In the assigning of positions, fitness and ability being sufficient, seniority shall prevail. Note that the word sufficient is the critical word. Generally, arbitrators have placed a very narrow interpretation on this. Thus, sufficient does not mean in comparison with other employees applying for the same job, but simply enough to start learning the new job. A large number of grievances arise out of disputes in the assignment of jobs by seniority. Some companies, however, find assignment by seniority as good as any other system for production work.
- Method of wage payment—This is a payday rule, establishing when and how frequently wages are paid.

- Union representation, stewards and visitation—The agreement usually has a rule giving union representatives full access to visit the property and recognizing the rights of local shop stewards to take off time for union work. Some agreements even provide that local shop stewards will be paid by the organization while carrying out union duties.
- Grievance procedure. Grievances are disputes arising from the interpretation or application of the collective agreement. They occur during the life of the agreement and are usually settled through an organization/union process of hearings and negotiations. Union agreements always provide for some method of grievance resolution. Usually it is a filing and appeal process, with the union having control over its representation of the employee. That is, the employee has the right to a union representative being present at each step of the grievance process, and the union has the obligation and duty to handle the grievances it finds appropriate and proper. Unions are given considerable latitude by the courts in deciding which cases they should pursue.
- Arbitration. In the event the organization and the union can't agree on how to settle a grievance, most agreements provide that unsettled disputes will be submitted to a neutral third party. This person is usually an arbitrator, who makes a final and binding decision on both parties. If arbitration is used this final step in the process assures closure of a dispute if the organization and the union are unable to do so by themselves. However, most unions and companies prefer to settle their own disputes through compromise or mediation. They tend to avoid arbitrations because (1) the process is expensive, and (2) they are turning their fate over to someone else. Some industries or companies have special arbitrators or "permanent" arbitration panels that have been pre-selected by agreement between the union and the organization. In these cases, the final step of arbitration is often viewed as less of a

threat to self-interest, probably because the parties are familiar with the arbitrators.

- Discharges—Discharge rules spell out the legitimate causes for discharges, how an employee is to be discharged, and the rights of appeal involved. They often have some particular circumstances that can result in immediate dismissal for major rule infractions. For example, in the banking and insurance industry, if an employee conceals prior criminal activity, the employee may be dismissed immediately. In the railroad and airline industry, employees drinking alcohol on the job are subject to immediate dismissal. Nonetheless, most agreements require adherence to the principles of Just Cause. Just Cause means that the disciplinary action is fair and equitable in its application.
- Bulletin boards—Collective agreements provide specific locations where union information can be posted as well as where organization job notices and changes are posted. The use of organization bulletin boards is a right won through the negotiations process.
- Jury duty—Most agreements have clauses providing that employees not only have the time off but also the right to be paid while on jury duty.
- New jobs—Creation of new jobs is a subject for negotiation under most labor agreements. Posting and the method of filling such jobs is also usually spelled out. Here is where the definition of competitive seniority is of utmost importance to the bargaining unit member in determining who gets the new jobs.
- Strike and lockout—The right to strike and lockout is regulated by law. In addition, most collective agreements have a "no strike" and a "no lockout" clause to prevent strikes or lockouts during the term of the agreement. The law does not require this, but most companies insist on the no strike clause as an assurance of stability so that the cost of labor

will be known for a defined period of time. In the railroad and airline industries (both are covered under the Railway Labor Act), collective agreements do not expire. To get around this, companies have insisted that a clause be signed establishing a fixed period of time during which there will be no strikes or lockouts.
- Waiver and alteration of agreement—This clause provides for exceptions to the agreement and how the agreement may be modified after a formal announcement. A "wage re-opener" might be an example. In such a case, only wages are discussed and arbitration is the usual mechanism to end the process.
- Safety and health—This clause usually places clear obligation on the employer to maintain a safe and healthful work environment. It also places a clear obligation on employees to follow safety rules and procedures. Many agreements include provisions for joint labor/management safety committees, assignments to committees, committee meetings and other steps to be taken to assure safety and health. A reoccurring problem regarding safety is defining exactly when an employee may walk off an unsafe job.
- New employees—This clause spells out the method of hiring and training new employees, special pay circumstances, and on-the-job training. This can be a potential area of conflict if the organization wants to hire new employees rather than retrain the old employees.
- Death in the family—This most commonly provides paid leave for attending funerals for a death in the immediate family, including grandparents and close relatives, and sometimes bereavement time for death in the employee's immediate family.
- Health and welfare—This commonly provides health, accident and life insurance programs for all employees covered by the agreement. It also may provide for a pension program in addition to Social Security.

The terms of the coverage, carrier(s) for the plan(s) and administration of the plan are usually covered in bargaining. In some industries there are joint labor/management trusts that administer pension, health and welfare programs.
- Wage structure, progression and rate—This clause spells out wage rates by position, length of service, step rates, cost-of-living adjustments, and so on. Changes in wages are usually negotiated near the expiration time of the collective agreement, although some collective agreements have wage-reopener clauses that may occur at specified times during the term of the agreement. However, management would prefer to have a consistent wage rate for the life of the contract so that the cost of labor in known in advance.
- Wash-up time—In situations where employees need to change clothes, wash up before or after working, or use special uniforms, there is usually a wash-up period stipulated in the agreement. The amount of time allocated is normally paid for by the organization.
- Duration of collective agreement—This spells out the exact dates covered in the contract, usually one to three years. By law (NLRA) agreements covered by that Act should run no longer the 5 years. Although, unions may attempt to decertify after 3 years of a more lengthy contract
- Management rights—Management rights allow managers to manage the plant and direct the work forces. They may be written very generally or they may be specific. Regardless of the format, management generally adheres to the residual rights doctrine. If it is still not bargained away, it is still a management right. Usually, but not in all collective agreements, management rights specifically cover the following subjects:
    - work to be performed

- how work is to be performed
- tools, equipment and machines to be used (except if a safety hazard is involved)
- money to be spend in performing the work
- organization structure
- selection of supervisory personnel
- need for increase or decrease of employees performing the work
- standard selection of employees.

All of these management rights, of course, are to be taken in the context of the previously stated rules in the collective agreement (Figure 9–3).

Policy and Procedures Manual

Organization-written policy/procedure manuals and employee handbooks are defined here as those statements of terms of work, benefits, and conditions of employment produced by the organization for its employees. They will be called *policy manuals*. In this chapter. These exist in union and union-free workplaces. In union workplaces, such policy manuals are usually somewhat abbreviated, since many of the collective agreement rules cover the

Figure 9-3. Collective Agreement Rules

Virtually all collective agreements cover the following subjects:

- Parties to the agreement
- A statement of purpose
- Recognition clause
- Coverage or scope
- Union shop
- Hiring hall
- Check-off
- Discrimination
- Hours of work
- Overtime
- Shift premium
- Holidays
- Call-in and reporting time
- Vacation
- Leave of absence
- Seniority
- Method of wage payment
- Union representation, stewards and visitation
- Grievance procedure
- Arbitration
- Discharges
- Bulletin boards
- Jury duty
- New jobs
- Strike and lockout
- Waiver and alteration of agreement
- Safety and health
- New employees
- Death in the family
- Health and welfare
- Wage structure, progression and rate
- Wash-up time
- Duration of collective agreement
- Management rights

247

subjects normally included in a policy manual.

The contents of an organization policy manual as used in a nonunion environment are not much different from those of a labor/management collective agreement in terms of topics covered and even many of the procedures involved. At one time, these policy manuals were not considered as biding as a collective agreement. However, more and more state and federal courts are interpreting policy manuals and employee handbooks as binding contractual agreements. The major legislative changes are occurring at the state rather than the federal level. The concept of employment-at-will is rapidly eroding. The idea used to be that the employer had the unilateral right to hire and fire for any reason not specifically in violation of the law. By violation of the law, it is meant a violation of an individual's protected rights. Things just aren't that way anymore. The courts and state legislatures are rapidly moving toward what is often called the *democratic workplace*. The idea of due process in the workplace is replacing the idea of employment-at-will. In many states, organization-written manuals are now treated as contracts. The absence of a manual can be even worse, since management and employees then must rely on implied or disputed understandings. That's why the supervisor's interpretation or administration of the manual is of critical importance.

Topics Included in the Manual

Most manuals address working conditions, such as vacation, wages, benefits, hours of work, leaves of absence, holidays, etc. Many policy manuals also include some type of grievance procedure although it may not be as specific or binding as those found in a union agreement. In fact, the five-step grievance process now being adopted and used by more nonunion companies is largely reflective of the form of grievance process found in most collective agreements. The primary difference in this and similar provisions is that in a

Figure 9–4. Comparing Topics Typically Covered in Collective Agreements (CA) and Policy Manuals (PM)

Topic Covered (Y=covered; N=Not Covered; S=Sometimes)

CA	PM	Subject
Y	Y	Parties to the agreement
Y	Y	A statement of purpose
Y	N	Recognition clause
Y	S	Coverage or scope
Y	N	Union shop
Y	N	Hiring hall
Y	N	Check-off
Y	Y	Discrimination
Y	Y	Hours of work
Y	Y	Overtime
S	S	Shift premium
Y	Y	Holidays
Y	Y	Call-in and reporting time
Y	Y	Vacation
Y	Y	Leave of absence
Y	S	Seniority
Y	Y	Method of wage payment
Y	N	Union representation, stewards and visitation
Y	S	Grievance procedure
Y	S	Arbitration
Y	Y	Discharges
Y	Y	Bulletin boards
Y	Y	Jury duty
Y	S	New jobs
Y	N	Strike and lockout
Y	S	Waiver and alteration of agreement
Y	Y	Safety and health
Y	Y	New employees
Y	Y	Death in the family
Y	Y	Health and welfare
Y	Y	Wage structure, progression and rate
Y	Y	Wash-up time
Y	N	Duration of collective agreement
Y	Y	Management rights

collective agreement the employee has the right to be represented by a union official. In an organization without a union, the employees are normally represented by a member of management. The question is how well are they represented by management? The National Academy of Arbitrators (NAA) has expressed concern of this issue for a number of years.

Policy manuals may well include programs that are union-like, such as employee/management committees to discuss issues and problems, complaint systems, counseling with assured anonymity, and so on. Some organizations set up these union-like structures to get employees involved and give them a sense of due process even though there is no formal union representation. However, in some cases, the organizations do not live up to the commitments they make in their own policy manuals.

Topics Not Usually Included in the Manual

Policy manuals will not include items particular to a collective agreement, such as recognition clause, union shop, check-off, discrimination as it relates to the union, union representation, stewards, strike, lockout, and the duration of the contract.

Figure 9–4 is a comparison checklist of a union versus a nonunion environment in terms of the topics covered by collective agreements and policy manuals. Again, the differences come in the specifics: how a rule is written versus how a policy is written. How someone is represented versus the position that she/he does not need representation. How due process is applied. Some see these as very significant differences while others do not.

Legal Considerations

In a union working environment with a collective agreement, you as a supervisor must realize that recognizing the union and following the agreement is more than the right thing to do, it's the law! The National Labor Relations Act, Section 1, sets forth the policy of the United States with regard to the right of employees to union representation and collective bargaining. It provides in part:

> *"Experience has proved that protection by law of the right of employees to organize and bargain collectively safeguards commerce from injury,*

impairment, or interruption, and promotes the flow of commerce by removing certain recognized sources of industrial strife and unrest, by encouraging practices fundamental to the friendly adjustment of industrial disputes arising out of differences as to wages, hours, or other working conditions, and by restoring equality of bargaining power between employers and employees."

Several of the legal considerations regarding union agreements were discussed previously, such as not interfering with a union representation election and not discriminating against employees due to their union membership/activity. In addition, breaching the collective agreement, like breaching most contracts, can result in costly and time-consuming arbitration or even more severe disputes. Supervisors who generate a lot of grievances make few friends on the higher levels of management. It's simply a bad supervisory practice. Supervisors who are unable to get along with a union are many times replaced by more accommodating supervisors.

The term *management*, as used in the collective agreement, usually means in practical terms, the supervisor. The supervisor is the one closest to the employees and is responsible for the day-to-day administration of the collective agreement. In essence, the supervisor legally speaks for management. Thus the supervisor must help protect the employer from any legal liabilities by making sure that the agreement is administered fairly and effectively and within legal restrictions.

Administering Collective Agreements

Administering collective agreements has many implications for the supervisor. Supervisors who have not worked in a union environment may fear the collective agreement, seeing it as a threat to the effective handling of their supervisory duties. Unfortunately, the union steward usually knows the agreement better than the supervisor. On the other hand, many supervisors who have spent their lives administering a collective agreement can't imagine doing their job any other way. An agreement gives structure to an otherwise dynamic and sometimes chaotic relationship.

Why Employees Join Unions

Understanding why employees join unions may help put things in perspective. Some of the many reasons employees join a union includes:
- security of association with others in the same condition, i.e., safety in number
- a desire to increase or secure their share in the economic system
- a sense of independence and control over their own affairs
- a means to understand and deal with the forces and factors at work in one's world
- the sociocultural heritage that assumes the need and right to belong to a union
- It's the thing to do.

Those explanations come down to: strength in numbers, more money, better benefits, and dignity and freedom from intimidation. Most people, sometime in their working life, have similar concerns in the relationship with their employer. Therefore, what is it that makes the difference? Why do some employees choose to go union while others do not? This chapter gives some of the information that helps answer these questions.

The Key

The supervisor is the key to the implementation of management/labor relations. It is the supervisor's responsibility to assure that the employer's rights are preserved in practice. The supervisor must also assure that the conditions of employment agreed upon are carried out fairly and honestly. In other words, the supervisor is also trying to assure that labor's rights are preserved in practice!

In the eyes of most employees, the supervisor is management. They will often look to the supervisor for interpretation of the collective agreement rules. Therefore, the supervisor must first know what is in the collective agreement and any other employer policies and procedures. The agreement cannot be ignored. It must be followed as it was intended to be followed.

To effectively administer the collective agreement, you will not only have to get to know the union representative but you will also have to understand that person's job. Sometimes this is a steward, a business agent, or whatever title the union uses. Get to know the union representative and strive for a good working relationship. Keep in mind that this individual is selected by the employees and works as an advocate on behalf of the union. Sometimes, the person may also be doing double duty, working full time for the organization and part-time for the union. Good communication with the union is invaluable, and most of the union contact you will have will be with the local employee representative.

In addition to the specifics of the union agreement that the supervisor must administer, the best way to avoid breaching the contract or the filing of grievances is to apply sound supervisory skills. These skills have been discussed throughout this book, but here are a few highlights:

- Strive at all times to bring understanding rather than confusion.
- Be consistent in all that you do.

- Communicate your expectations and act as a leader.
- Realize that what you get is usually what is given.
- Live up to your work.
- Treat employees as individuals and respect their differences.
- Learn to communicate with your employees: ask open-ended questions, listen actively, and talk in language the other person understands.
- Show enthusiasm about your employees.
- Give feedback and show appreciation.
- Personalize good things and depersonalize bad things.
- Help others be successful.
- Be fair, honest and impartial in the application of all rules and policies.

A lack of understanding between supervisor and employees is the greatest single basis of grievances. Supervisors fail because of people incompetence rather than technical incompetence. Does this mean that the number of grievances being filed in your area reflects on you? Yes, it does. At the same time, you do have to apply the agreement and get the work done. Theoretically you should be a 9-9 on the managerial grid, which means equal emphasis on employees and production. The best way to do that is to get to know your employees and keep them informed. Also keep in mind that the day-to-day administration of the collective agreement influences what will be brought to the bargaining table at contract negotiation time.

For example, if in choosing between two equally qualified employees for a promotion, you choose the one with less seniority and who also happens to be seen as your favorite, chances are seniority systems will be brought to the bargaining table the next time the contract is up for negotiation. And between now and then, you'll have a lot of grievances over the issue.

Fair treatment of and good communication with your employees under a collective agreement can also have safety implications.

Administration of the union agreement also has implications for the productivity of the organization. Adversarial relations may be inevitable at contract negotiation time. However, they need not be carried into the day-to-day workplace. Most workplace issues can be resolved with effective communication and understanding. They do not need browbeating from either management or labor.

Freeman and Medoff, both management people, in *What Do Unions Do?*, carried out an exhaustive study and comparison between union and nonunion work environments. The surprising results of their study were the general lack of differences between the two types of environments. One of their conclusions makes this very clear:

> *"Unionism can be a plus to 'enterprise efficiency' if management uses the collective bargaining process to learn about and improve the operation of the workplace and the production process....On the other hand, if management responds negatively to collective bargaining (or is prevented by unions from responding positively), unionism can significantly harm the performance of the firm."*

The issue, then is not so much whether the workplace is unionized or union free. The issue is how management and labor get along.

Brief History of Unionism

The study of the history of American labor provides invaluable insight for today's supervisor in understanding the philosophical viewpoints and behaviors of contemporary labor unions. Some of these philosophical viewpoints of today's labor unions are embedded in lessons learned from earlier labor unions in America. The history of American labor falls into four major periods. The early years, from 1865 to 1914, includes the formation of the National Labor Union, Knights of Labor, American Federation of Labor, and the Industrial Workers of the World.

The second major period encompasses the wartime cooperation of the AFL, the passage of the Norris-LaGuardia and Wagner labor laws, and the formation of the Congress of Industrial Organization. The third major period 1945 to 1960, involves the passage of the Taft-Hartley Act, the AFL-CIO Merger, and the Lardrum-Griffin Act. The final period, 1960 to present, witnesses the decline in union membership and the passage and implementation of the Civil Rights Act and WARN Act.

Between 1929 and 1933 gross national product fell from 104.4 billion dollars to 55.9 billion dollars. Wages and salaries paid dropped from 50 to 28.9 billion dollars in the same period. Unemployment was estimated to number as much as 15 million. The nation was now encountering the worst depression in its history. As a reflection of the condition of the economy, the membership of organized labor declined rapidly because union members could not afford to pay their dues. AFL membership totals dropped from 3,000,000 in 1930 to 2,100,000 in 1933.

In 1932, prior to President Roosevelt's administration, the Norris LaGuardia Act was passed which granted organized labor relief from federal court injunctions in labor disputes where no violence was involved. The Act guaranteed the right to strike for any purpose, the right to pay strike benefits, the right to picket, and the right to boycott without fear of court action. The Act also forbade federal courts from enforcing yellow-dog contracts. The significance of this act was that it protected organized labor from numerous previously enjoinable activities; however, the act did not provide any right by the union to demand employer recognition. This protected right of recognition would occur two years later with the passage of the Wagner Act.

After World War II, consumers anticipated the return of goods not available during the war because of wartime rationing and scarcities. However, an unprecedented wave of strikes occurred in 1946, and the public soon became hostile toward labor unions. Congress was determined to pass legislation that would protect employers and employees against unfair labor practices by union, and also protect the public against work stoppages that threatened the health or safety of the nation. To balance the power between union and management, Congress amended the Wagner Act under the Taft-Hartley Act.

After the passage of the Taft-Hartley Act, the AFL and CIO both realized that management had become equal in strength to labor. The time had come for unity instead of division. In 1954, a no-raid agreement was ratified by both AFL and CIO at their annual conventions. On December 12, 1955, the AFL and CIO agreed to merge into one united labor organization. This new merger was to be named the American Federation of Labor and the Congress of Industrial Organization with George Meany as president. The new constitution provided that all AFL and CIO unions would become affiliates of the merged organization, but their autonomies and integrity would be preserved.

From 1960 to the present, the AFL-CIO has continued to experience a decline in growth and membership. In 1960, union membership represented 23.6 percent of the total labor force as compared to today's 13.5 percent. This raises the question of why there has been such a decline in growth and membership. Part of this answer may be attributed to the widespread loss of manufacturing jobs inside the United States particularly when American multinational companies transfer their manufacturing abroad and use foreign workers. Unions adamantly opposed the passage of the North American Free-Trade Agreement (NAFTA) involving the United States, Canada, and Mexico. They feared that many jobs would be lost; however, the effect of NAFTA on the number of jobs lost is still relatively unknown.

Another factor for the decline in growth and membership is that unionized companies in Northeast and North Central states have closed and then transfer their operations to the right-to-work states in the South and Southwest regions of the United States. Still another potential factor was the firing of air traffic controllers and decertification of the Professional Air Traffic Controller Organization (PATCO) during the Reagan administration. This action taken by the federal government was viewed as an indication of the decline of power and prestige for labor unions. A final possible reason for the decline in union membership was that the service industry continued to grow; but workers employed in the service-producing jobs remained relatively non-union.

Unions continue to impact the policies and practices of non-union companies. This impact is known as the "spillover effect." To attract and retain qualified employees, non-union employers must offer competitive wages, benefits, and working conditions. Additionally, some non-union employers purposely offer higher wages and benefits to encourage their employees to remain union-free.

The primary area that has been influenced by unions is *wage levels*. Wages are mandatory bargaining subjects for which an employer and union must bargain in good faith. Within the context of a negotiated labor agreement, the wages of the various jobs are listed. Also, other contractual provisions will specify promotional levels of pay, overtime pay, shift premium pay, call-out pay, and even time-step increases.

Unions in Other Countries

The emergence of a global economy makes it important that supervisors are familiar with the labor relations systems that exist throughout the world. In recent years, there is no question that our economy has become more international as exports and imports continue to make up a larger segment of our gross national product. This expansion of international markets and trade can be attributed to the passage of the North American Free Trade Agreement (NAFTA) and the formation of the European Union (EU). This section examines the major features of the labor systems of those trading countries with the United States.

In January 1994, NAFTA came into effect and virtually removed all tariffs on the trade of goods amongst Canada, Mexico, and the United States. In essence, NAFTA liberalized trade between these countries and created the world's largest free trade area. The AFL-CIO opposed NAFTA because of their fear that many jobs would be eliminated as the result of US companies transferring their operation to Mexico and its low wage system. An excellent example is General Electric who has moved some of its operations to Mexico in order to reduce its labor costs and increased corporate profits.

Mexico is a highly unionized country compared to the United States and most unions are connected with the Institutional Revolutionary Party (PRI). Similar to the Wagner Act, the Mexican constitution and Federal Labor Law, guarantees workers the right to form and join trade unions. The majority of unions are in labor centrals and the Confederation of Mexican Workers (CTM) is recognized as the largest central. Unlike the AFL-CIO, the CTM fully supported NAFTA because of the belief that higher paying jobs would be created. However, real wages have remained relatively low since the Mexican peso was devalued in December 1994. It is interesting to note that union leaders have the authority to prevent the hiring of a new employee and to force the termination of an employee. In the United States, the supervisor is given the authority to recommend the hiring and discharge of an employee.

With two distinct cultural groups, English and French, Canada is also a highly unionized country compared to the United States. Favorable labor laws, within the various Canadian provinces, have yielded an increase in union membership since the 1960s unlike the decline in membership experienced by U.S. labor unions. Canada's labor relations system has been influenced by various U.S. labor unions and companies. For example, the Canadian autoworkers, one of the largest unions in Canada, was formerly affiliated with the U.S. autoworkers. However, there are distinct differences in the two labor relations systems especially in the collective bargaining arena. There are no mandatory or voluntary subjects in Canada. Unlike the right-to-work laws that exist in the United States, Canada has no such laws. Many Canadian labor federations, such as the Canadian Labour Council (CLC) and the Canadian Federation of Labor (CFL) opposed the passage of NAFTA. Like their U.S. counterparts, the Canadian unions feared that many jobs would be lost to Mexico with its low-paying jobs.

The European Union (EU), with its 15 member countries, was created to form a single market in Europe allowing capital, goods, and people to move freely amongst the member countries. In May 1989, the EU adopted the *Social Charter*, a declaration of a variety of fundamental rights including the right of workers to form and join unions. The Social Charter is merely a declaration of principles with legal enforcement determined by each EU country. In January 2002, the EURO was implemented to replace the currency of the member countries and formed a single European economy. Therefore, a single currency will promote a highly competitive and integrated European market.

Germany is one of the major countries belonging to the EU. Basically, there are 16 major unions in Germany, and I.G. Metall (engineering union) is recognized as the largest union. Germany's industrial relations system is unique compared to the United States. By German law, the key element of industrial relations is worker participation or codetermination (mitbestimmung). One major component of German codetermination is the work councils. These work councils are comprised of an equal number of members appointed by management and elected by employees and are involved in the day to day issues such as disciplinary actions, pay systems, holiday schedules, and safety regulations. Any operational changes, such as a lay off, must be negotiated between the work council and employer. Unlike the United States, collective bargaining is highly centralized with a majority of labor agreements finalized at the industry or regional level.

Once a labor agreement is reach with an employer association and union, this labor contract is then extended to other companies within that particular industry. Germany also possesses a formalized vocational education and apprenticeship training system. These apprenticeship programs are coordinated by a joint business-labor committee, which establishes vocational education standards and qualifications for each occupational field or trade. Keep in mind that the German work councils are involved in such issues as disciplines, work schedules, and employee work performance. In the United States, these day to day issues are typically the major responsibilities of a supervisor.

Another country belonging to the EU is the United Kingdom. The early trade unions in Great Britain were organizing approximately the same period of time that the Knights of Labor emerged in the United States. Of the EU members, Great Britain's industrial relations system is the only one that fairly resembles that of the United States. For example, Great Britain is the only EU country that has a mechanism for workers to vote on representation. The Central Arbitration Committee (CAC), similar to the National Relations Board, has the authority to conduct a union election.

Although Japan is not a member of the EU, it is also a leading trade country with the United States. Japanese unions emerged in the 1890s about the same time that the AFL was organizing and growing into national prominence in the United States. Japan has a unique and distinct industrial relations system. One such distinct characteristic is that Japan's enterprise unions can represent both white and blue-collar employees, with a foreman actively involved in union business. Another characteristic is the lifetime employment principle. In large Japanese companies, a new employee is hired after high school graduation and remains employed until retirement. There is no contractual provision to guarantee lifetime employment but rather a promise by the organization of no layoffs. Pay determination is also unique in that one's salary is based upon seniority.

Still another distinct feature in Japan's industrial relations is the role of labor-management consultation. To resolve labor disputes, informal consultation between labor and management is used unlike the formal grievance-arbitration procedures that are typically used in the United States labor relations systems. In Japan, supervisors are expected to conduct performance appraisals to determine pay and promotions. In the United States, on the other hand, a supervisor, in a unionized workplace, would rarely conduct employee appraisals. Instead, promotions are determined by seniority following the contractual provisions of the collective bargaining agreement.

Supervisors in nonunion settings however, usually conduct some form of performance appraisal. Since few companies have wage ranges, that is, jobs in the same classification paid at different rates within a range based on merit considerations, these performance appraisals are focused on promotion and performance counseling.

Case Study: A Union Environment

Background
A production employee with over 27 years of service was terminated for stealing organization products. During her unionized employment Joyce had a respectable work record with only a few minor disciplinary problems in the past, and those were years ago. Essentially, she was an employee in good standing with a good work record.

Situation
On Friday, after clocking out, Joyce was about to get into her car when one of the organization's security guards stopped her for some routine questions. The guard asked to search her to open her purse. Initially she refused, stating that her purse was private property and the organization had no right to invade her privacy. When she was reminded of a long-standing organization policy that allowed for random searches of employee's lockers, lunch buckets, purses and automobiles, while on organization property, Joyce allowed the search of her purse.

Upon opening the bag, the guard discovered organization products valued at approximately $180. During a subsequent meeting with her supervisor, Joyce did not deny her intent to steal the items, but pleaded that she had learned her lesson and was sorry for her actions. At that point, her supervisor suspended her until the case could be reviewed by the Plant Manager. After reviewing all the facts and talking to both Joyce and her supervisor, the Plant Manager discharged Joyce for stealing organization property, which was covered by language in the union contract which read in part:

"Any of the following shall be considered just grounds for immediate discharge without notice...
b) Dishonesty to the Organization.

Case Study

The Union filed a grievance and took the position that discharge for an employee, in good standing with 27 years of faithful service, was too severe a penalty under just cause standards.

The organization's position was that it has always terminated employees for stealing organization property regardless of mitigating circumstances. The organization felt there was no basis for an exception in this case.

Since the organization and the Union failed to reach an agreement on this case, the case was sent to an arbitrator, as called for within the collective bargaining agreement.

So, based upon the facts, did the arbitrator uphold the termination? If so, then on what basis do you think this decision was made?

Or, do you think that the arbitrator agreed with the union and returned the employee to work?

At this point, it may be helpful to jump to Chapter 10, Measuring Performance toward the end of the chapter and read the section on "just cause" before rendering your decision.

Conclusion

This chapter makes an important point that can be best understood when you have covered the full range of what a supervisor does. Good supervision is good supervision. Effective employee/management relations have more to do with effective supervisor/employee relations than any other factor even whether there is or is not a union. Also a good relationship between a supervisor and his/her employees is critical to the success of management in the areas of safety, productivity, morale, earnings, profitability and competitiveness. The relationship between the supervisor and the employee are the foundation of all of these issues.

It is very clear that the supervisor/employee relationship itself must be built on the foundation of some very fundamental concepts of the due process and democratic workplace. These foundation concepts include: integrity, fairness, mutual respect and open communication. We have laws that espouse and attempt to enforce these concepts. What we need are more supervisors, managers, employees and unions who will apply them. That is something to really look forward to.

References

Cohen S. *Labor in the United States*, 5th ed. Ohio: Charles E. Merrill Book, 1979, p 71.

Pelling H. *American Labor*. Chicago: The University of Chicago Press, 1960, p 152.

Fossum, *Labor Relations*, 42.

Kenney and Kahn ed., *Prime of Labor Relations*, 2.

Sleemi F. Collective bargaining outlook for 1995. *Compensation and Working*

Conditions, 47(1):19-39, January 1995.

U.S. Department of Labor, *Union Member Summary, News Release,* January 18, 2001, at http://stats.bls.gov/newsrels.htm.

Review Questions

1. Why should supervisors understand the historical development of American labor unions?

2. What are the major contributing causes for the decline in union membership?

3. What are some of the key differences in the supervisor's role in the United States compared to those of supervisors in Mexico, Germany and Japan?.

4. Why would employees prefer to work current employees overtime rather than hire new employees?

5. Why are employers forbidden from firing union organizers?

6. What constitutes the law of the workplace?

7. Why are closed shops illegal except in craft unions?

8. What can a supervisor do to insure success at that level of management?

9. How important is it for the supervisor and the union steward to get along?

10 Measuring Performance

by Michael O'Toole, PhD
Meredith Onion
Christopher Janicak, PhD

What Will I Learn in This Chapter?

This chapter explains:

- the purposes of an employee performance appraisal process.
- some of the reasons they fail.
- some characteristics of an effective system.

Overview

The performance appraisal system is made up of tools to assist supervisors effectively evaluate employee job performance. The appraisal process should lead to improved communication between supervisors and employees. These processes also provide an objective basis for recognizing employees' performance, from the less than acceptable, to superior and the range between. This is a unique opportunity for supervisors to accomplish one of their critical functions; the development of subordinates.

All managers are supposed to monitor the way employees work and assess how this meets departmental and organizational needs. These managers form impressions about the positive value of employees to their unit and seek ways to maximize that value through the employee's contribution.

The success of any performance appraisal process depends on the connection to business goals, to those of the individuals, and of the attitudes and skills of those responsible for its administration. The key to any performance appraisal process however, is how well expectations established within the process are communicated to employees so it will result in optimal performance.

Performance appraisal process can be used to assess various factors related to an employee's job and in turn be tied to a variety of systems. An employee's performance appraisal could be used for any or all of the following examples:

- salary administration
- performance feedback–of an individual or group
- training needs analysis
- consideration for analysis
- recognition of exceptional individual or group performance

- documentation for personnel decisions
- and many others.

Performance appraisal processes can also yield disappointing or even adverse results for a variety of reasons. Some of the more common reasons are:
- The manager failed to obtain adequate information about an employee's performance.
- or standards of performance are unclear to affected employees.
- Expectations or standards of performance are beyond the control of the employee to impact or control.
- No plan is established for the employee to implement for improving identified performance deficiencies.

The list can go on and on. There are probably some examples from your experiences, either giving or receiving performance appraisals that could be added to our list.

Many factors can address the key objectives as well as the reasons for the potential failures with performance appraisals. The first and most important step is to establish an effective performance measurement tool.

The employee(s) need to know what is expected of them. How much, how often, how long, with what degree of accuracy and within what budget limitations are they going to be held accountable. When these performance standards are established, they help to connect organizational and/or departmental goals into job requirements that communicate acceptable and unacceptable levels of performance to employees.

Most Human Resource (HR) professionals agree that there are four basic considerations when establishing performance standards: (1) strategic relevance, (2) criterion contamination, (3) criterion deficiency and (4) reliability.

Strategic Relevance

Strategic relevance refers to the degree to which a given standard of performance relates to the strategic objectives of the department and/or organization. For example, if a cost-cutting program has been established to position the organization as the industry's low-cost producer, then it is relevant to the manufacturing manager to use such a standard to evaluate performance. This standard is then relevant for both the manufacturing and purchasing departments to use such cost-cutting standards for evaluating the performance of managers and supervisors.

Criterion Deficiency

If a performance standard singles out or weighs too heavily to the detriment of other important, but perhaps less quantifiable dimensions criterion deficiency exists. If significantly more emphasis or weight is given to, say productivity, such that quality and customer service standards suffer, then our system would be suffering from criterion deficiency.

Criterion Contamination

Just as performance criteria can be deficient, they can also be contaminated. There are factors outside an employee's control that can influence his or her performance. A comparison of performance of production workers, for example, should not be contaminated by the fact that some have newer machines that other workers do. A comparison of the performance of traveling salespeople should not be contaminated by the fact that territories differ in sales potential.

Reliability

Reliability relates to the ability to sustain or demonstrate consistency of results over time. When we rate an individual's performance over time or at the same time by two independent raters, we can measure reliability. Reliability can be established by correlating the two sets of ratings.

One key to establishing reliability is to make sure you clearly define what it is you are going to or want to measure. For example an instructor once walked into the classroom and told his students that he wanted them to describe what followed. The instructor then proceeded to walk up and down the center aisle in the classroom, periodically scratched his head and "scrunched" his face. When asked to describe what went on, most students reported that the professor was in deep thought over some complex issue, while several others stated that he was troubled over something. The professor told them that they were all wrong. He stated what they should have reported was that the instructor walked up and down the aisle, scratching his head with a scrunched face. The exercise demonstrated that the students needed to restrict their observations to what they actually saw and not what they thought they saw! If we are trying to have a reliable measurement, it needs to be one that when examined by a number of individuals, there is little disagreement among them as to what they are measuring.

Legal Issues

Although not meant to be complete, the following points should be kept in mind when conducting a performance appraisal. Failures to consider the legal implications of performance appraisals and act accordingly will likely result in your employer facing all sorts of legal challenges from HR decisions. Many of these factors are discussed in Chapter 3, Supervisors, Employment and Workplace Law.

Note that:
- Performance evaluations must be job-related, with performance standards developed through and tied to job analysis.
- It is best to have a written copy of job standards to give to an employee

in advance of an appraisal.
- The standards to which an employee is to be evaluated must be objective and measurable. For example, we all know and can identify employees with a "bad attitude." However, the measure of attitudes is clearly subjective and should be avoided. Factors or issues related to productivity, safety, customer service, quality, etc. are more objective (measurable) factors.
- Those responsible for conducting performance appraisals need to be trained on how to conduct an appraisal and to use the appraisal form.
- The performance appraisal should not only cover those areas of poor performance, but also need to include specific corrective guidance to help ensure improvement.
- At the time of the appraisal, there needs to be an opportunity provided to the employee to disagree with the appraisal. This may include the opportunity to discuss their disagreements with the next higher level of management and/or with someone from the HR group.

Employers need to ensure that managers and supervisors responsible for conducting performance appraisals keep documented records of the appraisal. This way, in the event an individual employee or agency takes some sort of action, the individuals involved will have a good accounting of the facts. Otherwise we have to rely on our memories. With all that supervisors and managers handle each day on the job, it would be a stretch to remember what happened several months earlier.

Giving the Appraisal

Just as there are any number of job standards by which we can evaluate performance, there are several ways to give appraisals. Deciding which technique or approach to use can determine who should conduct the appraisal.

We can clearly have the traditional boss-subordinate appraisal as well as, peer evaluations, 360-degree-reversal appraisals, self-appraisal, team appraisal and even customer evaluations. To make matters even more complex we can design appraisal systems that use combinations of the above systems.

The boss-subordinate approach is perhaps the most traditional used to evaluate an employee's performance. Most of the time, the boss is in the best position to know what the employee is supposed to do, and what they actually did. In many cases it is not possible for the boss to directly know about all aspects of their employee's performance. In the case of a sales force not centrally located in the country, the supervisor or boss may not get enough opportunities to observe employees' behavior on the job to evaluate the job performance fairly.

When conducting *peer evaluations*, employees of equal or similar rank and who work together can be in a position to evaluate each other's performance. Because these individuals see each other from a different perspective, they are also able to provide a different insight into an employee's job performance than that of the boss. Some of the downsides or barriers to an effective peer evaluation system include:
- Evaluations are indications of popularity.
- Supervisors/managers are unwilling to give up process.
- Those receiving poor evaluations might retaliate against their peers.
- Those conducting evaluations rely on stereotypes or are influenced by personal bias.

Another form of peer appraisal is that of *team appraisal*. In those workplaces that have some form of team organization it may be very difficult to isolate any one employee's contributions. In these cases, the entire team's performance is appraised as a whole. To conduct individual appraisals may actually be counterproductive to the team according some in the field.

In some situations the team's appraisal is driven by some specific commitment of the organization, such as quality, production improvements or safety. In many of these situations an assessment is carried out at the system level whereas performance appraisals have traditionally been focused at the individual employee performance level.

Typically motivated by quality initiatives, an increasing number of organizations are using internal and external *customers* as a source of performance appraisal information. A long-standing example of an external customers' feedback used to evaluate staff has been that of the restaurant business. Companies such as Federal Express, UPS and Gateway Computers have begun utilizing external customers for evaluating performance of those employees in contact with customers.

Just think of the last time you had contact with some organization's customer service department by telephone. More often than not, you were notified that your conversation might be recorded for "training and coaching" purposes. The organization will sample enough customer contacts to identify either customer service representatives that need coaching or additional training with a specific issue.

In turn, internal customers include anyone inside the organization who depends on an employee's work product. As an example, a manager who relies on HR for selection and training services could be a candidate for participating in internal customer evaluations for HR.

A technique that has been used with varying amounts of success is that of the *360-degree appraisal.* As the name implies, 360-degree feedback is intended to provide employees with as clear a view of their performance by obtaining input from all directions or angles: supervisors, peers, subordinates, customers and anyone else the employee works with can contribute to the evaluation. There are several advantages to such a process, such as it is as comprehensive a view of the employee's performance as we can get. It therefore tends to reduce some of the biases mentioned a bit later due to the wide range of sources for providing feedback to the employee.

There are many disadvantages to such a system, not the least of which is the complexity of the system and the time necessary to collect the information. There could also be a feeling by the employee of being ganged-up on by the respondents. There is a good chance that the process could take on a "political" tone where groups of employees collude on ratings and give invalid evaluations.

Rater Error and Bias

Any rating system can contain certain types of error that need to be addressed in order to have a valid system. Two types of error most of us have heard of at one time or another are that of the halo effect and horn effect. The *halo effect* refers to favorable ratings based on a good first impression or some positive event. The *horn effect* is essentially the opposite of the halo effect in that an employee receives unfavorable ratings due to a poor first impression or one event, neither of which are representative of the employee's actual performance.

Another type of rating error is that of the error of central tendency. In an *error of central tendency*, a rater or group of raters refrains from assigning either high or low ratings, despite actual employee performance. What typically results with this type of error is that a group of employees in a department are all rated above average. In a large enough sample of employees, we should expect some degree of variation in employee performance. We should expect to see some employees rated excellent and some with poor performance ratings.

In contrast to the error of central tendency, there are two additional types of distribution error, which are referred to as either leniency, or strictness error. These errors are essentially mirror images of the same error. In the case of *leniency error*, a supervisor feels that his or her employees can do no wrong and will rate all employees "excellent." At the other extreme is the supervisor who feels that their employees are "not worthy" and rates them all unacceptable or below average.

One approach to reduce this type of error is to clearly define the characteristics and dimensions of performance and provide behavioral anchors on the rating scale. These behavioral anchors provide meaningful descriptions of behavior to guide the rater.

Another approach often used to negate these errors is to require a forced distribution. One form of a forced distribution is to require managers or supervisors place a predefined percentage or number of employees into the various performance categories. As an example, a manager may have 10 employees to rate and must put 10 percent or one employee in the excellent category.

Performance Appraisal Methods

Performance appraisal systems or methods have evolved significantly, with old systems being replaced with newer more sophisticated methods. Many of these methods have been changed to reflect technical improvements or legal considerations and are now more consistent with the overall objectives of appraisals. Performance appraisal methods can be generally grouped into those that measure traits, those that measure behaviors and those that measure results. Those that address traits continue to be popular despite their inherent subjectivity. The behavioral approaches provide more task-specific information to both the supervisor and employee and have been modified somewhat to be applied to the safety area in the past 10 years.

The results-based approach focuses on the measurable contributions that an employee makes to the organization.

Trait Methods

This form of appraisal is designed to measure the extent to which an employee possesses certain characteristics, such as dependability, creativity, initiative, or leadership. These are "measured" because they are considered important to the job and organization in general. We can see that most organizations desire employees who are dependable, take initiative, and are leaders within their work group. These methods are popular because for one, they are relatively easy to develop. But, due to the underlying approach of this type of performance appraisal, a significant amount of bias and subjectivity is often introduced into the system.

Some examples of trait methods used as an appraisal method includes the graphic rating-scale method, the mixed standard method, and the forced-choice method. What follows is a brief description of each of these methods.

Within the *graphic rating-scale method* each trait or characteristic to be rated is placed on a scale on which an evaluation a rater(s) indicates the degree to which the employee is identified with that trait or characteristic.

For example, it may be desirable to determine how dependable employees are as it relates to their jobs. It would be helpful to provide the rater a brief definition of dependability in order to reduce some of the bias and subjectivity in this method. In our example (see Figure 10-1), we define dependability as showing up to work, each day scheduled, on time. Within the rating scale, we further assist the rater by providing a number of options that indicate to what degree an employee is considered dependable. At one end of the scale, we might indicate that the employee meets all attendance requirements. As we move down the scale, there should be options that indicate the relative degree to which the employee is considered less than dependable,

Figure 10-1. Dependability:
Shows up to work every day scheduled at the appointed time.

Frequently absent and tardy	Absent at least once each month	Infrequently absent — tardy once each month	Infrequently absent and infrequently tardy	Meets requirements of attendance policy

Comments: This employee volunteers for overtime and has worked scheduled days off as needed.

with the inclusion of a comment box for some supporting detail.

A *mixed-standard scale* is a method that uses the same basic format as the rating-scale method with a few deviations. In this case, the rater is given three specific descriptions of each trait, instead of the single scale. These descriptions reflect the level of performance, for example, superior, average and poor. The rater, after reading the description, indicated whether the employee's performance is better than, equal to or worse than the standard.

For example, an "average" description for an employee's degree of cooperation might read as follows: *The employee is generally agreeable, but may become argumentative at times when given less desirable job assignments.* Works well with fellow employees. The rater(s) would indicate to what degree or extent the employee fits this description: better than, equal to, or worse than the standard.

The *forced-choice* method requires a rater to choose from statements, sometimes presented in pairs that appear equally favorable or unfavorable. These statements are designed to distinguish between successful and less than successful performance. With this particular method, the question of validity arises and when conducted properly is more costly than the previous methods.

Behavioral Methods

One technique to improve rating scale methods is to have descriptions of behavior along the scale. These descriptions allow the rater to better identify the point where the employee falls along the scale. Most behavioral methods have been developed to describe which behavior should (or in some cases should not) be observed in the job. This approach offers the opportunity for meaningful feedback and dialogue between the supervisor and employee for development and improvement by the employee.

There are several methods that can be used such as the *critical incident method, the behavior checklist method, the behaviorally anchored rating scale (BARS), and behavior observation scales (BOS).* Details about most of these methods can be found in any good textbook on human resources management. The key to all of these approaches is that descriptions if desirable behaviors are developed, often with significant input from employees. Since performance expectations are developed with this employee involvement, there is much greater acceptance of the performance appraisal.

In manufacturing and industrial settings, a *job safety analysis (JSA)* or *job hazard analysis (JHA)* is conducted to help build these descriptions of behavior at it relates to safety of a given job or task. This process requires that the sequence of critical or essential steps of a given job or task be identified with the assistance of those employees who perform the job.

Once these steps have been identified, the supervisor and affected employee(s) discuss the potential hazards that exist with each step of the job. Next, the discussion focuses on what actions or changes to the task will help eliminate or minimize the identified hazards. These actions may include the use of personal protective equipment or some other specific safety procedure such as a lock out prior to engaging in the task. After the JSA has been completed, it can then be used to conduct job observations of employees work on the job in order to provide feedback on their job performance as it relates to that specific job.

Results Methods

This method intuitively makes a lot of sense. The organization measures or evaluates what an employee accomplishes through their work. This approach appears to many to be more objective and enables the employee to have some control over the outcome(s). Typical results measures include sales figures, production output, customer complaints resolved, cost reduction and workplace injuries.

Like any measurement system, there are many approaches that can be used. In many organizations, the results are cast in stone and there is little discretion with exactly what is being measured. In others, the detail of what is measured is determined, within boundaries, by the employee and the supervisor. For example, we can measure the number of widgets produced within certain quality and cost specifications, which might include the percentage of good widgets shipped and percentage of scrap produced making the widgets. These boundaries will often be tied to goals or objectives established by the organization and the reward or compensation system is based on the achievement of specified goals.

One common method many organizations use to help set performance objectives for the employee is to use *management by objectives*, or some variation of this system. Management by objectives is an approach to performance evaluations first proposed by Peter Drucker in 1954. Using this approach, employees establish specific performance objectives consulting with the supervisor. These goals should support the organizational goals and objectives of the business. These objectives then become the basis for the employee's performance appraisal.

This approach, when established properly, begins when top management sets overall organizational goals and objectives. Each level of management in each functional area of the organization then can establish goals and objectives that support the overall goals and objectives set by upper management. These secondary goals and objectives will also support those of the subgroup, such as that of a division or manufacturing facility or functional area, such as HR or marketing. This process is completed at each level of the organization down to the first-line supervisor and in some organizations includes the production and maintenance workers. There are two key elements to the success of management by objectives:

1. Establish objectives that are both quantifiable and measurable.
2. Establish objectives that are in the employee's the control.

For example, consider the case of an employee in the purchasing department who is responsible for securing a wide range of products and services for their organization. One of the overall objectives of the organization is to reduce energy costs by 10 percent over last year's costs. Due to an unexpected reduction in output by oil producers in early spring (after the budget and objectives have been set), energy costs actually increased by 15 percent for the current year. This objective, although measurable, is clearly outside the control of our purchasing employee. In this case, this objective is not a good one to measure the performance of this employee's contribution to the organization and be used as part of the performance appraisal process. The same should hold if the energy costs went down by 15 percent due to an oversupply condition over which the purchasing employee still had no control.

Conducting the Appraisal Interview

There appears to be no set rules on exactly how to conduct a performance appraisal interview, there are guidelines that should increase the employee's acceptance of the results and a willingness to make changes to performance to improve in the future. The following are common guidelines that apply to not only performance appraisal interviews, but could also be applied to general interviewing.

Self-Assessment

Sometimes referred to as a 180-degree interview, it is sometimes helpful to ask the employee to prepare an appraisal of his or her own performance in advance of the formal interview. If for no other reason, this process gets the employee to reflect on their performance, including accomplishments, and shortcomings. In some cases an employee may actually be tougher on themselves than the supervisor. This clearly gives the supervisor an opportunity to "pump up" the employee and still offer suggestions on how to improve future performance. Researchers have found that employees tend to be more satisfied with the performance appraisal process when they have had input into resolving performance issues.

Participation

Whether self assessment is used or not, one of the keys to successful appraisal interviews is to initiate dialogue between the employee and supervisor that will help an employee improve his or her performance. The more the employee is part of that discussion, the more likely performance issues will be resolved and positive ideas for improvement will be generated.

Appreciation

Recognition is a powerful motivator. As an employee we all know how long it takes for the boss to find us when we make a mistake. Providing corrective feedback is necessary, helpful and part of the supervisor's role. But we need to ask ourselves, when was the last time the boss recognized the normal and expected performance of their employees. That answer may unfortunately be never. Experts tell us that it is important to let an employee know those areas in which they are doing well. This does not mean to heap praise upon an employee for expected performance, but rather on occasion just noting that the employee does a "good job." This action is one of the most powerful motivational tools available to a supervisor. Recognition does two things for you as a supervisor:

1. It allows you to reinforce your expectations for that employee's performance.
2. It signals to the employee that you actually notice when they do something correctly.

Remember, what gets measured, gets done!

Criticism

As noted, it is a necessary part of a supervisor's job to offer criticism of an employee's performance. Keep in mind that criticism; no matter how well delivered will generate some level of defensiveness. The key is to deliver the least amount of criticism to get the message across. There is a need to reflect on the message and decide (1) is it really necessary? (2) Keep the message in proper perspective; don't exaggerate. (3) Keep improvement the goal. It is very difficult to change a person or their attitude. Changing the employee's behavior is something within the control of employee and the goal of the supervisor.

Discipline

What do you do however, when an employee fails to meet performance standards? Those performance standards could be related to productivity, quality, service, safety, attendance or some other work-related factor.

One consideration is to initiate the disciplinary process. Supervisors need to use this tool with sensitivity and good judgment. The focus of a disciplinary action should not be to punish or seek personal revenge, but rather to improve the employee's future behavior. Disciplinary action is one method to initiate corrective action on the part of the employee to reduce similar performance in the future.

It is commonly accepted that disciplinary action taken against an employee should be based on the principles of "just cause." Just or proper cause means that the action taken against an employee meets specific tests of fairness and elements of normal due process. For example, employees should be given proper notification of their performance deficiency before adverse action is imposed.

Many union contracts specify a just-cause standard for discipline and discharge. Likewise, government agencies have been known to require employers to prove that their disciplinary actions taken against legally protected employees, as outlined in Chapter 3, were not discriminatory, but were for just cause.

Seven tests for just cause are as follows:
1. Did the organization give the employee forewarning of the possible or probable disciplinary consequences of the employee's conduct?
2. Was the organization's rule or managerial order reasonable and related to the safe operation of the organization's business?
3. Did the organization, before administering discipline to the employee, make an effort to discover whether the employee did in fact violate or disobey a rule or order of management?
4. Was the organization's investigation conducted fairly and objectively?
5. As a result of the investigation, was there substantial evidence or proof that the employee was guilty as charged?
6. Has the organization applied its rules, orders, and penalties even-handedly and without discrimination to all employees?

7. Was the degree of discipline administered by the organization related to (1) the seriousness of the employee's offense and (2) the record of the employee's service with the organization?

Using a just-cause standard for disciplinary action can be complicated. However, the supervisor who follows these guidelines in a conscientious way will likely create a defensible position for his/her actions, irrespective of whether it involves a unionized firm, non-unionized firm, or an area of potential legal discrimination.

Privacy in Discipline

If a supervisor decides to take a course of action that includes discipline, she or he should communicate the discipline to the affected employee in private. A public reprimand will likely humiliate the employee, embarrass you and lead to a loss of morale in the department.

Progressive Discipline

Progressive discipline provides for an increase in the severity of consequences with each offense. Although the type and severity of disciplinary action appropriate to a situation may vary somewhat, many organizations utilize some form of progressive discipline. A typical sequence of progressive discipline might follow the following: An oral warning (verbal counseling), written warning, suspension, and discharge. Keeping in mind our attempt to meet just cause, it is imperative that as part of our progressive discipline key steps include:

- At each step, the employee must be explained what they need to do to avoid further disciplinary action.
- Before discharge, it is clear to the employee that their job is in jeopardy.

- All steps of the disciplinary process are documented.

Measuring Safety Activity Performance

One area that many organization managers struggle to measure and provide good feedback on is the area of safety performance. Traditional measures of injury frequency and/or injury rates are reactive and trailing indicators that are of questionable valuable in correcting behavior. There is considerable discussion and debate on the value of these performance measures to supervisors.

The following section will give supervisors an opportunity to develop safety performance measures that are meaningful and likely to positively affect safety results. Two examples are measures of safety activity performance such as *frequency of observation* and *percent safe observations*. In many informal studies, frequency of observations per 100 employees has been shown to be a consistent predictor of accident frequency rates (Krause et al, 1990). An inverse relation holds here-when the frequency of observations are up, accidents go down, and vice versa. As the frequency of observations increases, the feedback about the job performance is more frequent and as a result, preventive steps are taken on a more frequent basis (Krause et al, 1990). Another old management axiom may hold here also: What gets measured gets done!

The percent-safe figures produced by observation are also good indicators; however. Management must be very careful not to put pressure on this indicator. This indicator is soft by nature, and employees must not be overly motivated to look good on this measure. Various involvement indicators can be quantified, such measures as frequency of attendance at safety meetings, number of employees trained to be Observers, and activity levels of safety committee meetings on specific projects (Krause et al, 1990).

Continuous Improvement Safety Process

The purpose of performance measurement is to continually improve. Zero accidents are the only worthwhile goal of a safety process, even though some may argue that it is not achievable (Daugherty, 1999). The steps of the continuous improvement safety process are the same as in the continuous quality improvement process: specify standards, measure compliance, and provide feedback on improvement. For safety, developing an inventory of critical safety-related behaviors and defining them in operational terms accomplish the first step of specifying standards.

To measure compliance, trained observers use the inventory of behaviors to rate the facility, producing a read-out in terms of the ratio of the safe-to-unsafe critical behaviors (Krause et al, 1990). Providing feedback on improvement then amounts to giving the workforce charts and reports of their progress on the inventory of behaviors.

In this way, the safety effort becomes a mechanism for continuous improvement, guiding itself by the incidence of unsafe behaviors rather than by injuries and regularly updating and focusing its inventory of critical behaviors to match developing safety issues. In addition, the analysis of persistent unsafe behaviors highlights management system issues, and problem solving addressed to such issues drives the organization culture toward stronger safety performance.

Safety performance can be measured and monitored the same as other indicators of productivity. This chapter presented the concepts of performance measurement program planning and implementation for the workplace. An effective safety program begins with the proper planning of a management structure. This management program includes the identification of the indicators of a successful safety program. Early on, the safety profession routinely measured safety performance in terms of accidents and losses. But today as safety is an important part of our everyday lives and jobs, the techniques used measure it have changed.

Evaluating the identification of safety gaps or deficiencies in the obtained data versus the desired outcomes is established in the program goals or benchmarks. Identification of these deficiencies can be achieved through the use of control charts and various statistical techniques. Depending upon the data collected, the appropriate charts can be constructed and trends identified.

Finally, the focus is on the elimination of unsafe acts and behaviors. Today, accidents, losses and monitoring safe behaviors are sources for data and a safety metrics program. Organizations are using a proactive approach of monitoring unsafe behaviors, instead of waiting for accidents and losses to occur, and then addressing them.

Goal-Setting

Since we are trying to support performance areas that are good or acceptable and improve those areas determined to be poor or deficient, setting up plans for supporting those efforts can be done through goal-setting with the employee. The following are several key points to ponder when establishing performance improvement goals:

1. Focus on the employee's strengths and have them build on that foundation.
2. Identify opportunities for growth within the employee's current job.
3. Key in on a couple of essential improvement areas rather than a complete rework of the employee.
4. Establish a plan of action for the employee and identify target dates and the role you as the supervisor will play as a supporting member of their team.

Conclusion

Remember, the purpose of this performance appraisal process is to document an employee's performance, both the strengths and weaknesses. Unless these issues are put before the employee to discuss, any problem areas are likely to continue and you, the supervisor, will be part of that problem. Improving employee performance is a team effort with active participation and support by both the employees and their supervisor.

Review Questions

1. Can you think of times when you conducted a performance appraisal/review that turned out less than desirable? If so, what were some of the short comings?

2. According to numerous Human Resource experts there are several important factors related to successful performance appraisals. Are they all equally important?

3. Most employees are most familiar with the traditional supervisor-subordinate approach to performance appraisals. Can you identify one small change to this approach that will often improve the process by identifying targeted improvements?

4. Other than with pith the performance appraisal process when else might a manager or supervisor fall victim to the "Halo Effect?"

5. What performance appraisal approach relies on specific descriptions of behavior along a scale?

6. What approach to discipline and discharge can a supervisor/manager rely on to guide their decisions in this important area?

11
Developing Employee Skills and Careers

by Michael F. O'Toole, PhD
Meredith Onion

What Will I Learn in This Chapter?

In this chapter we will address additional areas that will help you, the supervisor, develop your employees to their fullest potential within their current position and the organization. You will learn about:

- training—how to put into place on-the-job training and other learning experiences.
- leadership development—More than the supervisor leads the work group.
- academic education—the fact that learning never stops.
- coaching—how to assist and encourage individual employee development.

These focus points are critical for employee development because they represent areas where most employees need help. Your job, as always, is to assist your employees. Well done, it is the extra boost that can help an employee become a top performer and go far in work-related personal development.

Training

Few people can step into a new job, apply skills that they have never used before and perform the tasks of the job successfully the first time. Giving or receiving training is an ongoing part of most any job. As a supervisor, you should make sure that your employees are properly trained for the work assignments they are expected to perform. This may be you or someone from the department conducting training classes for your employees. Proper training helps to develop your employees by improving existing skills or giving them new skills to help them advance in their careers. One of the most powerful tools that a supervisor has to help in employee training and development is the supervisor's own good example. There are several approaches to training; on-the-job (OJT) training probably is the most common.

On-the-Job Training (OJT)

There are four key steps involved in effective on-the-job training, much like those in effective safety indoctrination.

1. **Prepare the employee for training.**
   - Explain the reasons for the training and why it is important.
   - If the training involves new procedures that are being introduced into the workplace, explain why the organization wants to use these new procedures.
   - Express your confidence in the employee's ability to learn and master the new information or skill.
   - Allow the employee to express any doubts or ask questions she or he may have.
   - Explain what the employee is about to experience during training.
2. **Explain the process.**
   - Explain the steps in the job or task the employee is to perform and

then show them to the employee.
- Show the employee **the correct way** to do the job or task. Don't tell or show the employee what not to do.
- The are many techniques for presenting this part of the training and which one you use will depend on your style of training, what the task is and whether there are many ways to do the same task. Some examples of these techniques are:
   - hands-on demonstration.
   - virtual reality.
   - DVD or videotape.
   - pictures.
   - simulations.
   - combinations of these techniques.

   Keep in mind that seeing is believing. Remember that you are constantly providing OJT by the example you set every day, so be sure that you set a positive example.
- Explain the job standards, including all quality requirements that will need to be met once the employee completes training and demonstrates proficiency.
- Break the job or task down into small, understandable steps, so that the employee can achieve success throughout the training and a base of success to build on.
- Don't expect anyone to master a skill by just reading an instruction manual. Written directions give background information that is important, but adult learning occurs best in the application of knowledge or skills learned. Just as reading this book cannot make you a better supervisor until you practice and apply the information presented, learning a skill cannot be achieved by just reading about it. Applying and practicing any skill is the only path to mastery.

In an environment where technology is constantly changing, OJT is a must. Training is an investment in the workforce that pays dividends in productivity. If you don't ensure that your employees have the necessary skills, techniques or procedures, your organization won't be able to compete in the global marketplace. Lack of or improper training negatively impacts performance, achievement of objectives and job satisfaction. A poorly or inadequately trained employee is an "accident" waiting to happen. Sadly many organizations fail to identify this deficiency when conducting an incident analysis and are therefore doomed to repeat the incident.

3. **Provide for tryouts**. Allow the employee to practice the new skill. As always, support and reinforce the positive and correct the steps not performed correctly. Be careful not to be critical or punishing to an employee who makes mistakes during the training process. Let him or her practice with your assistance and support. A little practice may not make it perfect, but practice and praise for successes usually does.
4. **Follow-up.** Gradually have the employee perform more and more of the job without your direct supervision or assistance. Continue to observe and provide feedback on their progress.

Training Programs for Employees

Don't send someone to training just because the training program exists. If one of your employees is generally doing a good job but may need some development in a particular area, consider a training program focused to address that development need. For instance, your administrative assistant may have good clerical skills but comes across gruff and less than courteous when on the telephone. If you have employees or customers getting turned off by your assistant's phone manner, you could send your assistant to a "Telephone Skills Workshop."

Another example may be if your machine operator is doing an excellent job in all assigned duties, but has expressed an interest in learning the skills to become a mechanic and work in the maintenance department. Or, perhaps that administrative assistant suggests that a new computer program will aid m in getting portions of the job done more effectively. If all the specific training and educational opportunities are not available from an in-house source, there are training and education providers like local colleges, trade schools and even some high schools. By providing the opportunity for employees to improve, expand or gain new skills or knowledge, you are helping develop employee skills and education. This will serve the best interest of your organization.

Formal Training Programs

Formal training programs, conducted by someone other than the supervisor or mentor, are also important in the development of employee skills. Your organization may have a training and development unit that offers program on-site. Often additional programs are offered off-site in the local community or via consultants who give specialized training both on-site and off-site. Any of these programs can be applied in a new job or as part of a promotion.

Find Appropriate Training

Find the appropriate training to fit the needs of you and the employee. In-house training is usually the most cost-effective, so consider using those available resources first. When deciding on the appropriateness of any training program, consider these factors:
- What is the stated objective of the program?
- Does the program specify what skills will be taught or enhanced?
- Who are the instructors? What is the level of their experience? Do they

have an appropriate background or certification necessary to be an instructor for this material?
- If from an outside source, is it a reputable firm?
- What references do they offer and who are previous clients they have conducted this or similar training? Will they let you talk to current or previous clients?
- What training method is to be used and is it appropriate for the material and audience?
- Where will the training be conducted? If off-site, is it convenient for the participants to get to?
- What is the length of the program and will the participants get an opportunity to practice their skills as part of the process?
- What type of feedback will be provided to the supervisor?
- What is the cost when compared to the benefit to be gained?
- How will the effectiveness of the training be measured?

Discuss Training Needs with Others

Your organization training specialist (or HR if there is no dedicated training specialist) should be able to help you locate programs to fit your needs and answer some of the questions listed previously. If the session(s) are off-site and more a continuing education mode, check to see if there is tuition reimbursement for participants. You may also want to consult with other supervisors at your location to see what they have done in the past. Networking in this fashion can be a great benefit, not only with this type of issue, but many others in the future.

Discuss Goals and Objectives

If you send your employees to a training session, take time before they attend to discuss the goals and objectives of the training and what they might expect while in attendance. Tell them to be prepared to report on the program and what they learned from it when they return. Be sure to conduct this debriefing with your employees and discuss what they learned. This session will also help you assess the value of this particular training for other employees in the future. Assist the employee(s) apply their newfound knowledge or skills. Use praise to positively reinforce the employee's demonstration of their new skills. Encourage the employees to share their new knowledge and skills and with others who may not have been able to attend the session.

Coaching

What is coaching? Coaching in the workplace may be a little different from that of the athletic coach but there are some similarities. In the workplace *coaching* is helping employees in a positive manner and developing them to full potential. Positive is the key here. Coaching does **not** involve yelling at your employees every time they do something wrong. Coaching also does **not** involve replaying the errors made for them or other employees at every opportunity to reinforce the message. Instead, coaching seeks to praise employees for their successes and use constructive feedback to reduce errors. If you and your "players" (employees) are to be successful, you as the coach (supervisor) have to be supportive to achieve a winning performance from your players (employees).

Key Elements of Coaching

The supervisor must perform the following key elements of coaching in the in the workplace:

- Establish objectives and performance standards or requirements.

- Provide nonthreatening advice and support.
- Listen to employees and probe for how they feel about their work and job requirements.
- Carry out coaching in the same way as you would a performance counseling or disciplinary session, in private.
- Work to inspire trust, confidence and respect. One of the key elements of inspiring trust confidence and respect is to be extending them to those you supervise.
- Try to be in a supportive and helpful role, rather than that of the Boss. Criticisms offered should be done to help, improve or prevent, not punish. It should be accompanied with advice on how the employee can build on known successes and skills to do the job right.
- Use good communication skills (see Chapter 6, Communication).
- Be patient. A good coach is patient even when it is the most difficult time to be patient.
- Use coaching to reinforce new skills, improve performance problems, or solicit ideas to solve a job or departmental problem.

Coaching and Career Development

The purpose of developing your employees' careers is to enhance their job satisfaction. This in turn benefits their organization. If an employee begins to feel trapped or dissatisfied with their current job assignment, productivity, safety and quality might suffer or the employee might leave for another job. No one wants someone getting hurt on the job, a decrease in production, poor quality, or the loss of a valued employee, all of which is costly. As a supervisor, you should always be on the alert for ways to enhance the employees' current jobs or develop them for advancement within the current organization. Development involves helping employees who are performing quite well but demonstrate interest or potential for a more challenging job.

As a supervisor, you can take the following steps to help develop your employees:

1. Get to know your employees. Find out their degree of satisfaction with their current job and what it is they really like to do at work. Unexpected performance problems from a high performer may indicate that he or she is just bored and needs new challenge.

2. Know the organization's policies and procedures for career development. What are the rules concerning internal transfers or promotions? What are the training and development opportunities are available. What type(s) of educational assistance is available from the HR? What type(s) of skills/knowledge will the organization need in 1, 3, 5 and 10 years into the future? Are there current skills that will be considered obsolete in the near term?

3. Meet with your employees at least annually to discuss personal development plans. These types of discussions are separate from performance-counseling and objective-setting sessions. Communicate the information you have acquired about the organization's career development programs and policies. Outline for each employee a career development plan to include action steps. For example, one of your maintenance mechanics may have expressed an interest in moving into the tool and die shop. To be qualified, however, she or he would need some experience with die set-up and machining. Is there a need for a machinist and what available training is available? Is there an apprentice program or skilled trades program in the area? If so, then a plan and a series of action steps can be developed to assist the employee realize his or her goal.

4. Develop action steps. Using the previous example, the action steps that the two of you agree on could be that the mechanic will:
   - spend one hour each day in the tool and die shop assisting one of the

machinists with their work.
- enroll in technical classes to read and understand prints and set various types of machines.
- be given simple assignments to be able to practice some of these newly developed skills.
- be assigned to one of the tool and die makes to mentor them in their development.
- establish performance standards for improved performance, including productivity, quality and safety.
5. Coach and encourage. Once the development plan has been outlined and set into action, the supervisor's should coach and encourage the employee to carry out the plan. Feedback and interim reviews of the action plan are important.

Leadership Development

As a supervisor, hopefully one of your goals is to develop leadership skills in both the employees that report to you, as well as your own. Leadership is an acquired skill, not something that you are born with. To develop and achieve one's career goals, individuals must have some demonstrable leadership capabilities. The importance of being a leader in the workplace has been stressed often. Since you are in charge of both your employees and yourself, you must take the lead. After all, your employees look to you for direction, guidance and expectations, all necessary for good leadership. Being good at it is the important part. Leadership involves having:
- good listening skills.
- integrity.
- a vision for the work group and the ability to communicate that vision.

- trust.
- fair and balanced approach to job assignments, praise and discipline.
- a good balance of knowledge and applied skills.
- the ability to delegate tasks and responsibilities along with the authority to get those tasks done.
- a detailed understanding of an organization's strategic management process.
- knowledge of the business and the competitive environment in which it operates.
- a working knowledge of the whole organization, not just your isolated piece of the business world.
- a positive attitude toward change.

To develop your leadership skills you need to identify which skills you already have and those that you need. Of those you lack, decide which ones you want to work on and find a positive role model in someone who possesses these skills. Practice behaviors you have observed in your role model. Get feedback from someone you respect and trust, perhaps even your role model. Be aware how your employees react to your new approaches. Continue to alter your leadership style until it is something that you are comfortable with and is effective. Practice some more!

Academic Education

In most communities there is some opportunity for taking more formal classes through a college or university. These institutions offer a variety of degree programs that lead to associate, baccalaureate, masters and even doctorate degrees. More and more colleges and universities are offering their courses in a variety of formats that include traditional day classes, evening classes, weekend classes, and in many cases distance education via the Internet or combinations of these formats. In any case, if you or your employees need or want to take college level classes, there is usually a way to meet those needs.

If you and your employees are not interested in a formal degree program, there are many institutions offering "*certificate programs*" that are the same classes as required by a degree program, but result in the achievement of a certificate of completion instead of a degree. Also, these certificate programs are targeted at providing the essential educational course work to meet specific needs of the business community. Another advantage of a certificate program is that the admission requirements are often lower or there aren't any. Supervisors should use HR to help identify an appropriate program, formal degree or otherwise, and make sure that the program meets both the employee's and organization's needs.

Development also can be used on a smaller scale. Sometimes offering an employee the chance to mentor a new hire can be enough to break up his or her job routine and show confidence in someone who has been doing a good job. Assignment of an employee to a new project can have a similar effect. Ultimately, of course, it is the individual's responsibility to develop his or her own career, but the supervisor can certainly lay the groundwork and be a supportive coach along the way.

Conclusion

Employee development involves many steps, including:

- selecting and matching the right employee for the right job

- proceeding through the very important first days and weeks when a new or transferred employee comes to the job
- providing safety and job training.

Find more information on topics such as safety, communication, planning, performance and discipline, in earlier chapters of this book. But the best way to develop employees is, of course by being a good supervisor.

Review Questions

1. What are the primary reasons for sending one of your employees to a formal or informal training session?

2. What is the key to coaching employees for improving performance and career development?

3. List three of the skills or abilities that characterize a good leader.

4. Is getting a formal degree the only way employees can get career development skills/education through academic institutions?

12 Developing Your Own Skills and Career

by Meredith Onion
Michael F. O'Toole, PhD

What Will I Learn in This Chapter?

Chapter 11 explored how you can help develop the careers of your employees. In this chapter, we'll focus on career development for you, the supervisor. Few people progress in their careers successfully without planning and taking action to get where they want to go. Life rarely presents prepackaged golden opportunities. If you don't plan and take the time to develop your career, no one else will do it for you, and you may find yourself at mid-career not being where you really want to be. This chapter focuses on how to take control of your career. It gives you tools to use to help develop your career, including:

- assessing your priorities and goals.
- designing a development plan/strategy.
- influencing your boss.
- time management.
- choosing a healthy lifestyle; and
- managing career setbacks.

Assessing Your Priorities and Goals

Without an objective or identified priorities, plans go astray. The first step in your career development then is to establish your personal priorities and goals.

Self-Assessment Tools

Several self-assessment tools are available to help you determine your priorities and goals. The Internet has numerous sites with career advice and assessment tools (see Figure 12-1). Your organization's HR department may also have some books or skills inventory tests to get you started. Find out what other career planning services your organization offers. Remember, it is in the interest of your organization to have you increase your skills and capabilities to perform more responsible jobs in the organization. They have a vested interest in helping you if our effort is focused on staying with the organization. Your local library is also a god source for career development information.

> **Figure 12-1. A Sampling of Internet Career Resources**
>
> - www.CareerShop.com
> - www.CareerBuilder.com
> - www.JobHuntersBible.com (by Dick Bolles, author of What Color is Your Parachute)
> - www.TheBusyExec.com (look especially for the career and professional development sections)
> - www.monster.com
> - www.Headhunter.net

Determining Goals and Career Priorities

Several factors determine what our goals and priorities are. Here are just a few to consider:

Figure 12-2. What I Like and Dislike About My Job

I Like	I Dislike	
( )	( )	Supervisory Responsibility
( )	( )	Relationships With my Coworkers
( )	( )	Relationships With my Subordinates
( )	( )	Relationships With my Boss
( )	( )	Geographic Location
( )	( )	Commuting
( )	( )	Small Organization
( )	( )	Large Organization
( )	( )	Benefits
( )	( )	Pay
( )	( )	The Industry
( )	( )	Opportunities for Advancement
( )	( )	Autonomy
( )	( )	Flexible Hours
( )	( )	Flexible Work Arrangement (ex., at home)
( )	( )	Daily Challenges
( )	( )	Constant Change
( )	( )	Routine
( )	( )	Safety Environment
( )	( )	Physical Surroundings
( )	( )	Indoor Work
( )	( )	Outdoor Work
( )	( )	Ongoing Education
( )	( )	Training Opportunities
( )	( )	Working With People
( )	( )	Working With Things
( )	( )	Union Environment
( )	( )	Nonunion Environment
( )	( )	Other_____

Figure 12-3. How Do I View Things?

1. What are my strong traits or highly skilled areas? List two traits and two skills?
2. What are my weaknesses or areas for development? List at least three.
3. What type of feedback have I received from my boss, peers, subordinates or peers that may be helpful in my development?
4. What expertise do I bring to this particular industry?
5. Do I have strengths that can transfer to a different industry(s)?
6. What other positions/careers interest me? List at least one.
7. What do I admire most about my boss?
8. What would I change in my boss if I could?
9. What are my family responsibilities and priorities?
10. Am I being fairly compensated?
11. Am I able/willing to relocate to another city/state/country?
12. Am I interested in continuing my education? Where? When? In what area?
13. What are my long- and short-term goals?
14. Do my goals and objective match those of the organization I'm currently working for?

- What do I particularly enjoy about my current job or jobs I have held in the past?
- What do I especially like or dislike about my current or past job? Figure 12-2 gives you a checklist of likes and dislikes to help you do a self-assessment.
- What do I especially enjoy or not enjoy about my current or past boss? Leadership style? Method of treating employees? Ability to delegate?
- What are my strong points or highly skilled areas? Initiative? Willingness to take on whatever is assigned?

- What are my weaknesses? Procrastination? Blame others? Worry a lot? Unable to delegate?
- What skills am I interested in developing? Communication? Confronting discipline problems? Delegating? A better understanding of international business implications?
- What other positions or careers interest me? Manager? Technician? Sales?
- What are my family responsibilities and priorities? Children's or spouse's education? Summer cottage?
- Am I interested in continuing my education? College? Graduate school? Technical courses?
- What are my short-term goals? For the job? For myself? Family?
- What are my long-term goals? For the job? For myself? For my family?

Figure 12-3 gives you a worksheet to develop the answers to these questions. Once you have identified these elements that are important and you are good at, rank them. Also list items that you really dislike or couldn't tolerate in a job.

Once priorities and goals are determined, investigate if these can be met with your current career choice, your current organization or if you need to consider a career change or change of companies.

Designing a Development Plan

Having established your priorities and goals, you can begin developing a plan to get there. The first stop is to do some investigating to determine what you need to do to achieve your goals. Let's assume that your goal is to stay with your present employer but to move into a middle-management position at one of your organization's overseas locations, within 3 to 5 years. Your development plan may look something like Figure 12-4. As you can see, the plan does not need to be detailed and complicated. It should cover your vision of what you plan to be, and contain some of the steps of how you plan to get there.

Notice that the plan shown in Figure 12-4 has a dual track. Track one is to make continuous improvement in the supervisory work you are already doing. Track two is to begin to find out more about what it takes to become a manager, and then implement a plan that will earn you managerial qualifications. Both approaches are necessary, since you are not likely to be promoted if you aren't doing a good job in your present assignment, regardless of any credentials you may gain.

> **Figure 12-4.**
> **A Development Plan/Strategy**
>
> Goal: I want to stay with my organization, but will seek an overseas managerial position within the next 3 to 5 years.
>
> Steps to be Taken:
>
> 1. Continue supervisor training/education to become the best supervisor that I can be.
> 2. Seek ongoing feedback from by boss, peers, subordinates and my mentor, concerning my supervisory skills.
> 3. Get to know middle managers in my organization to determine what their career paths look like.
> 4. Meet with the organization's recruiters who hire middle managers to determine what qualifications they look for when hiring for managerial and ex-patriot positions.
> 5. Research cultural practices and the language of the country I may be interested in moving to.
> 6. Attend evening college to secure my Bachelor's or Master's degree in Business Administration or filed specific to my career interests.

What Does It Take, and What Is It Like?

Whatever your goals or priorities, it is a good idea to find out what it takes to achieve them, and what the work involved is really like. Meet with people in the type of position you're seeking. Find out how they got where they are. Explore what other companies are like and what they have to offer. Talk with your friends or colleagues about the tasks and skills involved. Attend professional association meetings and educational seminars where you will meet others interested in the same things you are. Read books about the position you are interested in. Search the web for resources that could be helpful (see Figure 12-1). If you are considering furthering your education, meet with college or university representatives to discuss what the career paths of their alumni have been.

Developing Your Leadership Skills

As a supervisor, hopefully one of your goals will be to develop your leadership skills. Leadership is an acquired skill, not something you are born with. To move up in most organizations, you must have some demonstrable leadership capabilities. Refer to chapters 2, A Juggling Act, and 8, Leadership. The importance of being a leader in the workplace is key. Since you are in charge, you must lead. Being good at it is the important part. Leadership includes having:
- good listening skills.
- integrity.
- a good balance of knowledge and applied skills.
- the ability to delegate tasks and responsibility.
- a detailed understanding of an organization's strategic management process.
- knowledge of the business and the competitive environment in which it operates.
- a working knowledge of the whole organization , not just your isolated little piece of the business world.

- a positive attitude toward change.

To develop you leadership skills you need to identify which leadership skills you already possess and those that you are lacking. Of those that are lacking, decide which you want to work on, and find a positive role model in someone who possesses these skills. A mentor is also very important to your career development. A trusted mentor will be able to give you candid feedback regarding your leadership ability and may be able to give suggestions for development and/or improvement. If you haven't identified your own mentor, contact your HR group—your organization may have a formal mentoring program or may be willing to hook you up with an appropriate mentor.

Practice behaviors you are trying to develop. Get more feedback from you role model, mentor or current boss. Be aware of how people react to your new skills. Are you getting the response you want? Keep on practicing.

Taking Risks

Career development involves taking risks. Unless we want to maintain the status quo the rest of our lives, we will have to change from time to time, and changing means taking a risk. Risk-taking is scary for most of us, but it is a necessary, critical step to career advancement. You can minimize the amount of risk you must take and select the best risk options if you consider and plan carefully. These planning steps can help:
- Think about risks you have taken that have been successful. What made them successful?
- Think of some of the risks you took that didn't work out. Why did they fail?
- Observe people who are successful risk-takers. What do they do that

you aren't doing?
- Determine the ways you avoid taking risks. Be honest with yourself and ask someone you trust to help you look at this issue. Why were you avoiding the change? How many times did your caution prevent your possibilities for success?
- Take calculated risks, not just risk for risk's sake. Be cautious, but understand that risk-taking is a critical and necessary step to advancement.
- Evaluate and monitor your risk-taking.

Taking Responsibility

Many people simply wait for opportunity to knock. It seldom happens. If you really want to advance, you must take responsibility for your development plan and how you will implement it. No one will develop your career for you. Many people can help along the way, and many will if you show initiative. But ultimately, the responsibility is yours.

Don't procrastinate about developing your career plan. If you are dissatisfied with your current position or feel the need to enhance your career, stop talking and complaining and start doing.

Influencing Your Boss

Like it or not, we all need our bosses. If you plan to stay with your current organization, you won't get far without a good relationship with your boss. Even if you plan to move on to another organization, it will be much easier with a positive reference from your current boss. Don't assume the communication between you and your boss is a 50-50 proposition. Be willing to take all of the responsibility for keeping the lines of communication open and positive.

Assess Your Relationship with Your Boss

If you are going to be able to influence your boss in order to enhance your career development, you have to first take a look at exactly how the relationship between you operates.

- Do you interact with your boss the same way you interact with your staff and colleagues? Why not? Are you sure he or she wants it that way?
- Do you understand what motivates your boss? Do you understand his/her job, demands and pressures? Take some time to think about that.
- What are you boss' pet peeve, prejudices, and blind spots? Do you avoid stirring these, or do you sometimes goad a bit just to see the reaction?
- What is important to your boss? What are his/her priorities? For the organization? For advancement? For you fellow workers? For you?
- Is there open communication between you and your boss? Think about how you would describe it to a neutral person.
- What nonverbal signals do you receive from your boss? Has time for others, but never seems to have time for you? Always busy? Ready to talk?
- Do you know if your boss is at his/her best in the morning, the afternoon?
- Do you avoid interacting with your boss when she/he is tired, angry, frustrated, and preoccupied?
- Do you keep your boss informed on matters he/she wants to be kept informed of?

- Do you know what your boss's boss is like?
- Do you follow the chain of command?
- To what extent does you boss depend on you?

If you begin to build answers to these questions, you will have a profile of your boss and you. You should also begin to identify some areas where you need to change your behavior in order to have a better relationship. If you use the knowledge this simple checklist can give you, you will have the basis for improving the relationship and being able to influence your boss.

Getting Along with Your Boss

Remember that your effort is to influence, not to change. You will wear yourself out trying to change your boss, and in the end you won't succeed anyway. You can change yourself, however. The point is to have your boss as an ally who will be supportive of your career development efforts.

Disagreeing with Your Boss

Getting along with your boss doesn't always mean agreeing with his/her position. Disagreeing is often a very disagreeable business, but sometimes absolutely necessary. Of course, there is a right way to disagree or provide alternate solutions to workplace problems. Here are a few guidelines for disagreeing with the boss.

Rule 1. *Never, never embarrass or put your boss in a corner.* Telling your boss in the middle of a group meeting that his/her idea is a bad one probably won't ever work. Tactfully offering an alternate solution may, but it is best done in private.

Rule 2. *Get to know when and when not to argue a point.* Arguing the point in the group meeting might be O.K., but chances are, getting the boss alone will be far more effective. When is also a factor of timing. If your boss is best

Figure 12-5. Question

I am currently in a situation where I can't seem to really get along well with my boss. He isn't completely irrational, but I could use some help in how to approach him. What tips are there for getting along with my boss?

Here are a few quick tips for having a better relationship with your boss:

The Boss' Value
- Keep the boss looking good.
- Show respect for your boss' management style.
- Use active listening.
- A lot of enthusiasm goes a long way.
- Be respectful.

Taking Credit
- Always be accountable for your own actions and the actions of your employees.
- Share the credit for work will done, but recognize that sometimes the boss will want the credit.
- Work hard at being a team player.

Your Accessibility
- Be available.
- Demonstrate your loyalty.
- Learn good timing.

Your View
- Look at the big picture.
- Accept change in a changing workplace.

Your Work Commitment
- Always strive for excellence.
- Keep on top of your work.
- Communicate, Communicate, Communicate — there's not a boss in the world that likes surprises!
- Do thorough, careful work.
- Keep developing new skills.

Your Persuasiveness
- Learn how to sell your solutions to problems.
- Spring up after setbacks.
- Demonstrate your creativity.
- Control costs.

in the morning, then talk it over in the morning. Grabbing the boss in the hall on the way to an important meeting when he/she is preoccupied and rushed isn't good timing.

Rule 3. *Always know what issues or topics are and aren't open for discussion or dispute.* For example, if your boss has strong feeling about all supervisors wearing suits and not casual attire, it won't be worth it to try to convince her or him otherwise. However, if your boss is unsure about implementing flextime, you may be able to convince him/her that it is a good idea.

Rule 4. *Learn how to object without being objectionable and to disagree without being disagreeable.* If you propose an alternant plan to your boss and it doesn't fly, don't go away pouting. If you convince your boss that your idea is better than hers or his, share the credit and don't gloat.

Rule 5. *Treat your boss as a very important person.* Everyone likes to feel important. If you do that, he or she will be prepared to accept some disagreement from you.

Rule 6. *Get to know your job, what you can accomplish and the work environment before you try too much influencing or disagreeing with your boss.* If you really know your job, your boss will respect that knowledge and listen.

Rule 7. *Schedule meetings with your boss to establish or clarify goals and priorities—yours and his or hers.* This tends to at least reduce disagreement on priorities.

Rule 8. *Choose your battles.* You may disagree with your boss on a lot of issues—but not all of them will be worth letting him or her know about. No one likes to work with someone who constantly complains or disagrees with everything you say or do. Choose to disagree only when it's a really important issue, one that is worth your boss's time.

Time Management

Career development involves getting things done by effectively using your time. This means using your time to meet priorities in your current position and finding time to do some career planning. Everyone at one time or another has felt: *There just aren't enough hours in the day to get everything done.* Time management is very personal and what works for you may not work for someone else. The techniques offered here are suggestions. Try them out for a while, and then pick and choose what works best for you.

Figure Out How You Use Your Time

The best way to figure out how you're using your time is to keep a log for a few days or weeks. You don't have to run out and buy some expensive system. Keep notes in your calendar, palm-held computer or a blank piece of paper.

After you have kept a log for a few days, study it. Ask yourself:
- What did I spend time doing that I really didn't have to do?
- What could I have delegated instead of doing it myself?
- Is there someone I can train to do more so that I can delegate more?
- What did I do that wasted other's time?
- Did I spend time on high- or low-priority items?

Also, think about feedback you may have received from your current boss or prior boss about how you spend your time? Have they made suggestions for improvement?

Time Management—The Plan

If you want to manage your time, you will need to plan. For the purpose of time management, divide the planning into two parts: goals and time use.

Identify short-term and long-term goals. What would you like to do better with your time? For example, *I really need to spend more individual time with my staff?* Or *I'd really like to spend less time in meetings?* Or *I need to find more time to devote to professional development instead of always putting out fires.* All of these are legitimate goals, and all will take a rearrangement and reallocation of your time. How do you do it?

First, put the goals in priority order. What is most important, second and so on. Then list the steps that have to be taken to meet these goals. For example, in order to spend more individual time with staff, I would need to:

1. *Reduce the amount of time spent in group staff meetings.*
2. *Delegate shift scheduling to one of my team leaders.*
3. *Schedule lunch with each of my staff once a month.*

Prioritize the steps and work on the most important and achievable first.

Learn better methods of time use. Another form of planning is to make a list every week of your activities. Determine the priorities on the list and label them. Determine the least important activities and label them A, B and C with A being the most important and achievable, B the second and C the least. For obvious reason, this if often called the *ABC time management method.* Having identified your priorities, you then spend the majority of your time on the items you have identified as priorities. You do not move from "A" items until all that can be completed have been completed. After that, you go to "B" items. "C" items usually have to wait quite some time, unless something happens to change your priorities.

Time Traps

Time traps are what seem to take up your time in an unproductive manner. Try some of these tips to reduce the likelihood of time traps:

- Keep your priorities list within sight.
- Do the most important items first to reduce the stress and distraction and thus time wasted in putting them off.
- Work on top priorities in your peak time. If you're best in the morning, do them in the morning.
- Procrastination is a time trap. If it's a priority item, do it now. If it's something you can do on your way to something else, and will take up no significant time, do it now.

- Don't over-schedule your time. Leave time for the unexpected. Do save yourself some lunch and break time.
- Schedule a meeting with yourself from time to time. Close the door and ask not to be disturbed.
- Clear the unimportant tasks from your desk so you are not distracted.
- Use a calendar or note tickler system (either paper or electronic) that fits with your style and comfort level.
- Break larger tasks into smaller pieces. It's easier that way and gives you a sense of accomplishment.
- Don't be a perfectionist. Striving for excellence is one thing, but know when enough is enough.
- Set target dates for the completion of tasks or projects and hold your staff accountable for meeting them.
- Don't handle paper twice.
- Delegate, delegate, delegate.
- Take time to plan: 1 hour of planning saves 3 to 4 hours of execution time.
- Try to keep an even pace. Don't burn yourself out by noon.
- Don't open "junk" e-mail correspondence that you know you're not interested in.
- Learn to say "no."

Choosing a Healthy Lifestyle

You're probably wondering what lifestyle has to do with supervisors and career development. It is difficult to do your job and to develop yourself and your career ...not to mention juggling your career with your family demands, volunteer activities and hopefully some time for fun...if you are not at your best, physically and mentally It wasn't too long ago that we thought doctors were responsible for keeping us healthy. During the past 20-plus years, we've learned that although heredity and fate play a role, our own lifestyle choices make a huge difference in our ability to stay well.

The leading causes of death among U.S. citizens all have associated risk factors that the individual can personally control. One's lifestyle can either keep one well or make one sick. For example, cardiovascular disease has several primary risk factors:

- smoking
- high blood pressure
- high cholesterol
- lack of aerobic exercise
- heredity
- age.

Obviously, you can't do anything about your heredity or age, but you can:

- quit smoking (or never start).
- practice methods to maintain a safe blood pressure.
- maintain a low-fat/high-fiber diet.
- participate in aerobic exercise.

All of these measures have a major impact on avoiding heart disease or reducing its impact if you've been diagnosed with heart disease.

Healthy Choices

The following areas are all within your control and can help you be a peak performer.

Nutrition

What you eat is up to you. Maintaining a sound, balanced diet doesn't mean you have to eat only wheat germ and green leafy vegetables. The four basic food groups provide a simple framework for what is a balanced diet. The American Heart Association provides good guidelines for choosing within the food groups. You should also have your cholesterol checked to see if you should pay particular attention to your fat intake. Good nutrition is not only good for your physical well-being, good nutrition is also good for your mental health.

Smoking

Smoking is bad for your health. *A Report of the Surgeon General-2001, Women and Smoking*, in part states:

> "...Lung cancer, once rare among women, has surpassed breast cancer as the leading cause of female cancer death in the United States, now accounting for 25 percent of all cancer deaths among women. Surveys have indicated that many women do not know this fact. And lung cancer is only one of myriad serious disease risks faced by women who smoke. Although women and men who smoke share excess risks for diseases such as cancer, heart disease, and emphysema, women also experience unique smoking-related disease risks related to pregnancy, oral contraceptive use, menstrual function and cervical cancer."

Smoking is unhealthy for you, the people around you and a big waste of time during your workday. Consider quitting. Contact your local Lung Association, American Cancer Society or community hospital for smoking cessation programs. Also check out these websites:
- www.quitnet.org
- www.CDC.gov
- www.drkoop.com
- www.Nci.nih.gov

Exercise

Aerobic exercise for 20 to 30 minutes, three to four times a week is recommended. Aerobic exercise includes activities such as swimming, bicycling, jogging, rowing and walking. Choose an exercise that is the most enjoyable for you. If you dread exercising, set small goals for yourself and work your way up to the recommended level of exercise. If you overdo it the first few times, you may be too discouraged and sore to continue. Whatever you do, if you haven't been exercising, contact your physician before starting any type of exercise program.

Stress Management

Supervisors experience stress just like their employees, maybe worse.

Recognize Stress Symptoms

If you are going to control stress in yourself, you will need to watch for its symptoms. For example, frequent errors, trouble concentrating, can't make decisions, missing deadlines or meetings/appointments, temper outbursts, argumentative, sleeplessness, and fatigue are all signs of stress. Exercise, good nutrition and time management are all ways to prevent stress in the first place, but keep an eye out for these possible symptoms.

Stress Relief Techniques

In addition to the tips already mentioned (exercise, nutrition and time management), relaxation techniques such as deep breathing, head rolls, and stretching are also good techniques for reducing or relieving some of the immediate physical and emotional symptoms of stress. yoga, tai-chi, and/or a Pilates class are also very popular methods for stress management. Think about what relaxes you—music, fishing, cooking, reading, walking, etc—and find time to enjoy these activities.

Seminars

Take advantage of any stress relief programs your organization or community offers. Contact your organization's Employee Assistance Program (EAP) or Wellness Program for possible assistance. And never be afraid to ask for help from your physician or religious organization if life just gets too unbearable or if you think you're depressed.

Managing Career Setbacks

This chapter has focused on the many things you can do to help manage your career and career development. Like any best-laid plans, sometimes the plan goes awry. Any number of things can interrupt your career:
- involuntary lay-off
- someone else gets the promotion you had hoped/worked for
- new boss, new set of expectations
- company is sold, new vision, new set of rules, new career pathing
- termination for cause
- disability.

Terminations, whether for cause or not, are huge blows to your ego. These are never easy to handle and can be quite devastating, especially mid- to late-career. Allow yourself to feel bad, but also take whatever resources may be available to help you move on. Many organizations offer outplacement counseling and often people are reluctant to accept this type of help.

Maybe you're hesitant because you think, "*I've always been able to get a job on my own, and so who needs help?*" But the service can be emotionally supportive as well as providing practical resources for a well-managed job search.

Reach out to friends for support. In today's up and down economy, many people have been affected by a sudden job loss at one point in their careers. Find out how they managed to get through it. In addition to their tips for help, they will also be the basis for a network to look for the next position. The most effective means of locating a job is by networking with everyone you know.

We've mentioned in several chapters in this book, the importance of managing change. Changes to your career path may be one of the most important changes you'll need to manage. You can't prevent your organization from being sold, merged or acquired and every time this happens, there is a good chance you'll end up with a new boss, a new organization vision, or a new list of expectations for how you do your job. When change happens, fighting it or resisting it won't do you one bit of good. Learn to go with the flow. If you find that your new situation is simply unbearable or unpleasant, then certainly look for a new opportunity elsewhere. But in the mean time, do the best you can to embrace the new way of doing things and show that you can be a team player.

Last, but not least, and this may sound trite, look for opportunities that you will enjoy. So many people are in jobs, careers and industries that they don't even like, but they think they don't know how to do anything else. What may at first look like a career setback, may actually be a wonderful opportunity to break out of your usual routine to try something different that you may enjoy more. After all, life is short....

Case Study

Eliza Banks is feeling less and less motivated to get up in the morning to go to work. A Swedish organization recently acquired her company and all of the top management has changed, including her own boss. She used to feel good about her job, her performance and her career path with her current employer. She never really gave much thought to what she would do next—she just assumed the company would take care of her like they had in the past.

She'd started working with this telecommunications company right from high school as a receptionist. She worked her way up and is currently the supervisor of a team of service technicians. But now, her new boss is from Sweden and half the time, she can't even understand what he is saying, given his accent. His performance expectations are much higher than with her previous boss. She's not sleeping well, she's smoking more and she's tempted just to quit her job before she becomes any more miserable.

- Has Eliza been managing her career?
- What can she do now to manage the current situation with her boss?
- Should she just give up without another job to go to?
- What would you do if you were Eliza?

Review Questions

1. Who is responsible for your career development?

2. What resources are available to help you with career development?

3. What type of planning is important? For development? For influencing your boss? For time management? For a healthy lifestyle?

4. How healthy is your lifestyle and what goals can you set to improve your quality of life?

5. How can you manage career setbacks?

Appendix A
Safety in the Global Workplace

*by Ather Williams, Jr,
Laura L. Horian*

What Will I Learn in This Appendix?

This appendix presents the challenges and opportunities of working as a safety professional in a global organization through descriptions, examples and suggestions. Although this appendix is specifically written for the safety professional, supervisors with safety responsibilities will also benefit from this information.

Overview

All major organizations are, or will be, global in scope. That presents many challenges and opportunities to safety professionals educated in U.S. universities and corporations. Some of what is required to be successful in a global environment can be learned through study and observation. And some success is attributable to adopting certain perspectives and attitudes. We discuss the global safety organization in these areas:
- structure
- "global standards with a local touch"
- management challenges
- communication challenges
- opportunities for safety professionals
- advice for safety professionals going global.

Examples from Johnson & Johnson (where author Ather Williams, Jr., serves as Vice-President, Worldwide Safety & Industrial Hygiene) will occasionally be made. Readers who currently work in a global organization will be able to compare and contrast the challenges they face. Readers who do not yet work in an environment with global safety issues will become aware of the opportunities they will surely face in the near future.

The Structure of a Global Safety Organization

Safety functions in a global organization are not fundamentally different from those in a solely U.S. organization. Safety representatives work with operations and offices to manage occupational job risks. They may report directly to the manager of the operation, or may report to a corporate safety organization that assigns them to one or more operations. Regardless of the organization's structure or geographic scope of operation, safety professionals around the globe are driven by the same purpose: *to prevent and reduce work-related injury and illness.*

Like all safety organizations, those meeting global needs focus on the same criteria for success:
- **Structure**: how safety will be "installed" and maintained.
- **Tools:** what preventive programs and processes will be in place to ultimately incorporate safety into operational design.
- **Standards:** what global standards to strive toward, taking into account the local touch of governments, cultures, language, etc.
- **Competent People:** what technical and business skills are required to not only uphold current safety commitments, but prepare future safety leaders.
- **Measurements:** what measures will be used to demonstrate the investment value and success of safety efforts.
- **Accountability:** how accountability for a safe workplace will be established with line management and the safety professional.
- **Regulatory outreach:** how to influence governmental regulations for the good of all businesses.
- **Communicating:** ways to share cautions, best practices, and any other information that will help all regions succeed in reducing injuries and illness.

Global organizations may have the responsibility of maintaining safe work practices in dozens of different cultures. At Johnson & Johnson, the Worldwide Safety & Industrial Hygiene (S&IH) organization oversees the safety of employees in 190 operating companies in 51 countries. Safety professionals are part of a "shared services" structure in which they are paid by the corporate S&IH organization, but work at one or more assigned facilities. More commonly, facilities hire their own safety and/or environmental professional(s), perhaps with guidance from a corporate safety organization on what technical expertise is most needed. Samsung's Kiheung factory just outside Seoul, Korea, has 160 health, safety and environmental personnel on-site. Apparently that kind of person power pays off. Samsung has worked 250 million hours incident-free since 1991, earning them an entry in the 1999 *Guinness Book of World Records* as the world's safest workplace (Smith, 2000)

Corporations typically divide the globe into regions, and assign each a Regional Safety Director (or equivalent title). Each region is characterized by different regulatory environments, and different types of safety personnel—educated or trained; sole responsibility or shared responsibility; certified professional or safety coordinator. Here are some general regional characteristics:

- **North America:** Strong regulatory environment. Facilities often have one or more educated and trained safety professionals on-site.
- **Latin America/Caribbean:** Strong regulatory environment. Educated professionals in Brazil; scattered across other areas are trained safety coordinators with technical backgrounds (mechanics, engineers). Safety role is often combined with other responsibilities (e.g., facility management, plant engineering, security, medical).
- **Asia/Pacific:** Spotty to strong regulatory environment depending on the area. In Australia, most facilities have an on-site safety professional; elsewhere, scattered, trained safety coordinators.
- **Europe, South Africa:** Strong regulatory environment and high regard for technical skills. There are both educated and trained safety coordinators whose safety role is often combined with Environmental responsibilities.
- **Middle East, North Africa:** Spotty to strong regulatory environment

depending on the area. Middle East, Egypt, Morocco and North Africa are overseen by safety coordinators.

Some companies with U.S.-based headquarters will hire technical experts in the United States and move them overseas. Others will hire technical experts who are native to their region. The latter approach may be more effective, as safety experts native to their region understand the history, culture, language, and politics of their area. Additionally, many are trained in safety after having worked in manufacturing. For these reasons, line management and operators typically respect the decisions and technical leadership of safety representatives from their region.

Global operations that do not have the luxury of a dedicated safety representative, or ready access to a technical safety expert, offer an opportunity for U.S.-based safety professionals. Those with technical skills that are needed around the world are ripe for training or implementation assignments abroad. Safety professionals who specialize can be dispersed around the globe to target problems. For instance, if a safety professional has demonstrated success with an approach to confined space entry in her facility, she may be asked by the corporation to train facilities in other regions on that program. At Johnson & Johnson, one professional who specializes in potent pharmaceutical compounds was selected for a two-year assignment in Italy where such expertise was needed.

Global Standards with a Local Touch

Implementing a safety strategic plan requires commitment to *global standards with a local touch*. That means: all facilities adhere to the same standard, but their approach may be customized to "fit" their culture, and to maximize the area's available resources. For instance, when it comes to machine safety, Johnson & Johnson requires compliance with Zero-Access™ Machine Guarding. How companies accomplish that is up to them, and it can vary dramatically depending on expertise, resources and worker style. In the United States, laser guards are used on some machines. In other regions, a more traditional point guard is used. Other companies apply a similar philosophy, with a *corporate audit group* requiring *corporate compliance* or adherence to a *corporate policy*. Sites may negotiate how they reach compliance, or their timetable, but they are required to meet the policy. When facilities face particular difficulties in complying, they may be able to sign a variance for exclusion or they may secure resources from the corporation. Resources can be financial or human (e.g., the Regional Safety Director or technical experts are sent in to assist).

Another variable considered when applying a local touch to a global standard is lifestyle and affect on the community. An administrative solution may be selected over an engineering solution based on local employee and community values. For instance, an organization with consistent ergonomics strain may select job rotation to rest the hands rather than automation to remove the manual task completely–along with dozens of workers. Certainly, finances are part of the selection criteria, but so is the concern of putting people out of work. As with all business investment decisions, cost is a concern in making safety decisions. But employees and communities are also important parts of the equation.

Management Challenges

More important than finances, there must be leadership and commitment to make safety a value rather than a priority. Priorities change. Companies in different countries have different priorities that are determined by cultural, regional and financial issues. It seems that the further away from the home office, the greater the challenge to make safety a value for every employee. For example, a corporate mandate is issued for all companies to meet minimal machine guarding standards. Facilities with machine safety issues in, say, China are not profitable at the time the policy is issued. How does a safety professional reconcile that situation? Safety is everyone's responsibility. Regardless of geography, the financial issues must be known and understood.

Another safety challenge in a global organization is recognizing and prioritizing the greatest risks. Today, musculoskeletal disorders account for at least half of many companies' worker's compensation worldwide. With everyone in companies using computers, the population exposed to ergonomics risks is on the rise. While facilities are very ergonomics-aware in the U.S., Europe and Australia, in many parts of Asia/Pacific the medical community does not yet recognize ergonomics as a work-related illness.

Another serious safety risk worldwide is with those who drive company cars. For field sales and service personnel, their vehicle is their workplace. No matter how thorough the fleet safety program, companies cannot safeguard the vehicle workplace as comprehensively as they can their manufacturing, research and development, and administrative environments. It is in the field workplace that an employee is most likely to suffer a life-changing incident, or a fatality. Some companies do not have fleet safety programs, and some are very rudimentary (e.g., issuance of a few policies). Trying to hold fleet safety standards worldwide, across several thousand drivers, is daunting, especially given the cultural differences. For instance, J&J drivers in Brazil have a very sophisticated fleet safety program. But in some of the smaller Latin American countries that face political unrest, drivers are concerned about getting through neighborhoods without being assaulted. And in some countries, drivers licenses can be bought and sold, rendering a motor vehicle record search useless. There are parts of the Asia/Pacific region where field representatives drive two-wheeled scooters with no training, wearing little in the way of protective equipment. They are involved in more incidents, and suffer more injuries than in other locations because of balance issues, high traffic volume, and of course the unprotected structure of the two-wheeler. The solution for "fixing" this risk is more difficult than merely issuing a scooter safety standard. The scooter is the common, accepted mode of transportation in this area. Again, cultural, regional, and financial issues must be considered.

Acquisitions are also a challenge in a global organization, as they often pose several safety challenges at one time. Like many global corporations seeking growth, J&J acquires companies all over the world. Typically, newly acquired companies have six to eight times J&J's injury rate. Bringing those companies up to J&J standards quickly requires a clear understanding of the organization's operations, a specific improvement strategy, and ample financial and human resources to implement that strategy.

An underlying challenge to the global safety organization is maintaining the changing competency requirements of its safety professionals. Questions to consider are:

- Do safety professionals have the technical skills to address risks in their facilities? If not, does the organization have a training and development plan to improve their competencies?
- Do they have the business skills to influence management? Can they effectively present a safety business case that yields a call to action?
- Can they calculate the cost effectiveness of alternative solutions?
- Do they sufficiently understand business pressures to present safety solutions as a business *investment* rather than an *expense*?

All too often safety professionals complain of the difficulty in making management see that safety is good business. Traditionally, safety professionals sell safety using a humanistic approach (*"Your people are your most important asset"*) rather than a business approach (*"Safety improvements yield quality and productivity improvements, and reduce injury costs."*) The challenge is to provide safety professionals the training and tools they need to help management see beyond capital expense, and fully comprehend the cost savings of an injury- and illness-free workplace.

Communication Challenges

Communicating safety information in a culture other than one's own poses unique challenges beyond different languages. If safety professionals have the opportunity to train or to participate in a special project in a different country than their own, here are some things to consider when developing materials for a worldwide audience.

Use Media that "Fit"

Paper size, hole-punch and video formats differ around the world. Set margins to accommodate U.S. Letter (216 x 279 mm, or 8½ x 11 inches) **and** A4 paper (210 x 297 mm, or 8¼ x 11¾ inches). Create video masters that can be copied onto NTSC, PAL, PAL-N and SECAM formats. Make sure electronic materials are prepared in programs and versions that all geographies use.

Here are some general preferences by geography:
- Asia/Pacific: A4 paper; 2-ring binders; PAL and NTSC video formats.
- Europe/Middle East/Africa: A4 paper; 2-ring binders; PAL and SECAM video formats.
- Latin America/Caribbean: A4 paper; 2-ring binders; NTSC and

PAL-N video formats.
- North America: US Letter; 3-ring binders; NTSC video format.

Use Graphics

Graphic representations require little, if any, translating. Use photos or sketches to show the difference between right and wrong, or before-and-after. A graphic approach also reduces the chance for errors during translation. Simple graphics used well worldwide include:
- the international DO NOT symbol: Ø
- arrows to show direction
- hands showing how to hold something
- stick figures to show positioning or posture in a work area.

Write Clearly

To write clearly is to make meaning understandable to any potential reader. This seems obvious. But writing clearly for a global audience means making it easy for translators.

State ideas in one sentence. In an attempt to be clear, poetic, or to emphasize a point, we might write a sentence three different ways. When we do this, we are using shades of meaning to create an image. The non-native translator spends much time trying to find the shades of meaning in the redundant text. If certain information must be repeated, duplicate it exactly, so it only needs to be translated once.

One source of confusion for translators is using words with multiple meanings or multiple parts of speech. Here is an example of how the simple word *display* might cause confusion if translating for Argentina, France, and Austria (adapted from Jones et al, 1992):

When using words with multiple meanings, try to keep the use of each word to one part of speech throughout the document. For instance, if instructing to do something at a *table* (noun) avoid instructing to *table* issues in meetings (verb).

English uses for display	Spanish	French	German
Put up the *display* at the trade show	visualización	stand	Ausstellung
Change the contrast on the *display*	pantalla	écran	Bildschirm
Display the graphic on the screen	traer a la pantalla	afficher	zeigen
Observe the spreadsheet *display*	visualización en pantalla	affichage	Darstellung

Avoid jargon, acronyms, and abbreviations. Imagine translating *out-of-the-box thinking*! Yet we use that and other jargon freely. When translating the words that go into an acronym, the translated words may not begin with the same letters, producing a different acronym. Similarly, avoid abbreviations that can be misinterpreted or impossible to translate.

Be Sensitive to Cultural Differences

A few fundamental cultural differences to which we should be sensitive are gender, measurements, monetary values, dates and colors.

Gender

In the American attempt to be politically correct, we strive to include both genders (*he/she, s/he, he or she*). The extra words are cumbersome for translators. Try to use plurals (*they*) or the direct voice (*you, your*) rather than gender-specific terms.

Measurements and Money

All references to measurements should include U.S. and metric units. Similarly, references to monetary values should include the appropriate symbol: U.S. $, C$, F, £, etc. Also, be aware that many countries outside the United States use periods and/or apostrophes rather than commas to separate numbers (e.g., U.S. $1,000,000 vs. DM$1.000.000 in Germany vs. SFr$1'000'000 in French-speaking Switzerland).

Dates

In the United States we define dates in the order of month, date, year. The European convention is date, month, year. Neither way is correct. To avoid confusion, spell out the month rather than use an abbreviation or numerical representation (*August* rather than *Aug* or *8*).

Color

Be sensitive to that fact that other cultures may not associate colors with things or events in the same way Americans do. Not everyone associates a blue ribbon with the implied "first place" message. In the United Kingdom, for example, red ribbons are sometimes used to signify first or best. We may shade the drawing of a person's face red to signify anger or frustration. In China, red is associated with happiness.

Opportunities for Safety Professionals

This appendix already discussed the opportunity for temporary assignment in a region where expertise is needed to train or implement. These assignments can last anywhere from 2 months to 2 years. Because this type of arrangement is costly, it must benefit both sides. For this reason, it behooves safety professionals to develop technical skills, know the functions and needs of operations in other parts of the world, clarify the costs and benefits of their being assigned to a special project, and assert themselves as the optimal candidates.

The geographies covered by global organizations offer an array of rich possibilities. The people in Latin America are filled with joy, and are passionate about safety. Working with them reminds us of how important safety is to the health and happiness of every human being. Europeans place a high value on technical knowledge and skills, encouraging professionals to demonstrate their best performance. The diverse cultures across Asia/Pacific are fascinating. Its people are highly creative in developing safety methods that fully utilize their available resources. Americans can learn about the value of simple solutions from our Far East neighbors.

The reward in being a safety professional in a global organization is providing every employee equal safety. At J&J, there are about 98,000 employees, with 40,000 in the United States. That means there are 58,000 other employees across the continents whose safety can be influenced. Safety professionals have the opportunity to adopt the most stringent safety standards around the globe rather than merely comply with those in the headquarter's region. For instance, Europe is ahead of the United States in machine safety and ergonomics standards. Global representation challenges safety professionals to push their companies' safety involvement beyond compliance.

Advice for Safety Professionals Going Global

The simplest, most direct advice for any safety professional who intends to visit, train or work in a facility outside their own region is to know the region's culture and values. This is a greater task than merely learning a few conversational snippets in another language. Those seeking to be safety leaders should do their homework before talking safety in a foreign land. Here are some techniques for a smoother transition to another safety region.

In general:
- Study the history of the area to see if there are any deep-rooted issues (religious, political, etc.) that may affect how companies do business and/or how they value the worker.
- Study the culture to learn at least the fundamental differences in how they dress, eat, talk, etc. Learn the differences in body language and mannerisms. Learn words or gestures that inadvertently offend. For instance, the open-handed wave is an insult to Greeks. Crossing the legs and showing the bottom of the foot is an insult in the Thai culture. Global organizations often offer a cultural immersion course to help employees begin to understand the customs and body language of another region.
- Those interacting on the plant floor will need to know the native language or have an excellent translator. It is the only way to fully understand the situation during a needs assessment or an incident investigation.
- Observe the work style of those in other countries first-hand rather than make assumptions or take someone else's word for it.
- Learn the region's safety regulations to know how they compare to the corporate expectation, and to prepare for any gaps between what they are doing and what is expected of them.
- Be prepared for things to take longer, particularly the deployment of safety programs and processes. As those who have tried know, distributing a "safety training box" does not guarantee effective implementation. This is even truer when working across cultures. It is worth spending the extra time at the outset to make sure the region understands what is expected than to make several "emergency" trips to coach implementation.

- Expect more face-to-face meetings. In the United States, we rely a great deal on e-mails, phone calls, and conference calls to conduct our business efficiently. Travel to and from sites is time consuming and expensive. However, outside the United States., people seem to place a greater value on face-to-face interaction. In addition to demonstrating a concern for their issues, safety professionals who show up onsite have the opportunity to genuinely learn more about the site's needs, and what constraints it faces in trying to meet those needs.

Here are some other tips to consider when working in a non-U.S. facility, when offering solutions:
- Be sensitive to the site's financial position and constraints.
- Determine the technical competence at the site before suggesting solutions.
- Identify the technical resources available for proposed solutions. Safety representatives often have multiple responsibilities.
- Be open to alternative solutions. U.S. solutions do not automatically transfer abroad.

- When interpreting and comparing measurements:
  Be aware that injury/illness recordkeeping can be different abroad. For example, an injury that results in issuing a prescription painkiller is recordable in the United States. In England, that same drug may be over-the-counter, which means prescribing it for the same injury there is not recordable. We continue to be challenged by the need to create universal standards that accurately measure and compare regions.
- When calling attention to a safety issue:
  When witnessing an unsafe condition or someone engaging in an unsafe practice, talk to the supervisor privately. Ask for an opportunity

Case Study: A Global Safety Scenario

The case that follows is based on a real situation in which two U.S.-based safety representatives from Johnson & Johnson traveled to China to implement a safety training initiative.

Even though we had both visited dozens of facilities across the United States, and in Europe, we really did not know what to expect in China. We decided to go early, and learn as much as possible about their culture before making our first call on one of our company facilities. One of the things we did was visit a factory. It is not difficult to do this in state-owned facilities. We chose a high-productivity television factory. There was no heat in the facility. Women were wearing parkas while they worked. They sat in seats that were made "ergonomic" with cardboard and foam taped to the backs and arms. They soldered lead with no masks, respirators or ventilation. This prepared us for seeing our own factories, and gave us insight into how far we had to move them to meet J&J standards. We understood the potential size of the safety gap. We had a good idea of what to expect culturally. The experience removed judgement from our mind-set, and helped us understand that our task would be more difficult than expected. But we were now more prepared to prioritize risk.

When we did arrive at our site, we saw that it was under construction. The workers were wearing "flip-flop" sandals, and there were no hard hats. There were children at the site because workers bring their family to the job. The scaffolding was made of bamboo. Despite our charge to train on machine safety in the facility, we knew we had to address the potential danger to the workers and their families outside the plant. That was our first priority. We made suggestions on fundamental personal protective equipment, and had an interpreter explain the dan-

Case Study

ger of children at the construction site. They were very willing to make changes. Culturally, they accepted J&J as an authority. They immediately stopped construction workers from bringing families, and they started wearing hats, and shoes that covered their feet. The entire time we remained open to their rationale for doing the work the way they did, and consequently adjusted our perception of the need for steel scaffolding. Bamboo worked. Inside the plant, workers embraced any training we could provide. We did all of it in the local language, using an interpreter. Of course this made the training take twice as long, but it made it much easier for the workers.

Had we not prepared ourselves for the J&J experience by visiting the television factory, we would not have been aware of the cultural norms and expectations. We quite likely would have overreacted, judged, and imposed "American" solutions that were not culturally acceptable. Our research paid off.

to demonstrate how the unsafe condition or practice could cause an incident. For instance, at a J&J facility in Asia, a safety professional pulled out a metal money clip from his pocket to demonstrate how a magnetic interlock could be "fooled" into thinking the guard was closed even when it was open. Most people learn better by example, and a language difference makes this especially true. Examples, demonstrations, and pictures are better tools for explaining safety than written or oral descriptions.

Conclusion

Organizations that must meet safety needs around the globe may be structured in a variety of ways. And cultures, languages, politics, financial situations, and safety risks differ everywhere. But safety professionals worldwide all seek to prevent and reduce job-related injuries and incidents. The objective of world class organizations is to make safety a *value*. Staying focused on that overall objective will keep safety professionals true to their calling, and improve their likelihood of success. To prepare for an overseas safety training or implementation, prepare both technically and attitudinally. Make sure materials are easy to understand in any language. The more graphical they are, and the more examples they demonstrate, the better. Learn what challenges the region faces socially, economically and politically. Be prepared for things to take longer than planned, particularly in regions where translators are required to communicate instructions. Preparing to implement safety improvements globally is well worth the effort for the return gift of experiencing work life in other cultures.

References

Jones S, Kennelly C, Mueller C, et al. *Developing International User Information.* Digital Equipment Corporation, Digital Press, 1992, p. 43.

Smith T. The world's safest workplace. *Safety+Health,* December 2000, p. 57-59.

Appendix B
Resources for Supervisors

Professional U.S. Safety and Occupational Health Organizations and their Internet Websites

Please note that organizations do move their offices from time to time, change their telephone numbers and change Internet website addresses. The addresses and Internet websites for these organizations are current as of press dates.

- **AFL-CIO,** Website: **www.aflcio.org**
  815 16th St., N.W. Washington D.C. 20006, (202)637-5000. The coordinating labor organization in the United States–American Federation of Labor-Congress of Industrial Organizations–offers special safety features in their newspaper–AFL-CIO News–and at their website and union position papers on occupational safety and health.

- **Alcoholics Anonymous,** Website: **www.alcoholics-anonymous.org**
  General Services Office for the United States and Canada, 459 Riverside Dr., Box 459 Grand Central Station, New York, N.Y. 10163, (212)870-3400. Central coordinating office of Alcoholics Anonymous chapters.

- **American Association of Occupational Health Nurses,**
  Website: **www.aaohn.org**
  2920 Brandywine Rd., Atlanta GA 30341, (770) 455-7757. Professional association of occupational health nurses (formerly known as industrial nurses).

- **American College of Occupational and Environmental Medicine,** Website: www.acoem.org
    1114 N. Arlington Heights Rd., Arlington Heights IL 60004, (847)818-1800. Professional association of physicians specializing in occupational and environmental health.

- **American Industrial Hygiene Association,** Website: www.aiha.org
    2700 Prosperity Ave., Fairfax Virginia 22031, (703) 849-8888. Professional association of industrial and environmental hygienists.

- **American National Standards Institute,** Website: www.ansi.org
    11 West 42nd St., New York NY 10036, (212)642-4900.
    ANSI is the national secretariat for America's voluntary standards system, including workplace safety and health standards.

- **American Red Cross,** Website: www.redcross.org
    1621 N. Kent St., Arlington VA 22209, (703)248-4222. The national office for the American Red Cross in the United States.

- **American Society for Industrial Security,** Website: www.asisonline.org
    1625 Prince St., Alexandria Virginia 22314, (703)519-6200
    Membership organization of professionals responsible for company or business security.

- **American Society of Safety Engineers,** Website: www.asse.org
    1800 East Oakton St., Des Plaines, IL 60018-2187, (847) 699-2929. Professional organization of safety engineers serving industry, government and in academia.

- **American Society for Training and Development,**
  Website: **www.astd.org**
  160 King St., Alexandria, Virginia 22313, (703) 683-8100. Professional association for trainers in business and government.

- **American Trucking Associations,** Website: **www.trucking.org**
  2220 Mill Road, Alexandria VA 22314, 1-800-ATA-LINE. Offers programs, products and services for the trucking industry, including driver training kits and copies of federal Motor Carrier regulations.

- **Center for Substance Abuse Prevention,**
  Website: **www.health.org/workpl.htm**
  5640 Nicholson Lane, Rockville MD 20852, 1-800-843-4971
  Offers guidelines and helps businesses develop drug-free workplaces.

- **Centers for Disease Control and Prevention (CDC),**
  Website: **http://www.cdc.gov**
  1600 Clifton Ave., N.E., Atlanta Georgia 30333, (404)639-7394
  An agency of the federal Department of Health and Human Services which focuses on prevention and control of disease, injury and disability both on and off the job.

- **Code of Federal Regulations (CFR),**
  Website: **http://www.access.gpo.gov**
  Details of federal laws as compiled by National Archives and Records Administration, or 1-888-293-6498.

- **Department of Labor,** Website: **www.dol.gov**
  200 Constitution Ave., N.W., Washington D.C. 20210, (202) 693-4650

Washington D.C. National office of the federal department of labor.

- **Environmental Protection Administration (EPA),**
  Website: www.epa.gov
  1200 Pennsylvania Ave., N.W., Washington D.C. 20460, (202)260-2090. National office of the EPA.

- **Employee Assistance Professionals Association,**
  Website: www.eap-association.com
  2101 Wilson Blvd. Arlington Virginia 22203, (703) 522-6272. National organization of employee assistance professionals (EAPs). Offers a referral service to EAP facilities in many areas.

- **Equal Employment Opportunity Commission,**
  Website: www.eeoc.gov

- **ErgoWeb** Website: www.ergoweb.com/
  A leading ergonomics website established at the University of Utah.

- **Federal Register,** Website: http://www.access.gpo.gov
  The daily record of activity in federal laws and regulations in the House of Representatives and in the Senate.

- **Human Factors & Ergonomics Society,** Website: www.hfes.org
  P.O. Box 1369, Santa Monica California 90406, (310)394-1811
  Promotes exchange of knowledge about human characteristics that apply to the design of systems and devices

- **Institute for a Drug-Free Workplace,**

Website: **www.drugfreeworkplace.org**
1225 I St. St. N.W. Washington DC 20005, (202)842-7400. Coordinating agency for drug free workplace initiatives.

- **Job Accommodation Network,** Website: **janweb.icdi.wvu.edu**
at West Virginia University, 809 Allen Hall, P.O. 6012 Morgantown West Virginia 26506, (800) 526-7234. A free service for employees and people with disabilities, offering ideas for job accommodations, including safety-related implications.

- **Mine Safety and Health Administration,** Website: **www.msha.gov**
4015 Wilson Blvd., Arlington VA 22203, (703)235-1452. The federal agency dealing with safety in underground and open pit mining.

- **National Association of Manufacturers,** Website: **www.nam.org/**
1331 Pennsylvania Ave., N.W. Washington D.C. 20004, (202)637-2000. Membership organization of manufacturing companies in the United States.

- **National Center for Health Promotion,**
Website: **www.healthpromotion.com**
3920 Varsity Drive, Ann Arbor Michigan 48108, (734) 747-9579. The nation's leading provider of lifestyle programs. More than 300 health care institutions offer the center's programs to corporations and local communities.

- **National Council on Alcoholism and Drug Dependency, Inc.,**
Website: **www.ncadd.org**
12 West 21st. St., New York N.Y. 10010, (212)206-6770. Coordinating

organization for combating alcoholism and drug dependency.

- **National Council on Compensation Insurance, Inc.,**
  Website: www.ncci.com
  750 Park of Commerce Drive, Boca Raton FL 33487, (561)997-1000. National organization that performs workers compensation insurance ratemaking and regulatory service.

- **National Fire Protection Association,** Website: www.nfpa.org
  1 Batterymarch Park, Quincy Massachusetts 02269,1-800-344-3555. Professional association of industrial fire protection. Promotes use of NFPA standards and codes to combat fire problems.

- **National Institute of Occupational Safety and Health (NIOSH),**
  Website: www.cdc.gov/niosh
  200 Independence Avenue, Washington D.C. 20201, (202)401-6995. The research arm of OSHA, a unit of the Centers For Disease Control. Their research center and address for requesting publications is at 4676 Columbia Parkway, Cincinnati Ohio 45226 or 1-800-35-NIOSH.

- **National Safety Council,** Website: www.nsc.org
  1121 Spring Lake Drive, Itasca Illinois 60143, 1-800-621-7619.
  The international not-for-profit organization protecting lives and promoting safety and health of all persons, including safety and occupational health in the workplace. Conducts an annual conference, the National Safety Congress.
  The National Safety Council sponsors training sessions for supervisors and provides first aid and defensive driving courses. NSC Press publishes books on occupational and home safety and health.

- **Network of Employers for Traffic Safety (NETS),**
  Website: www.trafficsafety.org
  1140 Connecticut Ave., N.W. Washington D.C. 20036, (202)452-6005. Dedicated to reducing motor vehicle injuries and saving lives among employees by developing highway safety programs for workers who use vehicles.

- **Occupational Safety and Health Administration,**
  Website: www.osha.gov
  Department of Labor, 200 Constitution Ave., N.W., Washington D. C. 20210, (202)693-1999 (Office of Public Affairs). The federal department which administers and enforces the Occupational Safety and Health Act.

- **Occupational Safety and Health Review Commission (OSHRC)**
  Website: www.oshrc.gov
  1 Lafayette Center, 1120 20th St., N.W., Washington D.C. 20036, (202)606-5370. OSHRC is an independent federal agency and a review board that decides appeals by employers of citations and penalties resulting from OSHA inspections of the workplace.

- **OSHALOG** Website: www.safesoft.com
  801 West Main St., Charlottesville, Virginia 22903, 1-800-932-9547
  A software program that tracks injury and illness data to comply with federal OSHA Log requirements. Identifies immediate problems and long term trends.

- **OSHA Training Institute,** Arlington Heights, IL Website: www.osha.gov
  Click on "T", click on "Training Resources," Office of Training and Education Training Resources, click on "Alternative Training Sites"

(nationwide)

Offers training to managers, employees, union safety representatives in safety and health subjects at the location near Chicago and other locations around the country.

- **President's Committee on Employment of Persons with Disabilities,** Website: **www.pcepd.gov**

    1331 F St., N.W., Washington D.C. 20004, (202)276-6200 voice or (202)376-6205 TDD. A non-profit organization dedicated to helping persons with disabilities obtain and hold jobs, including safe placement on the job.

- **Prevent Blindness America,** Website: **www.preventblindness.org**

    500 East Remington Road, Schaumburg IL 60173, 1-800-331-2020. Sponsors the Wise Owl Club which honors employers and those workers who sight has been saved by the use of eye protection on the job. Sponsors programs to prevent blindness and preserve sight through education and research.

- **Risk and Insurance Management Society (RIMS),** Website: **www.rims.org**

    655 Third Ave., New York, NY 10017, (212) 286-9292. Professional society of persons with risk management, insurance, loss prevention and workers compensation responsibilities. Conducts an annual RIMS Conference.

- **Safety Equipment Association,** Website: **www.safetycentral.org**

    1901 North Moore St., Arlington VA 22209, (703)525-1695. A non-profit organization that offers third party certification testing and certifying a broad range of safety equipment products. Lists products certified and their suppliers.

- **Society for Human Resource Management (SHRM),**
  Website: www.shrm.org
  1800 Duke St., Alexandria, Virginia 22314, (703)548-3440; TDD (703)548-6999. The major association of human resources professionals with more than 140,000 members and some 425 chapters throughout the world. Holds a yearly international conference and exposition. Has a standing national committee on workplace safety and health.

- **United States Department of Labor, Occupational Safety and Health Administration,** Website: www.osha.gov
  300 Constitution Ave., N.W., Washington D.C. 20210, (202) 523-6091. The national office of federal OSHA which enforces the Occupational Safety and Health Act and its implementing regulations.

- **U S Chamber of Commerce** Website: www.uschamber.org
  1615 H Street N.W., Washington D.C. 20262, (202)659-6000.
  The world's largest business federation with more than 3 million corporate members.

- **Voluntary Protection Program Participants' Association (VPPA),**
  Website: www.vpppa.org
  7600-E Leesburg Pike, Falls Church Virginia 22043, (703) 761-1146. VPPA is a voluntary, nonprofit association that helps federal OSHA publicize and support those companies who have worksites accredited to the VPP program and which are worksites with outstanding low injury records.

- **Workplace Violence Research Institute** Website: **noworkviolence.com**
  1281 Gene Autry Trail, Palm Springs CA 92262, 1-800-230-7302. A commercial provider of workplace violence prevention programs.

International Safety Organizations

- **Canadian Center for Occupational Health and Safety**
  Website: **www.ccohs.ca**
  250 East Main St., Hamilton Ontario Canada L8N 1HG, 1-800-668-4284 (Telephone number is open to U.S. and Canada).
  The national center for occupational safety and health information that relates to Canada. Web site offers text in English and in French.

- **Canada Safety Council** Website: **www.safety-council.org**
  1020 Thomas Spratt Place, Ottawa, Ontario Canada K1G 5L5, (613) 739-1535.
  Offers programs in English and in French on occupational, traffic, home and leisure safety

- **Industrial Accident Prevention Association (of Ontario),**
  Website: **www.iapa.on.ca**
  250 Yonge St., Toronto Ontario, Canada, M5B 2N4, (416)506-8888.
  Industrial safety association of the Province of Ontario.

- **British Safety Council** Website: **www.britishsafetycouncil.co.uk**
  70 Chancellors Blvd., London W6 9RS, England, (44)020-8741-1231.
  Information on best practices in safety, occupational health and environmental matters.

- **Ergonomics Society of Australia,**
    Website: www.curtin.edu.au/society/esa
    Curtin University of Technology, GPO Box U1987, Perth West Australia 6845, (08)9266-7819.
    Curtin University acts as secretariat for the Australian ergonomics society.

Glossary of Frequently Used Terms

Acronyms

The full text of the acronym and the explanation of the term can be found under the full-text word or words in the glossary immediately after the list of acronyms.

ADA	Americans with Disabilities Act
AIHA	American Industrial Hygiene Association
ANSI	American National Standards Institute
BLS	Bureau of Labor Statistics
CFR	*Code of Federal Regulations*
CDL	Commercial Driver's License
CIH	Certified Industrial Hygienist

CSHO	Compliance Safety and Health Officer
CSP	Certified Safety Professional
dB	Decibels (as used in noise control and hearing loss)
EMR	Experience Modification Rate
EPA	Environmental Protection Agency
FOM	Field Operations Manual
FR	*Federal Register*
GAO	General Accounting Office
HCA	Hearing Conservation Amendment
HPD	Hearing Protection Device(s)
Hz	Hertz (a measurement of noise levels)
JSA	Job Safety Analysis
LOTO	Lock Out, Tag Out
LWCR	Lost Workday Case Rate
MSDS	Material Safety Data Sheet(s)

NSC	National Safety Council
NIOSH	National Institute for Occupational Safety and Health
NRR	Noise Reduction Rating
OSHA	Occupational Safety and Health Administration
OSHAct	Occupational Safety and Health Act
OSHRC	Occupational Safety and Health Review Commission
PEL	Permissible Exposure Limit
PPE	Personal Protective Equipment
ppm	Parts per million (as in industrial hygiene measurements)
RIMS	Risk and Insurance Management Society
RTK	'Right-to-Know' (federal Hazard Communication) Standard
SHRM	Society for Human Resource Management
SIC	Standard Industrial Classification
STS	Standard Threshold Shift (in hearing loss)
TTS	Temporary Threshold Shift (in hearing loss)

TLV	Threshold Limit Values
TWA	Time-Weighted Average (in noise exposure)
USC	United States Code
VPP	Voluntary Participants' Program

The following words are common safety and occupational health terms supervisors should know.

Abatement–An OSHA term, abatement is the elimination or correction of a safety or health hazard violation that led to an OSHA citation.

Abatement Verification–The process by which an employer informs OSHA, affected employees and their representatives that a hazard cited by OSHA has been corrected. OSHA itself may choose to conduct the verification.

Action Level–As referenced in OSHA regulations, means employee exposure to certain airborne concentrations, averaged over an 8 hour work period. If employee exposure exceeds this level, action is required to eliminate or control the contamination.

Acute–A sudden symptom or condition or an adverse effect on the human body.

Accident–A situation or incident in which an employee is injured on the job or through work-connected duties. May also describe damage to company property, vehicles, materials or refers to nonoccupational events.

Accident or Injury Investigation–Usually a formal process where the immediate supervisor of the injured worker and possibly others determine the cause of the incident which resulted in an injury and the steps required to prevent recurrence.

'Accident Repeater'–Also known as an 'injury prone' worker. An employee who is believed to have more than the normal or average number of injuries on the job compared to persons with the same job responsibilities.

American Industrial Hygiene Association (AIHA)–Professional organization of industrial hygienists in the United States.

American National Standards Institute (ANSI)–An international standards setting organization.

Americans with Disabilities Act (ADA)–A federal law which gives increased protection to persons with disabilities and requires employers to provide accommodations to otherwise qualified applicants and employees.
http://janweb.icdi.wvu.edu/ (Job Accommodation network)

Audiogram–A record of hearing level from an audiometric test measured at several different noise frequencies.

Audiometric Room–A room that is intended for the testing of a person's hearing, insulated against outside noise.

Baseline Audiogram–An initial audiogram against which future audiograms are compared.

Benchmark–A surveyor's term which has since been applied to satisfactory business conditions which employers can use as a guide to improve their operations, including hazard detection and control activities.

Bloodborne Pathogens Standard–A federal OSHA standard requiring protective measures for workers who handle blood products.

Bureau of Labor Statistics (BLS)–The agency responsible for collecting, compiling and analyzing work injury and illness statistics.

Carcinogen–A substance that causes cancer.

Certified Industrial Hygienist (CIH)–An industrial hygiene professional who has met the required educational and work experience and has passed an examination for certification as a professional in that field.

Certified Safety Professional (CSP)–A safety engineer or safety professional who has met the required educational and work experience and has passed an examination for certification as a professional in that field.

Chemical Inventory–A list of the hazardous chemicals known to be present in a work area or facility.

Chronic–An adverse health effect on the human body with symptoms which develop over long periods of time.

Code of Federal Regulations (CFR)—Published annually in paperback volumes *CFR* is the compilation of the general and permanent rules that have been previously published in the Federal Register. OSHA regulations are included in Title 29 of the *CFR*.

Closed Container—A container sealed by means of a lid or other device that neither liquid nor vapor will escape from at ordinary temperatures.

Commercial Driver's License (CDL)—A driver's license for operators of trucks with 26,001 pounds and above gross vehicle weight and vehicles designed to carry 16 persons or more, such as busses.

Compliance—The state of meeting all of the requirements of the law.

Compliance Safety and Health Officer (CSHO)—An OSHA official who is authorized to inspect the workplaces of employers.

Confined Space—Refers to a space which by design has limited openings for entry and exit, unfavorable natural ventilation which could contain or produce dangerous air contaminants and which is not intended for continuous employee occupancy.

Controls—Actions taken to eliminate or control risk.

Corrosive—A substance which eats away, corrodes or disintegrates the skin.

Cost-Benefit Analysis—The comparison of the costs of a business endeavor (such as work injuries and illnesses) to the benefits derived from a safety and health process (lower workers compensation costs, less downtime, less building and product damage, etc).

Decibel (dB)–A unit for measuring the level of sound.

Dermatitis–An inflammation of the skin.

Designated Representative–Any individual or organization (often a labor union) to whom an employee gives written authorization to exercise the employee's rights under certain labor and safety laws.

Documentation–The record of compliance that an employer should maintain.

Dosimeter–A device affixed to a person (by an industrial hygienist or OSHA inspector) to determine the accumulated noise or chemical exposure over a designated period of time.

Drugs–Any substance other than alcohol that is considered a controlled substance under federal regulations 49 *CFR (Code of Federal Regulations)* 40. Controlled substances include marijuana, cocaine, opium, PCP or amphetamines.

Emergency Action Plan–A plan for a workplace describing what procedures the employer and employees must take to ensure employee safety from fire or other emergencies.

Emergency Escape Route–The route that employees are directed to follow in the event they are required to evacuate the workplace or seek a designated refuge area.

Employee–One who is employed in the business of his or her employer affecting commerce.

Employee Exposure Records–A record containing information such as environmental monitoring, biological monitoring, material safety data sheets of materials to which the employee may have been exposed in the workplace.

Employee Medical Records–Refers to a record of the health status of the employee which is made or maintained by a physician, nurse or other health care person or technician. May include medical questionnaires or histories, medical examination results, medical opinions and diagnoses. Employee medical records must be kept separate from employee personnel records and kept in locked cabinets.

Employer–Any person engaged in a business affecting commerce who has employees. May be owners of the business or hired managers who act as agents of the employer.

Energy Control Procedures–(As referred to in the OSHA Standard on Control of Hazardous Energy). A written document that contains items of information an authorized employee needs to know in order to safely control hazardous energy during servicing and maintenance of machines or equipment.

Energy Isolating Device–(As referred to in the OSHA Standard on Control of Hazardous Energy) Any mechanical device that physically prevents the transmission or release of energy, including manually-operated electrical circuit breakers, disconnect switches, line valves and blocks.

Environmental Protection Agency (EPA)–A federal government agency responsible for enforcing clean air, water and toxic substance control acts and other federal environmental laws.

Establishment–A single physical location, as defined by OSHA, where business is conducted or services or operations are performed; also the place where employees report for work, operate from or from which they are paid.

Experience Modification Rate (EMR)–Another indicator of high or low workers' compensation experience and expense, the EMR is used by insurance companies to determine workers' compensation premiums. The insurance carrier estimates the financial losses expected over a period of time (typically 3 years) and these are later compared to the actual losses encountered by a company (the claims against the insurance policy) based on a complex formula which considers the type of business the employer is engaged in.

Exposure–The reasonable likelihood that a worker is or was subject to some effect, influence or safety hazard; or in contact with a hazardous chemical or physical agent at a sufficient concentration and duration to produce an illness. Also, frequency and length of exposure to a hazard.

Exposure Monitoring–A term used in industrial hygiene, generally the measurement of the exposure an employee would undergo to air contaminants without the use of a respirator.

Facilitator–A person who assist others, usually line managers, in carrying out their responsibilities; a staff person such as a safety coordinator.

Federal Register (FR)–The official source of information and notification of proposed rule making by the federal government, including OSHA and any standards, regulations and other official matters, including amendments, corrections, insertions and deletions from any federal agency.

Field Operations Manual (FOM)–The manual provided to OSHA field personnel explaining federal safety regulations in more detail and providing recommended course of actions to handle inspections, employee complaints, etc.

Fire Brigade–A group of employees selected by the employer who are knowledgeable, trained and skilled in at least basic fire fighting operations for the employer.

First Aid–As defined for purpose of recording injuries and illnesses for the OSHA Log, any one time treatment and subsequent observation of minor scratches, cuts, burns, splinters and so forth, which ordinarily require medical care. Under this definition, such treatment and observation are considered first aid even though provided by a physician or registered professional personnel.

First Report of Injury–The initial notification to an insurance carrier or other agency that a worker has been injured or has suffered an occupational illness during the course of employment. The report includes details about the employee, how the injury occurred, initial medical treatment, and the like. This report activates medical payments for any treating health care providers, possible temporary or total disability payments for the injured worker. The OSHA 101 Form can also be used as a first report of injury.

General Accounting Office (GAO)–The General Accounting Office of the Federal Government which audits government activities, including OSHA and EPA programs, for cost effectiveness.

General Duty Clause–Section 5 (a) (1) of the federal OSHAct which provides that employers provide a work environment "...free from recognized hazards that are causing or are likely to cause death or series physical harm to his employees...."

Grounding–Electrically connecting an object to ground, preventing sparks and shock.

Handrail–A single bar or pipe supported on brackets from a wall or partition, as on a stairway or ramp, to furnish persons with a handhold in case of tripping.

Hazard–Any real or potential condition that can cause injury, illness, damage or death.

Hazard Assessment–The determination if a workplace condition is hazardous and, if so, the likelihood that the hazard will cause some form of injury or illness to a worker.

Hazard Communication means the identification of hazards, the end result of special measures and activities conducted by employers. The purpose is to reduce and eliminate adverse health effects due to unnecessary exposures to hazardous materials

Hazardous Chemicals–Any chemical which is a potential physical hazard or a health hazard.

Hearing Conservation–The prevention or minimizing of noise induced hearing loss through the use of hearing protection devices and/or the control of nose through engineering or administrative procedures.

Hearing Conservation Amendment (HCA)–An amendment to the federal OSHA Standard (1910.95) on Occupational Noise Exposure dealing with employer responsibility to establish a hearing conservation program for employees exposed to high noise levels, as defined in the standard.

Hearing Level–A measured threshold of hearing at a specified frequency, expressed in decibels relative to a specific standard of normal hearing.

Hearing Protection Device(s) (HPD)–Ear plugs, ear muffs or other protective devices designed to protect employee hearing from exposure to excessive noise.

Heatstroke–A severe, oftentimes fatal, condition caused by the body's failure to regulate its internal temperature after prolonged exposure to extreme heat.

Heimlich Maneuver–A first aid measure for choking, a technique to dislodge meat or other food items that may become lodged in a person's throat, threatening that person with a choking death.

Hertz (Hz)–A measurement unit of noise level.

Incentive Programs–The awarding of tangible awards (cash, prizes, etc) or intangible awards (plaques, certificates, etc) for no or low accident performance or for positive safety behaviors.

Imminent Danger–An OSHA definition of any condition where there is reasonable certainty that a danger exists that can be expected to cause death or serious physical harm immediately, or before the danger can be eliminated through normal enforcement procedures.

Industrial Hygienist–A professional who determines what health hazards are involved in the workplace, how much and how the worker is exposed and then recommends steps to control the exposures.

Job Safety Analysis (JSA)–An observation and recording process by which a job is studied to determine the hazards involved and ways to safely perform the job by work procedures and/or the use of personal protective equipment

Label–Any written, printed or graphic material displayed on or affixed to containers of hazardous chemicals.

Line Manager–See 'Management.'

Lock Out–The use of locks or locking devices to positively secure the control devices which release hazardous energy (ie. electricity, hydraulics air, water etc).

Lockout Device–(As referred to the OSHA Standard on Control of Hazardous Energy). Any device that uses positive means such as a lock (either key or combination type) to hold an energy-isolating device in a safe position, thereby preventing the energizing of machinery or equipment.

"Lock Out, Tag Out" (LOTO)–An informal term for the federal OSHA Standard on the Control of the Release of Hazardous Energy.

Loss Control–The profession which deals with the control of potential losses of industrial accidents, building damage and environmental factors. Loss prevention activities are those which would eliminate, control or reduce the potential loss.

Lost Work Day Case (LWCR)–An OSHA definition of injuries or job illnesses which involve days away from work or days of restricted work activity, or both.

Management–Those persons who are responsible for the mission or objectives of the business or organization. Line managers are those directly responsible for the success of the business–production or operations managers, sales managers, and the like. Staff managers are those who assist line managers in carry out their duties effectively– quality control managers, production planning managers, purchasing agents, human resource managers, safety managers and safety coordinators.

Management Systems–Those mission statements, policies, procedures and control mechanisms that, coming together, drive the managing of an enterprise. In safety, those system elements that make for a successful hazard detection, elimination or control process.

Material Safety Data Sheet (MSDS)–A compilation of information required under the federal OSHA Hazard Communication Standard on the identity of hazardous chemicals, health and physical hazards, exposure limits and precautions to be taken when working with these chemicals or materials. Employers who use hazardous chemicals must have an MSDS on hand for each chemical with the MSDS available to employees in the workplace.

Means of Egress–A continuous and unobstructed way of exit travel from any point in a building to a public way and consists of the path of exit, the exit and the path of exit discharge.

Medical Surveillance–Many of the chemicals regulated by OSHA have requirements that the employer conduct medical surveillance on employees to assure that chemical exposure is within acceptable limits and not excessive, as detailed in each standard.

Medical Treatment–Under OSHA's definition, includes treatment of injuries (excluding first aid treatment) administered by physicians, registered professional personnel or other health care persons.

Monitoring–Periodic or continuous surveillance or testing to determine the level of compliance with statutory requirements and/or pollutant levels.

National Institute of Occupational Safety and Health (NIOSH)—The federal unit focusing on research in occupational safety and health, a branch of the Department of Health and Human Services.

National Safety Council (NSC)—An international, not for profit organization, promoting personal safety on and off the job.

'Near-Miss' Incident—A workplace incident where no person was injured but could have been injured and where property, equipment or product damage occurred.

Noise-Induced Hearing Loss—Progressive hearing loss which results from exposure to continuous noise over a long period of time.

Noise Reduction Rating (NRR)—A measure of hearing protection which indicates how much noise each type of hearing protection will prevent or reduce.

Occupational Illness—An OSHA definition of any abnormal condition or disorder, other than one resulting from an occupational injury, caused by exposure to environmental factors associated with employment. It includes acute and chronic illnesses or diseases which may be caused by inhalation, absorption, ingestion or direct contact.

Occupational Injury—Any injury such as a cut, fracture, sprain, amputation etc., which results from a work accident or from a single instantaneous exposure in the work environment.

Occupational Safety and Health Administration (OSHA)—A federal agency, part of the U.S. Department of Labor, which is responsible for developing, implementing and enforcing safety and health standards and regulations, including the federal OSHAct.

Occupational Safety and Health Review Commission (OSHRC)–An independent review body outside the Department of Labor that reviews and decides on employer appeals of OSHA penalties and abatement dates.

OSHA Log–Also known as the OSHA 300 Log, this document requires designated employers in most industries to record work-connected fatalities, lost work day cases, recordable injuries and illnesses. The summary section of the Log is to be posted on a facility notice board for the month of February each year.

Outside Contractors–Companies which provide construction, maintenance and repair services to employers. These are companies independent of the employer with their own staffs of workers.

Parts per million (ppm)–A unit of measurement or way of expressing tiny concentrations of pollutants in air, water, soil, human tissue, food or other products.

Permissible Exposure Limit (PEL)–Refers to the maximum air contaminant concentration a worker can be exposed to on a repeated basis without developing adverse effects.

Personal Lock–A lock for which the worker personally controls the key, as used in lock out, tag out procedures for the control of hazardous energy.

Personal Protective Equipment (PPE)–Specially designed equipment which protects the worker from injury or occupational illness. Includes items such as hard hats, safety eye shields, prescription safety glasses, gloves, work aprons, safety shoes, and the like.

Point of Operation–That point at which cutting, shaping, boring or forming is accomplished on material.

Presence-Sensing Device–A safeguarding device designed, constructed and arranged to create a sensing field that signals the clutch or brake control to deactivate the clutch and activate the brake of the press when any part of the operator's body or a hand tool is within such a field or area.

Probability–Likelihood of an event occurring.

Pull-Out Device–A safeguarding mechanism attached to the operator's hands and connected to the upper die or slide of the press, that is designed to withdraw the operator's hands as the dies close, should the operator's hands be inadvertently within the point of operation.

Recordable Cases–An OSHA term describing all work-related deaths and illnesses and those work-related injuries which result in loss of consciousness, restriction of work or motion, transfer to another job, or require medical treatment beyond first aid.

Regulatory Compliance–Meeting requirements of federal, state, county or local laws and regulations regarding safety in the workplace.

Restriction of Work or Motion–As defined in the regulations for posting to the OSHA Log, refers to a situation where an employee, because of a job related injury or illness, is physically or mentally unable to perform all or any part of his or her normal assignment during all or any part of the workday or shift.

Risk–Chance of exposure to a hazard occurring. The assumed effect of an uncontrolled hazard, appraised in terms of the probability it will happen and the maximum severity of any injuries or damage.

Risk and Insurance Management Society (RIMS)–Professional association of risk and insurance managers.

Risk Decision–A decision to accept or not accept the risk associated with the potential adverse actions.

"Right-to-Know" (RTK)–A term applied to a variety of laws and regulations that provide for the availability of information on chemical hazards. An informal name for the federal Hazard Communication Standard.

Safe Work Practices–Those techniques and work habits, determined by the employer, which allows the employee to perform job duties with a minimum of risk.

Safety–The protection of the physical and mental well-being of employees on the job.

Safety and Health Audit–A systematic examination of safety and health activities to check their accuracy against established safe work practices or working conditions.

Safety Block–A prop, when inserted between the upper and lower forming dies, to prevent the slide from falling on its own weight.

Safety Can–An approved container, of not more than 5 gallons capacity, having a spring-closed lid and spout cover and designed that it will safely relieve internal pressure when subjected to fire exposure.

Safety Coordinator–A person, usually in a smaller organization, who has the staff responsibility of assisting line managers with implementing and maintaining an effective safety process.

Safety Management–The accomplishment of a safe workplace through others.

Safety Professional–A professional person who identifies, evaluates and eliminates or mitigates hazards to an acceptable level in all aspects of human behavior.

Safety Process–A continuing series of activities, many of which are never ending, that integrates safe work practices and the identification, elimination or control of unsafe conditions into the daily business processes of the organization.

Safety Rules–Those job procedures, determined most often by the employer but often with worker input, which the employee performs with a minimum of hazardous exposures.

Society for Human Resource Management (SHRM)–Professional society of human resource managers and professionals.

Solvent–A substance, usually liquid, capable of dissolving or dispersing one or more other substances

Sound Level Meter–An instrument designed to measure the sound pressure level of noise exposure.

Sprinkler System–A system of piping designed in accordance with fire protection engineering standards and installed to control or extinguish fires.

Standard Industrial Classification (SIC)–A classification system developed by the federal Office of Management and the Budget to classify establishments by the type of activity or business in which they are engaged. Each establishment is assigned an industry code for its major activity which is determined by the product manufactured or service rendered.

Standard Threshold Shift (STS)–A change in hearing threshold relative to the baseline audiogram of an average of 10 decibels or more at 2000, 3000 and 4000 Hz (Hertz) in either ear.

'State Plan State'–The federal OSHAct permits states and territories to establish their own state OSHAct, in lieu of coverage by the federal Act, as long as the state requirements are as strict as the federal requirements. At this time 26 states and territories have elected to establish their own state plan OSH coverage. Often called a 'state plan state'.

Subpart Z–The section of OSHA regulations dealing with toxic and hazardous substances, *CFR* 1910 Subpart Z.

Substance Abuse–Excessive use of alcohol or of illegal drugs.

Tagout Device–(As refereed to the OSHA Standard on Control of Hazardous Energy). Any prominent warning device, such as a tag, that can be securely fastened to an energy-isolating device in accordance with an established procedure. The tag indicates that the machine or equipment to which it is attached is not to be operated until the tagout device is removed in accordance with the energy control procedure.

Task Lighting–Illumination to improve task brightness and contrast, thereby reducing eyestrain and the potential for headaches.

Temporary Threshold Shift (TTS)–Progressive reduction with the passage of time of a measured hearing level, usually when the cause of the hearing loss has been removed

Threshold Limit Values (TLV)–Represents the air concentrations of chemical substances to which it is believed that workers may be exposed daily without adverse effects.

Time Weighted Average (TWA)–Refers to concentrations of airborne toxic materials weighted for a certain duration of time, usually 8 hours.

Toxic–Harmful to living organisms.

Toxicity–The degree of danger posed by substances to animal or plant life.

Toxic Substances–A chemical or mixture that may present an unreasonable risk of injury to health or the environment.

Trade Secret–Any confidential formula, pattern, process, device, information or compilation of information that is used in an employer's business, providing an employer with an economic or marketing advantage over competitors who do not know or use it.

United States Code (USC)–Describes the public, general and permanent laws of the United States

Ventilation–The act of admitting fresh air into a space in order to replace stale or contaminated air.

Volunteer Protection Program (VPP)–A voluntary association of employers who have met the standards for membership in the OSHA-sponsored organization by expanding worker protection beyond the minimum required by OSHA standards.

Willful Violation–A violation of the OSHAct, standards or regulations where the employer either knew what he or she is doing constitutes a violation or is aware that hazardous condition existed and made no reasonable effort to eliminate it.

Work Environment–Consists of the employer's premises and other locations where employees are engaged in work-related activities or are present as a condition of employment.

Workers' Compensation–A no-fault system of medical and disability benefits provided to workers injured on the job, in lieu of the worker having to sue the employer for lost wages and the cost of medical benefits. Administered at the state level in the United States.

Index

Academic education, 306-307
Accident reporting, 72
Affirmative action, 66-68
Age harassment, 60-61
Aging workforce, 128-131
Avoiding employment law claims, 64
Baby Boomers in workforce, 126-127
Bargaining unit, 85
Career development for supervisors, 311-333
Career development plan for supervisors, 316-317
Career goals for supervisors, 313-316
Career setbacks, managing, 331-333
Changing workplace, 207-212
Child labor, 80-81
Coaching, 106, 302-305
Coaching and career development, 303-305
Collective agreements, 238-247
Collective agreements, administering, 251-252

Communication, 147-173
Communication, one on one, 167-169
Communication, groups, 169-172
Communication, verbal, 150-153
Communication, nonverbal, 153-158
Communication, written, 159-165
Developing employee skills and careers, 295-308
Disabled in workforce, 129-130
Disciplining a protected class employee, 66
Discrimination, in employment, 37-69
DOT regulations, 37
Diversity in the workplace, 119-142
Employee orientation, 195-196
Employee rights under OSHA, 73-74
Employee training goals, 301-302
Employee unions, 252-255
Employment law, 37-40, 42-69
Equal Pay Act of 1963, 83
Essential management skills, 93-94
Exempt employees, 82-83

Exit interviews, 198-200
Foreign labor unions, 258-262
Foreign managers, 135-139
Harassment, 59-64
Hazard communication *(see OSHA Hazard Communication Standard)*
Hazards or risks, 10-12
Healthy lifestyle, 327-330
History of labor unions, 255-258
HR and feedback, 106
HR and moral support, 104-105
HR and motivation, 105
HR and workforce planning, 105
HR as bureaucrat, 96
HR as complaint department, 97
HR as disciplinarian, 95
HR as fixer, 96
HR as functional and technical expert, 101
HR as holder of people values, 95
HR as last resort, 97
HR as mediator, 103-104
HR as organization resource, 102
HR as roadblock, 97-99
HR as rule maker, 94-95
HR as terminator, 98-100
HR data and metrics, 102
HR perspective, 103
Human resources, 93-114
Influencing your boss, 320-324
Interviewing job applicants, 184-193
Keeping employees, 195-198
Law, employment *(see employment law)*
Law, workplace *(see workplace law)*

Leadership, 203-233
Leadership, authoritarian, 220-222
Leadership, democratic, 222-223
Leadership development, 305-306
Leadership, hands off, 223-226
Leadership, key elements, 213-215
Leadership styles, 220-227
Leading a meeting, 169-170
Listening to feedback, 149-150
Listening, actively, 165-167
Managing change, 7, 111-112
Measuring employee performance, 271-292
Measuring safety performance, 289-291
Mentoring, 106
Minimum wage, 81
Motivating employees, 216-219
Multicultural workforce, 130-137
National Institute for Occupational Safety and Health (NIOSH), 28
National Labor Relations Act (NRLA), 4, 238, 241, 250-252
National Safety Council, 28, 69, 72
Nonexempt employees, 81-82,
OSHA, 28
OSHA Hazard Communication Standard, 78-79
OSHA Regulations and the OSHAct, 69-79
OSHA Self-Inspection Checklist, 75-77
OSHA violations, categories of, 71-72
OSHA visitations, 74-77
OSHAct, 12, 28
OSHA-required training, 72-73
Overtime, 81-83,

Partnering with HR, 93-114
Performance appraisals, 271-292
Performance appraisals, legal issues, 274-275
Performance appraisals, giving one to an employee, 275-278, 284-289
Performance appraisal, methods, 279-284
Policy and procedure manual, 247
Racial and ethnic diversity in workforce, 125-126
Reasonable accommodation for religious discrimination or disability under the Rehabilitation Act, 57-58
Recruiting employees, 177-181
Reference checks, 193-195
Reverse discrimination, 68-69
Risks, or hazards, 10-12
Screening applicants, 181-183
Safety, 8-12
Sexual harassment, 59-60
State and local laws, 51-54
Stereotypes, also see class assumptions, 56-57
Stress management, 330-331
Supervising in union environment, 237-265
Supervising mixed culture workforce, 140-142
Supervisor and human resources, 93-115
Supervisor and union contract, 86-87
Supervisor, as advocate for the workforce, 29-30
Supervisor, as assessor of industry trends, 22-24
Supervisor, as keeper of, rules and procedures, 25-27
Supervisor, as leader of the frontline, 24-25
Supervisor, as maintainer of a safe and productive workplace, 28
Supervisor, as representative of the organization, 31-32
Supervisor, as trainer of employees, 29
Supervisor, defined, 1-6,
Supervisor or manager, 5-6,
Supervisor, frontline, 19
Supervisor, roles, 19-33
Supervisors and safety 8-12
Supervisors, risk and responsibility for career development, 319-320
Supervisory style and needs of a diverse and global workforce, 226-233
Teams and work, 212-213
Time management, 324-327
Title VII of the Civil Rights Act of 1964, 37, 38, 43-44
Training, 297-302
Training employees, 299-302
Training programs, 297-302
Understanding cultural differences in workplace, 131-135
Union organizing activity, 85-86
U.S Rehabilitation Act of 1973, 37, 47-48
U.S. Age Discrimination in Employment Act, 1967, 37, 46-47
U.S. Americans with Disabilities Act, 37, 48-50
U.S. Bankruptcy Code, 37

395

U.S. Civil Rights Act of 1964, 37, 44-45
U.S. Civil Rights Act of 1964, Title VII, 37, 43-44
U.S. Civil Rights Act of 1991, 37, 45-46
U.S. Coast Guard regulations, 37
U.S. Constitution, 37
U.S. Equal Pay Act of 1963, 38, 83
U.S. ERISA/COBRA, 37
U.S. Fair Labor Standards Act, 37, 80-84
U.S. Family and Medical Leave Act, 37, 50-51
U.S. Immigration Reform and Control Act, 37
U.S. National Labor Relations Act, 37, 84-87
U.S. Occupational Safety and Health Administration (OSHA), 37, 38, 69-79
U.S. Pregnancy Discrimination Act, 1978 (Amendment to Title VII), 38, 44
USERRA, 37
Voluntary guidelines, 79-80
Women in workforce, 124-125
Workplace law, 37-39, 40-42, 69-87